WEDNESDAY AT FOUR

Books by Mrs Robert Henrey

THE LITTLE MADELEINE (*her girlhood*)

AN EXILE IN SOHO (*her adolescence*)

JULIA (*further adolescence*)

MADELEINE GROWN UP (*her love story and marriage*)

MADELEINE YOUNG WIFE (*war and peace on her farm in Normandy*)

LONDON UNDER FIRE 1940–45 (*with her baby in London during the air raids*)

HER APRIL DAYS (*the death of her mother*)

WEDNESDAY AT FOUR (*an afternoon in London and a journey to Moscow*)

WINTER WILD (*clouds on the horizon*)

SHE WHO PAYS (*background to a near 'revolution'*)

LONDON (*with water-colours by Phyllis Ginger*)

PALOMA (*the story of a friend*)

BLOOMSBURY FAIR (*three London families*)

THE VIRGIN OF ALDERMANBURY (*rebuilding of the City*)

SPRING IN A SOHO STREET

MILOU'S DAUGHTER (*she goes in search of her father's Midi*)

A MONTH IN PARIS (*she revisits the city of her birth*)

A JOURNEY TO VIENNA (*her small son becomes briefly a film star*)

MATILDA AND THE CHICKENS (*the farm in Normandy just after the war*)

WEDNESDAY

AT FOUR

by

MRS ROBERT HENREY

LONDON
J. M. DENT & SONS LTD

Printed in Great Britain
by
Lowe & Brydone (Printers) Ltd., London
for
J. M. DENT & SONS LTD
Aldine House · Bedford Street · London
© Mrs Robert Henrey, 1964
First published 1964
Reprinted 1971

ISBN: 0 460 03535 5

I

I WAS in Normandy when the communication, forwarded from my London flat, was pushed through the letter-box at the top of my home orchard, that same letter-box which earlier in the year had been used by a thrush for her nest. It was a large square envelope, which I took to be from the Tate Gallery, which sends me invitations for the Private Views of its exhibitions with flattering regularity—this in spite of the fact that something invariably happens to prevent me from going. Spoiled by the Tate's delicate attentions, I am apt to leave this familiar missive to the last of my mail, giving substance to the adage that familiarity breeds contempt.

The envelope on this occasion did contain an invitation, but not from the Tate Gallery; and it was not in the true sense an invitation—but a command. I was 'commanded' to attend one of the three garden parties which the Queen was holding that summer in the grounds of Buckingham Palace. I turned the card over once or twice in surprise that the Queen, through her Lord Chamberlain, should have thought fit to issue this invitation or command to me who had so little reason to expect it. Indeed, I am afflicted with such a deep-rooted dissatisfaction with myself as a person that my first thought was to dismiss the matter out of hand, so that nothing should stand between myself and the quiet monotony of those summer days when I was trying to discover a new tranquillity of mind.

'I shall not go,' I thought. 'Who will miss me in the crowd?'

That morning I was taking Georgette, my farmer's young wife, and Brigitte, their eight-year-old daughter, to Caen, where Georgette was to consult a specialist. Her husband was busy in the fields and I was proud to be driving these two little women in my small car. Georgette could of course have taken her husband Jacques's car, which was larger and faster than mine, but she was, I think, afraid to venture alone so far from the tracks and lanes which surround our two homes.

Though I have held a licence since before the days when it was necessary (at least in England) to pass a test, I am still conscious of a natural timidity which makes me over-cautious when in charge of a car, and which is by no means any longer typical of the average woman driver. I retain, along with a swiftly diminishing number of other women, those failings which once made woman-kind somewhat ridiculous in the eyes of men. My nerves are too often taut. I am terrified of unwittingly doing something wrong which could conjure up a member of the mobile police like a demon in a fairy tale to deprive me of my licence, for in spite of my tendency to give way too quickly to emotion I derive a greater sense of freedom from my small car than from anything else I know. In fact I can no longer envisage life on the farm without it. I use it to run down to market or to go down to the beach to bathe, to call on my friends or to bring back somebody's child from school. But while driving it I suffer from that same over-sensitivity which makes me in the recurring crises of my life give way to passion or tears.

The mere fact that Georgette had asked me to drive her daughter and herself to Caen, admitting that she would feel safer with me than by herself, gave me the sweetest sense of confidence. We made a thoroughly relaxed trio and we felt, perhaps a little smugly, that we were being much more careful than all the other drivers on the road. Those who swung out on to the wrong side of the highway to pass us at great speed, looking back over their shoulders in anger, were mad. But it was high summer, the smooth surface of the road glistened and burned like hot steel, and flags were flying in all the villages we passed through because on the morrow it would be the Fourteenth of July.

In due course we reached the River Orne and caught a distant glimpse of church spires—the city of the thousand spires, as Marcel Proust called Caen. At the first bridge we turned right and a few minutes later drew up in front of a modern block of flats. This was where the specialist had his consulting-room. Brigitte was a child so well versed in country lore and knew so many things about it which I did not, that at home she often used to put me to shame. She was always telling me that our cows had recognizable face like people, though to me they all looked alike. Now this same Brigitte found herself for the first time in her life in a lift which went into action by the pressing of a button. When I put a finger on the button and we began our ascent she looked at me in admiration, and the curious thing is that I felt flattered as if I had really done something worthy of the wonder I could read in her eyes, and then as quickly I felt ashamed, as if I had taken advantage of her simplicity.

Though it was only 8.30 a.m. the waiting-room was full. Conversation was interrupted while chairs were found for us, and we prepared ourselves for a long wait. Every now and again a door opened noisily and a man appeared and called out: 'Next patient, if you please!' There was something almost terrifying about the loud voice and the hurried but meek response of the victim who was swiftly drawn into the unknown. Then conversation broke out again, for these country town patients were eager to discuss their maladies, their gardens, the beauties of rebuilt Caen, the width of its tree-lined avenues, the height of its apartment houses and the splendour of its shops and stores. I had the feeling that merely to live in this resurrected town was enough to give its inhabitants an impression of wealth, happiness and security, and to efface, for those old enough to have lived through it, the nightmare of battle and aerial bombardment.

When Brigitte became restless, her mother suggested that while she was waiting for her turn I should take the little girl for a walk in the town. We walked hand in hand for a time, not knowing where we were going, until we came upon a very modern-looking church which we entered by a side door, so that we found ourselves almost immediately at the foot of the altar. Here we knelt down to make a short prayer that the painful trouble in Georgette's back, which was the reason for her visit to the specialist, might prove to be less serious than we feared. The little girl obediently repeated the words after me. Her devotion for her mother was infinitely touching, but she was surprised that one could pray otherwise than in set prayers recited at night before going to bed. Her face lit up with wonder. As we left the church she said with the delight of discovery: 'The ones I know have to be learned by heart, and they all have a beginning and an end. Nobody told me people could invent their own.' This glimpse of something so novel in her existence gave her more joy than all the wonders of the gleaming city. We turned into a square where there was a small lorry filled with yapping, barking dogs of different breeds and sizes. Their master called them out and

started to race them round the square. 'Perhaps they are performing dogs,' said Brigitte. 'Why don't you ask the woman? I
am sure she is the man's wife.' When we asked the woman she
said: 'No, they are not performing dogs, but simply dogs my
husband and I have rescued from being taken to the pound and
probably destroyed. For instance, we were driving into town the
other day when we saw that big white one being led off by a
gendarme at the end of a rope. It didn't take us long to understand. We overtook the gendarme and asked him to hand over the
dog to us. We said we would give it a good home. Believe me, we
can sleep safely in our bed at nights. No burglar will come near
our house. Our dogs are devoted to us and guard us well.' Her
husband gave a long low whistle and the dogs all came to heel,
and we watched them being driven off in the small lorry.

Brigitte was worried about her mother, but she had been
thinking also about the lift, and was anxious this time to press the
button herself and see if it would work for her as well as for me.
When the mechanism obeyed her she was ready to believe in
magic.

Georgette gave us good news. Her condition was much less
serious than she had been led to believe. She would have to put a
board under the mattress at night—taking care that it was on her
side of the bed so that her husband could sleep in comfort—and
she was advised to lie down once or twice during the course of the
day on a rug on the floor. Brigitte, sensing her mother's relief,
exclaimed exultantly: 'I prayed a special prayer for you!' She
added in the same breath: 'And I pushed the button and made
the lift go up!' These two miracles had become fused in her
mind.

When I had returned to the farm that summer I had taken back
the four hens which were all that remained of the flock I was
compelled to disband after my mother's death. During the winter
Georgette had kept them at her place. These four hens had been
quick to feel at home again, and I was so attached to them that I
hated the idea of leaving them even for a day.

The invitation to the royal garden party had begun to worry
me again. I had in the course of years attended many splendid
occasions. As a young married woman I had, with my husband,

interviewed many of the great ones of the earth and covered social
and political events in different parts of the world for the newspaper in which we wrote a column. But if I had been present so
often at historic moments and events it was not because of myself
but because of the newspaper I represented, and there came a time
when I began to fear this overshadowing of my timid personality.
This phase in my life was over and I had learned the hard lesson
that few are the times when one is wanted for oneself. And now
suddenly this precise thing was happening. I was being asked for
my unimportant self—and by no less a person than the Queen of
England.

As soon as this fact became clear my attitude changed. The
honour was not so great as if I were being given a personal
audience. I would be only one in a crowd; but still, whichever
way I looked at it, the invitation was to me as an individual, and I
even had permission to bring my husband, so that for once I
would be in a position of having something important to offer to
the person I loved. A stranger, and yet not altogether a stranger,
was asking me into her house and into her garden, and such
kindnesses were not—at all events so far as I was concerned—so
common that I could treat them lightly.

So my mind was made up. I would accept with humility.

There remained the question of my hens.

In the evening Brigitte came to bring me the milk. Her mother,
she said, was in the hay fields, which was not the best possible
thing for her back, but the weather had turned fine and time was
valuable. When I told Brigitte that I hoped her mother would not
strain herself, the little girl answered like a grown woman: 'Well,
anyway, her morale is much better. That ought to help.' She
added, with that quick turn of mind that I found endearing: 'I
would like to go down to the sands with you.'

She was already half way to the car and soon we were sitting
side by side driving along the lanes. I was still thinking of the
hens, and I said to Brigitte:

'Have you noticed the golden sandals that the little Parisian
girls are wearing this summer?'

'Oh yes, I have!' exclaimed Brigitte. 'Nathalie Durville and
Anne Poirot wear them. They must be very expensive.'

'I have to go to London for a day or two,' I said, 'and I am
worried about my four hens, so I thought that if you would come

and let them out in the morning and give them their bread and milk, and put them safely to bed in the evening so that foxes could not get at them, and if you were to water the roses in my garden and put out food for the sparrows and the tits, and if you were to collect the eggs every night and lock up carefully, I would buy you a pair of golden sandals to say thank you.'

Brigitte wriggled in her seat.

'Thank you!' she said.

'They would not be a present,' I explained carefully. 'You would have earned them. Think about it and let me know tomorrow.'

Now that I was convinced that this invitation was in some way a recognition of something, however small, achieved by myself, I was bursting to talk about it. But I had been taught in childhood that pride is a sin, and it has become second nature in me to repress the slightest upsurge of self-satisfaction, to the point that bitterness often replaces joy. I remembered also a certain visit I once paid to a person whose talent I greatly admired, whose literary fame came from hard work and sound values—truly an erudite person. While waiting in the drawing-room my eye had been caught by a gold-rimmed invitation card. It was from royalty and was vulgarly displayed on the mantelpiece. I said to myself, waiting for the great writer to come in: 'May I never be guilty of such ostentation!' And such is my narrowness of mind that some of the admiration I had for this writer—but happily not all—was taken away. Thus in my own case I would have liked to keep my happiness locked inside me and ponder it in my heart.

But the devil that is always in us caused me to meet Patsy. She is half English, and for this reason I could not help telling her the news. She congratulated me and then went on to say: 'Come to Montauzan this evening for coffee. My uncle Owen and his wife Gladys will be there, and we can talk about my other uncle David, whom you know, and who this year is spending his holiday in Wales.'

Vanity of vanities! Scarcely was I seated in Patsy's drawing-room that evening when I opened my handbag and drew out the invitation. Quickly it was passed from hand to hand.

'I shall pay for this,' I thought. 'I have committed the sin called pride.'

The orchard was dark. I put the car away and entered the empty farmhouse. Was it this thing about pride that made me think back to my childhood? I switched the kitchen light on and turned almost mechanically towards the door of what had been until so recently my mother's room—fourteen months ago, to be exact. Roses grew on her grave in the tiny churchyard at Auberville. My son had fashioned a cross out of a sixteenth-century oak beam taken from the old cider press at the bottom of the orchard. How smooth and shining was the oak, which wind and rain could no longer harm! I had bought the plot beside hers for a small sum in the hope that one day my husband and I would join her there. But how pleased she would have been about this invitation to take tea in the Queen's garden! We were apt to laugh at the almost childish interest she invariably took in the members of the royal family, and I could still see her seated at the kitchen table, the light playing on her copper-coloured hair as she studied one of those glossy albums that are produced to commemorate state occasions. Yes, we were sometimes almost unkind about it, but she saw in the British royal family a reflection of the country where she had spent her happiest years. Paris had meant anxiety, cruelty and near-starvation. London, even when she and I had been alone together, had seemed like a land of plenty. I now wished bitterly that I could have given her the happiness of this news, for though she did not often show it I think she was probably proud of me. Tears were the price I paid for my show of pride. I never seemed able to capture happiness for long.

The invitation was for Wednesday at four.

On Tuesday night I drove to Le Havre and left my car in a garage by the dockside. The next morning my husband was waiting for me at Waterloo, and I said: 'Whatever shall I wear? Do you realize I shall need a hat?'

Was a garden party like the royal enclosure at Ascot? House parties, dances, Virginia Water, cotton dresses and cartwheel hats all floated through my mind. There was an old house near

Egham—or was it Sunningdale?—where I had danced once on a summer's night. The ceilings were low and oak-beamed. The doors and windows were thrown open to frame rose trees in full bloom in the garden. The Prince of Wales and his brother Prince George were there: that Prince of Wales who was later to become king and abandon a throne for the love of a woman, and that Prince George whose destiny it was to die while still so young and so good looking. I remember he wore a red carnation in his buttonhole. We danced all night and then at dawn, while the cars were being fetched, we drifted into the hall and stood in front of a fire whose burning apple logs sent up a pungent smell to join the scent of roses and Chanel No. 5. Who could have foreseen on that dewy morning as the cars crunched on the gravel to fetch these royal sons away that what promised to be a straight line would shudder and change course? How long ago it all seemed!

'I don't want to disguise myself,' I said to my husband. 'I want to remain *me*.'

The previous season Mlle Chanel had made me a navy blue suit with gold buttons, and as it had been made under her personal supervision, and was impeccable, I decided to wear it with a blouse of white tie silk on which were large blue spots. My husband, who has an eye for such things, brought me back from the office a small white plastic beret which to my surprise could not have suited this ensemble better. A crocodile handbag bought some ten years earlier in Paris, black and white Ferragamo shoes made for me in Florence and a red umbrella with a cane handle from Fenwick's—a Christmas present I had never got down to using— these completed my outfit. Thus, perhaps unconventionally equipped, I set off with my husband soon after three, a diamond brooch half hidden by the knotted bow of my blouse.

For what is now nearly half my life my London home has been within a stone's throw of the Green Park. As I have seldom been without a Pekinese, which I exercise morning and night by walking it twice or three times round the park, I have come to think of it as my own domain, and I look at the trees through expert eyes, comparing their growth and foliage.

What I please to call my domain is bordered to the north by the great arterial way which is Piccadilly, to the east by those noble houses which include Spencer House, Bridgewater House,

Stornoway House and the town house of Lord Rothermere, and to the south by Buckingham Palace and, on the other side of Constitution Hill, the tall brick wall of the palace gardens.

How often have I idly wondered about life on the other side of the wall.

I doubt if it had ever struck me that I might one day be invited to penetrate that mysterious oasis in the heart of London which in my dreams appeared as remote as the fountains and cherry trees in the gardens of the Emperor of Japan, But I remember that during the last war a stray bomb blew away a piece of the wall and all the leaves off a plane tree at the edge of the Green Park. It was very curious in high summer to see this lone tree naked as in winter while all the other trees were in their summer best. And I recall being even more surprised when it burst into bud just as all the other trees were shedding their leaves.

With only the Green Park to traverse it did not seem right to hire a car or hail a taxi-cab to take us to Buckingham Palace. So I was easily prevailed upon to walk, though I was not accustomed to walking along the gravel paths in the sort of shoes that I was wearing on this occasion—such thistledown shoes and such very high heels!

It is a familiar sight to me to see the royal standard above Buckingham Palace bob up and down between the leaves of chestnut, Turkey oak and maple, against every kind of changing sky at times streaked with white horses. Once, when I was walking across the wide lawn in the middle of which are those two majestic lime trees that some say date from the days of the early Georges, a helicopter rose from the other side of the wall with a whir and flutter of metal blades like an immense version of a child's top. The Duke of Edinburgh was in it, and it passed only a few yards above my head, frightening my Pekinese (then a puppy) and causing it to race with its tail down towards a clump of hornbeams whose massive strength doubtless gave him the illusion of safety. Then peace returned to both sides of the wall and, the Queen remaining at home, the royal standard went on fluttering at the top of its white pole.

But now let us hurry, in spite of my excitement, in spite of my shoes that were obviously a mistake. The joy of an afternoon like this should not be darkened by a determination to hurry along rough paths on high heels. These, however, are my favourite shoes. It is not their fault if lately I have become something of a country bumpkin.

Yes, let us hurry, because knowledgeable people say that if one arrives early one has time to explore the gardens before the Queen comes down.

The pavement in front of the palace railings was lined with a thin crowd holding guide-books and cameras. Until a short time ago the sentry boxes were here and one can clearly see where the stone is worn away by the banging of soldiers' boots as the sentries marched and noisily turned, this way, that way, incessantly, until their feet must sometimes have ached and bled. Was this toy-soldier business magnificent or ludicrous? Often, watching it, I had the strange feeling of being wafted across space and time to the days of Frederick the Great at Sans-Souci. Tall soldiers, bright uniforms—how they amuse children and frighten grown-ups!

A policeman held out his hand for the invitations, carefully checking them. Boy scouts in the forecourt ran to open the doors of cars and help people out. Now we passed into the inner courtyard or quadrangle and the sun was momentarily hidden by stonework. Then we went up the steps into the Grand Entrance Hall.

Here were cream pillars fluted with gold, veined marbles from sunny climes, glimpses past crimson silk ropes of ceremonial stairs leading to picture galleries and private apartments, rich sofas upholstered in damask too beautiful to sit upon, pink and white fuchsias, so aristocratic that their delicate bell-shaped heads drooped right down over giant porcelain bowls; then more steps and more pictures and statues along the Marble Hall and a distant vista, through another guest room, the famous Bow Room, of green lawns and the flamingoes arching and twisting their long necks as they stood delicately poised on the reed-covered shores of the lake.

Little girls reading fairy tales on wet afternoons must have conjured up pictures just like this of a queen in her palace, of a fairy prince, of the whir of wings, of a magic garden where the flamingoes were princesses transformed by a spell. Do we not all dream of spending an hour in a queen's palace just once in our lives? Now here we were, our wishes come true, and by one of the windows facing the quadrangle boy scouts were counting the invitation cards and checking the numbers printed on the back, and the mayor of a midland town was saying to the mayoress to hide his nervousness: 'If only the rain holds off! Have you ever seen anything like this?'

The corner by the boy scouts suddenly appeared familiar to me. I had been here before. My brain in some dream had paid this corner a visit. How could this mystery be explained? Then I recalled most vividly a scene in a colour film of the wedding of Princess Margaret—the Queen leading the royal party up those very stairs to the east gallery. The past was thus superimposed on the present. I felt as if I were seeing ghosts.

'I think we had better be moving along,' said the mayoress to the mayor.

There was really no hurry. We could take our time. The guests were made welcome and could walk at their ease in the palace of the Queen.

I thought I might feel shy, but I was infinitely less so than when I was first taken to the home of my future mother-in-law. Their vicarage, a farmhouse in the days of Charles I, had a garden which ran down to the Thames. Lilies of the valley grew wild, there was a mulberry tree over two hundred years old, and kingfishers fished amongst the reeds. The house and garden were exactly opposite Kew Palace, in the grounds of which poor George III chased Fanny Burney.

Before George III became insane he had bought what was then Buckingham House for a matter of £21,000. It was left to his son to do something about it. When the Prince Regent became king he decided to abandon Carlton House, which had been his town residence, and ask Nash to convert Buckingham House into a palace. This proved such an expensive business that he pulled down Carlton House to defray the expense. Thus we lost the gateway to the two Regent Streets. Though a thousand workmen hurried on the new palace, even working overtime by candle-light, George IV did not live to see it finished. Seven years later young, timid Victoria came to the throne and moved into the palace.

Here was her portrait in the Marble Hall. This in a sense is the house which she made. Her spirit, and that of all those German relations, those princes and princesses of royal blood, pervades every part of it. For instance, Maria Alexandrina, Queen of Hanover, seemed almost present in the Bow Room, while in a glass case stood the Mecklenburg-Strelitz table service of early Chelsea porcelain. Brave because I was with my husband, I found myself leading him into an adjacent room which also opens on to the gardens. It is a very fine room known, I believe, as the Household Dining Room, but more truly a sort of museum to commemorate the Emperor Louis Napoleon and his lovely but tragic Empress Eugénie. There are life-sized portraits of each of them, either by Winterhalter or after his style, and a great many pictures and souvenirs of our joint campaign in the Crimea, that brief moment when the French and English were not quarrelling. Somewhere back on my mother's side there was a Zouave of whom I have a faded photograph which I keep in a pencil box I used at school. A member of my husband's family, Lord Wantage, had stood with the colours at Alma and won the V.C. I have heard it said that it was the first, but I'm not sure. The following spring he was chosen by the Prince Consort for the post of equerry in the newly formed household of the young Prince of Wales. Here, on a table by the window, I now saw his picture. He was standing in a group of people and suddenly the room took on a friendly atmosphere, as if somebody were stretching out a hand and saying: 'You're not entirely a stranger here.'

We walked out into the garden almost dazzled by the afternoon light. On the lawn were three marquee tents where tea would presently be served. Our tent was set at right angles to the other two and this was where most guests would have their tea. One of the two facing us was for members of the Diplomatic Corps, the other for the Queen's entourage.

As we stood for a moment on the steps leading down to the lawn, I recalled lines in Virgil's *Aenid* about the building of Rome. Edifices rising up to reach the sun. There is something that makes the heart miss a beat in the sight of a noble city reaching up to the light. Here as I stood on these steps my little gasp of surprise was not so much for the beauty of this wide stretch of grass, for the lake so much larger and more irregular in shape than I expected and for the ocean of trees with their multicoloured foliage waving gently in the wind, as for the two great pillars of a new world, the Hilton Hotel in Park Lane and the gigantic Portland House in Victoria Street, which rose like mighty sentinels on either side of us. By some freak, some quirk of perspective, they appeared much nearer to us than they really were. I had the strange impression that they had been invented on purpose to lend grandeur to this dream of George IV and his architect Nash, and though I told myself that it was foolish, still as I saw them from where I stood they seemed to represent for me the pure lines and dazzling whiteness of Roman columns.

We crossed the lawn and went down to the lake where the delicate, long-legged flamingoes dipped their toes into the cool water. Their pinkness was of a shade that seemed almost unreal. There was an inlet or harbour at the water's edge where a rowing boat with shipped oars was moored. Somebody behind me said that it was here that Prince Charles learned rowing from his father. We decided to explore the whole garden and took a path which wound past azalea bushes and copper beeches and rare shrubs from the Himalayas in a direction which, if my judgment was right, was about half way between Hyde Park Corner and Victoria Station, but the outside world, except for an occasional streak of red bus flashing through the leafy branches of a tall lime tree, was so carefully hidden away by banked coppices and mounds that we might have been in the heart of the country. We walked for about forty minutes or even more and I began to rebel, for one can have a satiety of botanical specimens, stretches of lake, rose-beds and Greek temples, and I had the feeling that we should get left behind after the gates closed and be found asleep under a conifer in the morning. I wanted to go back to where the crowd was to see the Queen.

The band was playing an old-fashioned waltz and there had been great activity on the big lawn during our absence. Human avenues had been formed, two or three of them, along which presumably the Queen and her family, breaking up into separate groups, would soon walk slowly in the direction of the tea tents. As I am very small it would have been hopeless for me to fight for a place—undignified also. I stood aside for a moment and watched what was going on.

A lot of important-looking gentlemen in morning coats and

top hats were taking counsel together on the fringe of the crowd. As they were all wearing the same coloured carnation in their buttonholes, I concluded that they were there for some special purpose. Several of them ran forward a few steps, appeared to consider something carefully and then hurried back to their fellows. They looked happy but anxious. I heard one of them say: 'The sun has gone in and it may rain. So we must try to run to time.'

On the edge of a gravel path was a group of women who I felt sure must have been their relations—mothers, wives, daughters. They were tall and fair, and their cool, assured voices were the voices of ambassadors' wives in British embassies abroad. I had seen them in Madrid, in Lisbon, in Paris and The Hague. They receive one in beautiful drawing-rooms where there are signed photographs of the Queen, the Duke of Edinburgh and Sir Winston Churchill in well polished silver frames that stand on Sheraton side tables.

As my husband had momentarily deserted me, I walked over to this group of ladies who, true to their upbringing, gave me the sort of smile that says: 'Come and make yourself at home.' They talked not so much to one another as to all their friends at the same time. Their English was exquisitely poised, but not at all affected, and it was clear at once that they knew everybody and all the ropes. I gathered that the anxious-looking gentlemen were Gentlemen at Arms who on state occasions (such as the Opening of Parliament) wear plumes. Lord Cobbold, the Lord Chamberlain, crossed the gravel path to a farther lawn to receive the Queen and the royal family. Suddenly the band struck up the National Anthem and everybody stood to attention. From where we were the Queen, the Queen Mother, the Duchess of Kent and Princess Alexandra looked in their summer dresses like a bouquet of flowers. The Queen was dressed in exactly the same colour as the flamingoes by the lake, and she was so small and slim that I found the scene infinitely touching and burst into tears. The sound of 'God Save the Queen' was deafening and seemed to sail over the top of Buckingham Palace—away, away, over St James's Park to Nelson standing on his column in Trafalgar Square. When it was all over people relaxed and the Queen, followed by the Duke of Edinburgh, talked to one or two people on this special piece of lawn on the other side of the path.

Presently they began to walk towards us. The Queen Mother was in white and the Duchess of Kent in emerald green with a hat that frequently demanded attention from her gloved hand because there was a wind blowing up and dark clouds were hurrying across the sky. The ladies beside me watched the scene.

'I remember during that last summer at Delhi——'

'Did you really dine at the White House? What did the President say?'

'I positively know that my nose is shining, but one just can't do anything about it here, can one? It's like in church——'

'Well, here they come. . . . Give me a ring tonight. I'm dying to hear about your journey. . . .'

The royal party crossed the path in front of us. The Queen Mother gave us all a beaming smile which seemed to embrace the entire world. I have a photograph in Normandy of my son, aged eight, presenting her with a bouquet at the Royal Command Performance which followed the making of his film *The Fallen Idol*. Her smile on that night of triumph seemed to leap across the years, and I found it again in front of me, just as warm, just as delightful. She had a way of allowing her smile to linger a moment so that you felt the warmth of it in your eyes. The Queen had already started to go down one avenue, very slowly, having people pointed out to her as she went, stopping a moment to have a word with them, and now the Queen Mother was about to enter the second avenue. They would meet presently in a sort of fairy circle in front of the diplomatic tent.

But here was Lord Louis Mountbatten.

One day earlier in the year I had met a very charming woman when I was walking with my dog in Green Park. She also had a dog, but hers was one of those beautiful Mexican creatures known as chihuahua. We therefore took to sitting together on the same bench facing the palace wall.

I soon discovered that this gifted person had been a close friend of Lady Louis.

If, in my youth, I could have been anybody else but myself I would without the slightest hesitation have chosen to be Lady Louis. I saw her for the first time at Brook House, one of the last great private mansions in Park Lane to remind us of what this street must have looked like in the days of its aristocratic prosperity. Eventually it had to come down like the rest and modern flats were built on the site, the Mountbattens reserving themselves a penthouse at the top.

There was some sort of committee meeting with a fork luncheon, and afterwards, when the others had gone, my husband and I remained for a little while alone with Lady Louis and Lady Brecknock. It was in winter and fog shrouded the trees in Hyde Park, but in the vast room the chandeliers were lit and gave the impression of warmth and sunshine. We were all very young, and I even remember the hat I was wearing. I had liked it very much when I put it on in the apartment in Beauchamp Place where we were then living, but by the end of the afternoon I hated it.

Lady Louis was wearing a summer ermine coat which seemed sculptured on her slim, beautifully proportioned body. It was a very new fur at that time, light, silky, chestnut-coloured, and worn in the afternoon. Her small hat was tilted off the forehead and she had fastened a large diamond clip against the brim. These clips also were very new and had replaced the diamond brooch. They were to become the rage in what one might call the Prince of Wales society. Lady Brecknock, slim also and very blonde, had a silvery laugh that set me curiously at ease. I remember her taking me by the arm to show me some picture she was interested in. I think we had only been there a short while when we were joined by the then Begum Aga Khan, a young woman with the clearest blue eyes, wearing a black velvet suit, the collar of which was of white ermine. Her black velvet beret was worn at a rakish angle and on to its brim she also had fastened a diamond clip.

Lady Louis and Lady Brecknock had been to the first night of Richard Tauber's *Land of Smiles*, in which, of course, he had sung his famous 'You are my Heart's Delight', and while explaining all this to us Lady Louis quoted the words in German so naturally that I doubt if she ever realized that she had changed from one language to another. Her French was impeccable, and if anyone expressed surprise at how fluently she spoke so many tongues, she would answer that just as there were five senses—sight, hearing, smell, taste and touch—so the blood of five nationalities flowed in her veins.

The King of Spain used to stay at Claridges when he came to London, and as Lady Louis had become his cousin by marriage

Alfonso XIII used to walk down Brook Street and ring the bell at Brook House, where he would be invited to lunch. Lady Louis showed us how she could make the big dining-room smaller and more intimate by sliding doors. 'That', she said, 'is how I like to capture my cousin, the King of Spain.'

After that we used to meet her dancing the blues at Ciro's or the Embassy Club. On such occasions she often wore one of those tight-fitting dresses by Molyneux in her favourite tints of aquamarine.

A most impressive spectacle was before me. The Queen and the Queen Mother, each continuing slowly along converging avenues, were about to join up in the magic circle now surrounded by Yeomen of the Guard. These rugged men looked just as though they had stepped out of the reign of Henry VIII. They were gorgeously attired with the Tudor rose embroidered all over their uniforms and rosettes flopping over their shoes.

'Have they come from the Tower, darling?'

The woman beside me looked up anxiously at her tall husband.

'Not at all,' he answered importantly. 'Nothing to do with the Tower. They are the Queen's Bodyguard of the Yeoman of the Guard.'

'Like in Gilbert and Sullivan?'

'Hush, dear. They might hear you.'

'What do they do in ordinary life? They seem so fierce.'

'Smoke their pipes by the fire, I expect, and watch TV.'

I was standing just where the Queen's avenue joined the grass circle. The Gentlemen Ushers showed fresh signs of perturbation. They grasped their slips of paper and ran this way and that, anxiously looking at their watches. The chief of the Yeomen of the Guard was a powerfully built man and his splendid appearance was made even more impressive by the clear cut face and strong neck that were visible above the white ruff of his uniform. Clutching his murderous looking partizan he exchanged a few polite words with one of the Gentlemen Ushers who wore a black patch over one eye.

'Not too bad, I must say. Not too bad. Actually we may be a

moment or two ahead of schedule, but it's the devil to keep the way clear. Madam, do you mind? Of course. Of course.'

The Queen was coming. Another usher arrived. His eyes swept along our row and suddenly fixed the timid little woman on my left. What on earth had she done? What was her crime? He was a typical military man and I pictured him on the parade ground suddenly noticing that one of the soldiers had arrived without a rifle or a belt. Now he was preparing to do something. I trembled for my neighbour. But there was now no anger in his expression. He pointed a weather-beaten index finger at the regimental brooch the timid little woman was wearing and exclaimed:

'The Buffs, eh? The Buffs? Capital! Capital!'

His white moustaches, for he was rather old, shook with violent approval and his whole face had a conspiratorial smile. His cheeks and the tips of his ears were tinged with a becoming flush . . . but quick as a flash he disappeared.

'Retired senior officers—lieutenant-colonels and above. That's what they are,' said a voice behind me. 'Possibly his own regiment. The brooch was sure to catch his eye.'

This swift-moving scene left me pensive. Why must we all have our pasts shut up inside us like closed books? This timid little woman whom I would not have noticed otherwise had not quite closed her book. A stranger with white moustaches was able to look quickly into it and discover part of her secret. How quickly he struck! Possibly she would remember the scene to the end of her days.

The Queen is fortunate. As is the custom on all such occasions there were gentlemen near her whose duty it was to point out guests and say: 'This one did this. That one wrote a symphony. The person you are going to shake hands with next built a bridge. The one with dark hair discovered a new drug. The woman with white hair is a saint.'

She smiled at each one rather sadly as if in spite of her youth and the freshness of her face her mind was full of understanding.

But now it was tea time and the tents were full of food.

Down by the water the flamingoes had been busy.

They had waded, delicate leg by delicate leg, across the shallow water and were now grouped at the back of the royal tent, in which there was an opening. They gazed curiously through this opening at the Queen, who was wearing their precise shade of pink. The Queen was herself such a slim and delicate figure that she looked like some beautiful reflection of them—or was it they of her? Nothing I saw that afternoon could compare with the ethereal quality of this scene or to the seeming unreality of it, which gave one the impression of living in a fairy story.

The Queen's guests glanced furtively at the uncut chocolate cakes, but few of them were brave enough to break the spell.

I had not noticed until now how many of the guests came from distant lands and wore their native costumes. I saw Japanese girls crossing a little bridge over the lake, three at a time, giggling and twittering while they hardly touched the ground with their tiny feet. Girls from the Philippines wore multicoloured blouses with wings on their shoulders and their young men wore blouses, also of silk, so fine that they looked like moonbeams. The infinite variety in costume no longer made it necessary for European men to wear traditional morning dress. I was glad that my husband came in a dark lounge suit. I felt more certain that he was mine and not a stranger in disguise.

Rain began to fall lightly and the Queen decided to go home, but she did so with seeming reluctance, and several times turned to talk again to one or other of her guests. Then somebody put up a man's umbrella and she walked under it across the private strip of lawn in front of the royal tent.

The chief of the Yeomen of the Guard was standing by the wicker gate, looking very proud. The Queen went past, and then the Duke of Edinburgh. I have seldom seen anything like the salute of the chief of the Yeomen of the Guard. I thought he was going to disrupt the whole of his gigantic frame, but I swear that the Duke of Edinburgh winked at him; and then the chief of the Yeomen of the Guard gave a huge smile. It was at these moments that the Duke was at his best.

I stayed a moment drinking tea and eating chocolate cake. The waitresses who had been serving in the open air all donned light plastic capes over their uniforms, and from a distance looked like moths fluttering across the grass. The rain was not enough to bother about, however, and we decided to walk home across Green Park.

It was time for me to see what was happening on the other side of the wall!

We re-entered the Bow Room, crossed the Grand Entrance Hall with its cream and gold pillars and fuchsias in porcelain bowls, circumnavigated (because of my high heels) the gravel of the quadrangle, traversed the forecourt and, passing out by the iron gates, became once more normal citizens of London.

The rain had stopped, but Green Park smelt of moss and damp grass. The plane trees on either side of the path leading to Piccadilly appeared taller than when I had seen them last and their foliage was so thick, forming an arch above our heads, that the evening light was filtered, as in a wood.

It was as if Green Park had suffered some slight change. Many of the trees are forest trees and have grown to great height, and there seemed a stillness here, a mysteriousness that was quite the opposite of what we had seen on the other side of the wall, where much of the beauty of the gardens is due to sheets of calm water and light.

Here, under the maple trees, lovers sauntered hand in hand and talked in low tones to each other. The habitués sat on benches. When one lives in Piccadilly or in the purlieus of St James's one gets to know most of the habitués, who nearly all have dogs which need to be exercised. On my way home it seemed strange to me to meet so many of my friends sitting here as if nothing had happened to make this particular day different from any other. When we experience something important or wonderful it is natural to want others to understand and share our emotions.

'What a noise that loudspeaker is making,' said a woman in grey.

'They're calling the cars,' I said, 'on account of the garden party. I saw a palace servant in the Marble Hall right opposite the portrait of the Prince Consort talking into a machine. He was giving out the names.'

'There must have been a great crowd. Did you see Lord Louis Mountbatten?'

'Yes—why?'

'His younger daughter Pamela is in King's College Hospital expecting another baby. I hope it's a boy. They have already prepared the nursery—white organdie trimmed with emerald green. The father thought of it.'

'It seems strange——' I began.

'What? About the organdie? It's very pretty, and fathers take a great interest these days.'

'No—strange to think that Lady Louis's daughter is already a young mother and expecting her second baby. The wedding seems such a short time ago. By the way, does she speak French?'

'Impeccably. But then she's good at everything. When she has had her baby she plans to visit her aunt, the Queen of Sweden. Then perhaps she will go to Russia. Lady W—— has just come back from Moscow and was enchanted. Absolutely enchanted——'

'I can well understand that. I would hate to die without having gone there. If I could be granted a second wish——'

'You haven't told us about your first?'

'My first? Oh, I think I have just had it.'

'Then tell us. What was it?'

'No, that would be unwise. Telling might spoil it.'

'Oh, look! How very amusing!'

'Where?'

'The young man in the black overcoat who has a corgi on a lead.'

'Is there anything unusual about him?'

'Let us wait and see!'

Half a dozen deck chairs were piled against a thorn tree. The young man took one of them, set it up and, divesting himself of his black overcoat, folded it carefully and laid it on the chair. He was wearing livery of which the buttons shone brightly in the evening light. As it was warm he also removed the jacket of his livery. Then he released the corgi.

A suspicion crossed my mind.

'Whose corgi is it?'

'The Queen Mother's. I expect they are busy today.'

2

MY HUSBAND had decided to spend a week on the farm, so we set off together on the Friday by the night boat to Le Havre, where I found my car waiting at the dockside.

The early morning drive through the back streets of the city, across the suspension bridge at Tancarville and from there through sleepily awakening villages, brought me great peace of mind. I responded to the sights and smells of the Pays d'Auge— old women milking in orchards; half-timbered houses roofed with small iridescent slates of a kind I have never seen elsewhere or thatched with straw or reeds and crowned with irises; long low cider presses with rickety outside stairs leading to hay-lofts which are curiously gabled at one end; gardens filled with old-fashioned roses; cafés which are stopping-places for long-distance buses, as they have been for many a long day; smells such as the smell of river mud and sea brine; of milk being carried in churns on the saddles of donkeys; of hot crisp bread stacked in tall osier baskets in not-yet-open bakers' shops. All this was what I had come to think of as home, and as if to welcome me the mist which had hung over the estuary on our starting forth was lifting, and by the time we reached Honfleur the sun was warm enough to add colour and excitement to the setting up of stalls and parasols in that small market which, situated beside a famous and ancient hostelry, is at its busiest on a Saturday morning.

We took the old road by the sea, less steep than the Côte de Grâce and flanked by tall trees but too winding and narrow for modern traffic. Lucie Delarue-Mardrus, who sang the praises of this part of the world better than anybody since Flaubert and Maupassant, lived here when she wrote *L'Enfant au Coq*. I had not taken this road since Chamberlain declared war on Hitler at the end of that nerve-wracking summer of 1939. I recalled sitting

on a terrace overlooking the estuary and knowing—yes, knowing
—that the lights were about to be extinguished for the second
time in my life; aware of what it meant, helpless and mortally
afraid. I had a baby in arms at the time. It was a desire to redis-
cover the terraced garden that brought me back now. That other
time we had come here on a hot afternoon in a hired car. None of
us had any doubt that the thing was about to happen, the sombre,
inescapable tragedy into which we would be inexorably drawn.
The Continent, unlike England, was alarmingly certain of the
inevitability of war. Yet that utter darkness we envisaged, that
tunnel of marching feet, of Gestapo men and extermination
camps, did not engulf all of us, and today it seemed long ago,
unreal, and slightly absurd, like seeing the ghosts of people
fleeing from Uhlans during the war of 1870 or hiding Royalists
during the Terror. Our fears had merged with the fears of past
generations caught up in events we had not known but only read
about. Soon who would care what we had thought when Hitler
was about to invade Europe? Meanwhile I would be wiser to
concern myself with trivialities, like wondering whether Georgette
had remembered to fill up the Aga, and if it would be radiating
its usual welcoming warmth.

A straggling row of Edwardian villas built on the edge of the
sand is the beginning of our village when one drives in from the
direction of Deauville. They are boarded up in winter, but
summer residents who live in bikinis or shorts can almost jump
out of their beds into the sea at high tide. At low tide they are
separated from it by nearly half a mile of golden sand, along
which people like to ride on horseback in the early morning. In a
few more years the sand dunes will no doubt be covered by
cement, but for the moment sand blows from the sea across the
highway and poppies grow between tufts of coarse grass and
little mounds of powdered sea shells.

By twenty minutes past eight I had parked my car in the triangle
formed by two cafés, their outside tables and the side window of
the baker's shop. I had arrived well before the passing of the bus
from Le Havre to Caen, and though I could hardly claim to have
done the journey in quick time—Jacques Poirot would have
thought me as slow as a snail—I felt that my initiative in leaving

the car at Le Havre and driving it back was a satisfactory achievement. Most other women would have taken this sort of thing in their stride. In American stories young women drive along the highway at eighty miles an hour. I was happy when I reached my destination safely. Speed was never my ambition. Perhaps I was fortunate in continuing to find obstacles to surmount. I had wanted to surprise my husband, and now his pleasure was as great as mine. Moments like these compensated for the inevitable disappointments of life.

Our baker's pretty young wife was sitting at the cash desk. Her husband arrived, wiping flour off his hands and arms, and she called to him to choose me two long loaves of bread baked lightly the way I liked them. For her it was just another morning. The holiday season kept her busy from dawn till after ten at night. She thought that I had come straight down from the farm as usual.

Driving down the track that Raiteault had built so cunningly across my orchard, I peered through the branches of the apple and pear trees for a glimpse of my house. I was always afraid that it would have gone, or that something might have happened to it during my absence. But there it was, with the sun gleaming on the slates, the half-timbering winking at me from behind the rose trees, the swallows lined up on the telephone wires, my four hens perched on the long green wooden seat at the foot of the peach tree. The cows, all twenty of them, were huddled against the stable wall. They looked at us intelligently from under their low eyelashes as if to say: 'It's going to be a hot day. We're glad of the shade. Where on earth have you been?'

We left the car in the patio out of their reach and ran into the kitchen.

Yes, the Aga was alive and the house had a feeling of being just as I had left it. Georgette and her daughter had been here after milking time—they would have milked in the home orchard up by the walnut trees—and everything had been made spick and span for my homecoming. The chairs had been polished, the table against the window was laid ready for breakfast.

I put on water for coffee and started to unpack the bags that my husband had brought in from the car. There were paint boxes for Brigitte, my farmer's daughter, and for Nathalie Durville and Anne Poirot, and a box of crackers to celebrate Philippe Poirot's third birthday in September. These had been the most difficult to find. Shop assistants could not understand why I wanted to stock in so early for Christmas. At the Scotch House in Knightsbridge I had bought a length of tartan for Patsy, who wanted to make an autumn skirt. She wanted something with red in it, so I chose a MacGregor, and for myself I took a length of Lindsay, because through my husband I had some right to it and I liked its sombre shades. From the Scotch House I had gone to Harrods, where I bought a superb Chinese marriage blanket, orange on one side, shocking pink on the other, trimmed with wide bands of grass-green shiny satin. They were the most beautiful blankets I had ever seen and whenever I wanted one Harrods ordered it specially from the manufacturers in the midlands.

My husband was already examining his rose trees and exclaiming about the lavender that grew in massive ciumps and was alive with bees. We welcomed them because they pollinate the apple trees, but there was no longer the hive behind the slates under my bedroom window. A blackbird had stolen it for her nest. A large hungry family had been brought up there. In the autumn I would have to see what damage they had done.

We breakfasted at the table I had recently moved near the kitchen window. I felt an urge after my mother's death to change things round so as not always to be seeing the empty chair at the place where she used to remain motionless, her poor hands folded on her lap. From the table where it now was, I could see through the open window into the garden where, because I no longer had any cats, birds of every kind came to delight me. My husband approved of this slight alteration, and that was something else I was glad about. The kitchen appeared larger and one could pass more easily through the always open door into what had once been my mother's room, but which I had now turned into a sewing-room and boudoir to save me from continually having to go upstairs. There was a tall Norman cupboard, on the top of which (like the peasants used to do) I put jam as I made it from the fruit in the orchard. When I was little, jam was a treat and a recompense, not to be handed out lightly, and my grandmother used to keep her pots locked away, the key hidden in a pocket in her underskirts.

The kitchen garden, of which I was proud a month ago, with the grass clipped, the paths weeded, vegetables in neat rows, had

suddenly become a jungle. Grass grew so fast and tall that I really
believed that if I had the patience to sit down in front of a tuft of
it, I would see it grow as one does in slow-motion films.

Death hit our village twice that summer in quick succession:
first, our beloved Dr Lehérissey, perfect example of a Norman
country doctor, secondly, without warning and in all the splendour of his herculean strength, Raiteault, our big-hearted woodcutter. He knew more about trees than any man I have ever met
and, with the carpenter, Longuet, was a great comfort to me
exactly a year earlier when my mother died. That May morning
he and his men had lifted my mother's oak coffin from the hearse
and reverently placed it in the tiny medieval church at Auberville
where she lay under the blanched beams until after Ascension Day.
I thought of him as so strong—tough like the mighty trees he
felled.

He was felled as suddenly and as quickly as he brought down
an oak with the axe. He was taken to Caen in an ambulance; the
next morning he was dead. His strength had been a source of
constant amazement to me. His wrists and torso were like those
of Tarzan, but he was gentleness itself and I never knew him
refuse to do a kindness.

When I needed an urgent piece of work done, like the building
of my road or the clearing of my garden, he would arrive the next
morning very early, long before I was awake, before even the
cows were milked, with a gang of three or four men whom he
would have recruited from neighbouring farms. Whatever had to
be done was accomplished with the speed of a magical task in a
fairy story, so that by nightfall one came to expect the palace to be
built or the road finished.

He took it for granted that he would be rewarded on the same
noble scale, and indeed I never knew my husband argue with
Raiteault—their regard for each other was too deep. It was
enough that as soon as we sent for him he would appear like a
genie waiting for our command. He would split three-foot logs
and stack them with such precision that they looked end-on like
squares on a draughtboard. The last time he was with us I heard
my husband saying to him: 'Are you sure, M. Raiteault, that this
is a piece of elm?', and Raiteault's deep-throated laughing answer:

'Oh, M. Henrey, believe me, if there's anything I know about, it's wood!'

Now the grass in my kitchen garden had grown half as tall as a man, hiding the red currants and the black currants and the gooseberries on the bushes, throttling the strawberry beds —and there was no Raiteault to come with his men and cut it down.

So it was not long before I heard the sound of a sickle cutting grass rhythmically under the pine trees which skirt the kitchen garden, and I knew that my husband was trying to do the work of four men. So I took up a sickle and went to join him.

When my son was still quite small we had planted a row of Norway spruce just inside the railings dividing the south end of the kitchen garden from the orchard. Our first idea was that they would give us a plantation from which we could draw on Christmas trees, which are not indigenous to this part of the country. Rather to my surprise they immediately took to the soil, and did so well that in due course they began to reach considerable height, so that we were loath to cut any of them down. Except that they formed a picturesque curtain and may to some extent have cut the wind, they were of no financial profit to the farm. Our neighbours, who had the age-old peasant regard for money, considered them an interesting folly. We had relatively so much land to play about with that we were always experimenting with trees. Doing something merely for the fun of it seemed a reasonable way of compensating for much of the necessary but rather dull expenditure which any undertaking such as ours entails. The sort of tree planting we embarked on was too uninformed and haphazard to prove a real success. The sudden remembrance of a much-enjoyed chestnut soup inspired my husband to send for two dozen young trees from Agen, in the Lot-et-Garonne, but of these only three survived and one was planted much too near the hedge. The fact that his mother had made remarkable quince jam, from quince trees that had flourished amazingly because their roots were continually flooded by the muddy water of the Thames at Kew, made him put young quince trees down in the dampest part of the home orchard. None of these prospered, however. On the other hand the walnut trees we planted did splendidly. Some peach trees gave fabulous fruit, then died. Plum trees were unpredictable. Cherry trees grew so fast that we could never find enough ladders to reach to the top, and the birds were up earlier than we were in the morning.

All this is to explain what my husband was doing with a sickle under his Christmas trees and why I went out to help him.

Wherever we worked, whether in the flower garden in front of the house or in the kitchen garden, the cows, if they happened to be in the home orchard, would invariably come to see that we were doing. We would look up to find them peering over the barrier trying to attract our attention. Their desire for human companionship was quite surprising. If we were in the flower garden they would try to nibble at the climbing roses through the wire netting. If a rose was imprudent enough to poke its lovely head over the top of the barrier it would be eaten—foliage, thorns and stem. Thorns were no deterrent. But if our cows enjoyed eating our roses it was in part because they enjoyed being near the house. If we had forgotten to close a gate I think we would have found them in the kitchen. During a drought I was naïve enough to take out a pail of water. The animals that drank from it followed me ever afterwards with signs of affectionate gratitude. Even in stormy weather, when they were apt to go mad and career down the orchard in follow-my-leader fashion and then turn round and come up again, they never frightened us. One had merely to call gently and they would either stop or dance to one side almost comically as in a ballet, for in spite of their size they were light on their feet. There was no reason, of course, why they should not be friendly. They were extremely privileged and, even if we did not count them sacred as in India, they were accorded great consideration. Our farmers would milk them in the orchard in which they happened to be. Nobody herded them into a cowshed. Georgette and the woman who helped her at milking time talked to the cows with marked politeness, never raising their voices, not even getting angry if a cow accidentally upset a churn. They would be treated thus till they became old or sterile. Then the world could become cruel. They ceased to have a place in society.

In a different way the thing happens to humans and I was always terrified of my own physical powers declining. What would happen to my domain when I could no longer dig, hoe or wield a sickle? Would I also become a drag on society? The scythe frightens me. I would not dream of using it, but I rather like the sickle. However, I lack the suppleness which comes naturally to a man when he uses it. I tire my wrist. I exhaust myself and am then appalled to contemplate how little I have done and how quickly that little will need to be re-done. How could I ever keep up the kitchen garden without the occasional help of Raiteault and his goodly men?

Raiteault had been removed from us, as I have already said, in the course of a half-year which had been saddened by the death of Dr Lehérissey. The good doctor had played such an important role in my life that I could not fail to be deeply affected. He had remained at the farmhouse during the whole terrible night preceding my difficult confinement. But this was not nearly all. During our flight to England in 1940 he arranged for us to be given hospitality in a small manor house he owned in the Cotentin south of Cherbourg. After the battle of Caen five years later he was the first to send us news of the farm, a few lines scribbled on a sheet of paper to say that though it had been emptied of all its contents, by some miracle the house had remained intact. He had tended my mother, once saved my husband's life. Mado, one of his daughters, was married to Gaston Duprez. He was in many respects the essence, the flavour of the village, and in recent years when he was no longer able to follow his profession he had been during the summer months the king-pin of our reunions on the sands. We would all sit at his feet while he told us stories of his youth, of all the families he had known. There was not a castle, a manor house, a farmhouse, not even a tumbledown barn or a cider press for fifty miles round that he did not know about. Here he had seen a man dying, there he had brought a baby into the world, there he had put a broken leg into splints. As a young doctor he had criss-crossed the Pays d'Auge on a bicycle, then in a pony trap, and then, as he grew older and more financially important, in his car. His understanding of the Norman mind was as subtle and as affectionate as his knowledge about Norman chests and cupboards, Calvados and cider, customs and beliefs, fairs and market places, barrels and casks, duck-shooting and trout-fishing, legal quibbles and rights of way. He was a gourmet and a *raconteur* and an excellent husband, though nothing of a prude. The handling of money bored him, for he came of a class and of a generation who thought that there were so many more exciting things to do than count it and worry about it. At first

B

sight his wife gave the impression of being extremely witty but a little scatter-brained. In fact she was almost a financial genius. She combined small talk about her maids and what she was going to concoct for dinner with penetrating views about the Bourse or the value of farmland. She was also apt to turn disconcertingly from thoughts raised by the reading of a volume of romantic fiction to what had struck her during the perusal of the Officiel de la Bourse. The doctor's wisdom, so striking in all matters, was not least on such occasions. He left her to follow her hunches, entrusting his earnings to her, so that indeed their partnership was most complete.

In the doctor's early days these small seaside resorts so near to Trouville and Deauville attracted a mixture of aristocratic and artistic families who owned their own villas. Playwrights, singers, novelists, actors, musicians—all those who were responsible for the brilliance of the Paris of their day came to relax here. Our country doctor, therefore, could count on having at his table many of these as well as the great lights of the medical profession who followed the people they most admired. Dr Lehérissey recalled glittering nights at the Casino, memorable theatrical occasions which he never succeeded in witnessing to the end. Somebody was certain to come to him during the evening with a message that a patient on some distant farm needed him. Then it would be the lonely and probably muddy journey along narrow, cart-rutted lanes, under arches of elms, skirting orchards in which apple trees made eerie shapes in the night.

I never knew a man so completely happy in his retirement. He liked those mornings on the beach when we all arrived to laze in the sun in front of the bathing-tents. Every summer brought a new batch of children, and though he would quote Julian Huxley on the problem of over-population he was the tenderest and most indulgent grandfather. The women knitted, gossiped, read or dozed in this magic circle, but whatever we did we had one eye on the children and one ear attentive to what the doctor happened to be saying. Thus I remember snatches of his monologues. Once he said that for a doctor to read a book which was not a medical treatise was in some respects a theft, because in the medical profession one never caught up with all there was to learn. I used to tell him how depressed I was at being so stupid with a car. My pride suffered. I hated seeing people slip their cars swiftly into a narrow space along the kerb and never turn a hair when a policeman put out his arm or made some sign. He encouraged me, saying that though he had driven by day and by night for three-quarters of a lifetime, in good weather and bad weather, but mostly in mud and hail or rain, there was always some little thing more to learn. What he liked most was arriving in the middle of the night at some lonely farm where a light would be burning in the bedroom, often a candle or an oil lamp, but 'a sign that my presence was needed', he would say, and that would be enough to make up for his tiredness and loss of sleep. There would be long waits if the baby was slow to arrive. The family would give him strong coffee with a drop of Calvados, an owl would hoot and the night hours pass. Dawn would break. The men would sit round the table, sometimes polishing their guns for the opening of the shooting season, when they could go duck-shooting or looking for a pheasant or a hare. As the bottle went round, tongues would be loosed and stories told—those stories which the good doctor stored up in his mind and now brought out for our amusement as we sleepily listened to him on the sands. 'I have driven a car since the days when the sight of a car was a rarity,' he once said. 'The day I bought my first one I hadn't the faintest idea how to drive. The man who was to give me a driving licence came in to sit beside me. He showed me the gears and said: "You do this and that," and put his hand over mine. We went as far as the bridge over the River Touques and from there up one of those steep, narrow streets leading to the church in the old part of Trouville. There were pony traps and governess carts and peasants driving donkeys with produce for market. The car was boiling over by the time we reached the top of the street, so we turned round and came down again, and back over the bridge and so home. My shirt and collar were limp with sweat. "Well," said the instructor, "we've got back safely. That's all that matters. So here's your driving licence and a very good morning, doctor." A trifle primitive, maybe, but I drove for sixty years and it's only recently because my sight is not what it used to be that I've given up.'

Occasionally, when we stayed late on the sands and Mme Lehérissey had gone home to make lunch, I offered to drive the doctor back, and he always accepted joyfully. He was not the man to criticize. On the contrary he would say the nicest things, and

he once added: 'We all get it into our heads that there are things
we ought to do better. The solution is to do that thing as often as
possible in the most difficult conditions. As a young doctor
certain problems terrified me. A candle would blow out in the
middle of a complicated confinement. I was called to deliver
women who lived more or less with their animals on lonely
farms. A cow or a horse might wander into the tumbledown
hovel where the woman was in bed and over would go the table
on which I had put my instruments. As likely as not I would find
myself in the dark. But those were the hazards of a country doctor's profession, and when I look back on them I merely see what
was amusing or colourful. One is even apt to regret the un-
hygienic but picturesque. The important thing was to do it over
and over again so that it became second nature.'

These often repeated trips into what we sometimes called the
'interior', the rich dairy land behind the sea, filled his mind with
rare local knowledge. One summer on the beach I deplored the
fact that I had grown more broad beans than I knew what to do
with. I feared to see them grow hard. 'Bring me a few,' he said.
'I never can buy any at market and they are a favourite dish of
mine. At one time farmers' wives used to plant them between
their rows of potatoes. The theory was that the pests that attacked
the potatoes had a liking for the leaves of the broad bean, and
if they found them near at hand, they went on those instead.
So when I had left my patient I was often taken into the
kitchen garden and offered a basket of broad beans. In that way I
learned to appreciate them.' Encouraged by the doctor's story
I would take some to his wife in the early morning when I was
sure to find her in her kitchen, a big airy room that opened
out on to a veranda. The doctor would not be up yet, but the
grandchildren, Estelle and Didier, would as likely as not be
drinking their morning coffee out of bowls, as the custom
still was.

These houses in the villages always struck me as cold in
summer. The chimneys had been swept, stoves taken down and
the winter's supply of coal or wood not yet delivered. It was often
in small things that I learned to appreciate my own house with its
big, old-fashioned hearth. On blustering, damp days—and it was
too often either one or the other even in the height of summer—
I would go out into the orchard and pick up dead twigs or

branches from under the hedges or apple trees and make a fire. When my husband was there he would often burn large logs that would keep a friendly blaze going through the day and half the night, but I found them heavy to handle and was haunted by a strange sorrow for all the forest trees that must have been consumed, during the last four hundred and eight years, in this giant fireplace with its great supporting pillars of Caen stone. I hated to see a tree cut down. On the other hand when a dead apple tree was uprooted by the wind—and this was always happening in the orchards—I would be the first to think of it in terms of wonderful, sweet-scented firewood. Like my mother and my grandmother I would put on an apron and drag the unwieldy, moss-covered branches back home.

Looking through the books in Patsy's library—I was standing on one of those ladders specially designed to enable one to reach the top shelves—I came across a volume entitled *John Halifax, Gentleman*, by Mrs Craik. Not unnaturally I am interested in the works of women writers, and was surprised not to have heard of Mrs Craik. Fortunately there was a brief biography. Born at Stoke-on-Trent, she married in 1864 a partner in the publishing firm of Macmillan and produced nearly fifty books of novels, essays and verse.

I borrowed the volume and read it that night in bed. The England of exactly a hundred years ago seemed further away than I had hitherto imagined: The hero—a Quaker, whose dialogue was enriched with the charming 'thee' and 'thou'—was a tanner by trade and his path was chequered by those two nightmares of the past—hunger and overwork. But what pasture for the novelist! These harbingers of illness and premature death upon which Mrs Craik, in common with other writers of her period, drew for her emotional scenes can no longer affect us, at least in the same way. Her world is more remote than that of the peasant who four centuries ago built my house. Or perhaps I suffer from this delusion because my fireplace has not changed its appetite for consuming tree trunks, whereas John Halifax, Gentleman, has no longer his counterpart in this modern age. I fear that Mrs Craik would be shocked beyond measure by our literature of brutality and sex. But at least in this year of 1963 she has had yet another reader in myself. As I put the book down and switched off the light it struck me what a pity it was that she could not have known of our brief encounter at the end of her first hundred years of modest fame.

On market days a man stands behind his stall, wearing a smock. He knows that people will stop and exclaim: 'Ah, those were the days!' When he has gathered a dozen people round him he cuts off thin slices of dried sausage and offers them to the crowd on pieces of crusty home-made bread. 'Back to the simple life!' he cries. 'None of your pharmaceutical food!' His sausages sell briskly and he cashes in on the same sentiments that make people flock to a five-ton lorry disguised as an old-fashioned mail coach with horses made of painted wood riding astride the bonnet.

At 4 p.m. Brigitte, sheltering under a tiny red umbrella, came down the orchard with a miniature tea-set under her arm.

I laid the table by the window in the kitchen and we pretended to be ladies having tea in the parlour. The tea was Earl Grey, from Fortnum and Mason, and as Brigitte by now had learned to scald the teapot and put in just the right amount, the party was a great success. After it was over I said to her:

'You can put your tea-service away in the cupboard if you like. As it's still raining you'll have enough work holding up your umbrella.'

Brigitte had not yet learned the art of hiding her feelings. Her expression became clouded. I detected apprehension and deep thought.

'No!' she said after a moment. 'One never knows. After all, it's mine.'

I watched her hurrying home across the orchard, clutching her tea-set in its cardboard box, holding up her red umbrella which bounced up and down like a poppy on its stem. Then the rain stopped, the sun came out and I decided to go into the kitchen garden and look for a lettuce.

When Mary Tudor was reigning in England, the occupants of my house put up a three-roomed building in which the women baked their bread. The outside is half-timbered and inside one can still see the big oven. As it stands in the kitchen garden we use it as a tool shed.

Three years ago a women's magazine offered to send its readers some rose trees at half price. I sent for two which I planted on either side of the bakery door. One, like the seed in the parable, must have found stony ground, for it withered and died; the other took a liking to the soil and prospered exceedingly, putting forth roses of delicate salmon pink. The grass here, as everywhere else, had grown too high and I was just wondering what to do about it when something moved against the wall, low down at the side of the rose tree, and I had the sensation of being watched.

I remained quite still for a moment. Then I bent down and parted the tall grass, bringing into view the top part of a large white cat whose grey ears, cocked up, made it look as if it was wearing a fur bonnet. My mother had a mania for describing animals as if they were dressed-up people. I must have inherited this trait from her. The cat didn't move, but it looked at me with huge anxious eyes and I then became aware of two more pointed ears lower down beside it. I gave a small gasp of surprise. The mother made off like an india-rubber ball bouncing through the grass, her offspring streaking behind her.

'The thieves,' I thought. 'They were after my garden peas.'

The trouble was that my husband had merely cut the grass under his Christmas trees. He invariably did what interested him most. The trees, he said, were there for ever; the peas grew up and were eaten.

Only a year or two ago I could work for a whole morning cutting grass with the sickle. Nothing depresses me so much as the thought that every summer I tire more quickly. I love to hurl my energy into this type of work. Cut grass smells delicious and a cabbage patch all ready for planting gives me a greater sense of achievement than a dozen foolscap pages covered with my writing. From time to time a toad would leap out from the still uncut grass and then turn round and look at me with his big intelligent eyes. I once saved a toad from the claws of a cat, and when I held it in my cupped hands I was surprised to feel its little heart beating so fast. I like them because, though they are ugly and cold to the touch, their heads have a human expression.

They show fear, affection and gratitude. On another occasion, when Raiteault and his men were clearing the garden, something came swiftly towards me. It was a snake. It stopped a couple of yards away from me and appeared to consider my presence. As upon first seeing it I had not felt particularly afraid, I found myself calmly looking for the V which spreads terror in the human mind. Was this an adder? I could recognize no marking on its head, and the fact that it remained sunning itself at my feet suggested that it had a clear conscience. I forebore to call out to Raiteault, who would doubtless had slain it with a giant's slash. But as it slid back into the long grass I imagined some unfortunate toad being faced with imminent death, and I recalled the heart that had throbbed in my hands.

My family deplored my love for sound radio and TV. I was told that this is a sure sign that I was no creative artist. This I was willing to concede. I liked to have my radio on in the middle of the night. I wanted the whole world to come into my room, and it amused me to think that I brought voices from Russia and Poland, from Italy and Spain, not counting England and France, to the nightjar perched in the cherry tree outside my window and the bat that flew in guided by his own radar. The noise mitigated my fear of death, and I had never abandoned a childish desire to learn something new. All these unknown men and women were hurling truths at me, and I imbibed bookloads of knowledge.

The TV. I bought for my mother gave me—now that I was so often alone—infinite pleasure. I built my evenings round it. At 6 p.m. I went into the big room, made a blaze in that monumental chimney and set my modest supper at one end of the dining-room table. Then I switched on a reading lamp, the one that stood by the portrait of Lady Wantage (whose husband won that V.C. in the Crimea), and when the egg was boiled I turned on the TV.

At Easter I started making a green pullover. The wool was what the French call Zephyr, but what in England might be mistaken for Shetland. It has the thinness of two-ply, but is not twisted. Its beauty has brought it into disgrace. Women no longer have the time to knit with thin wool, and Mme Alin, who keeps the haberdashery shop in our village, decided to get rid of her stock at half price. 'And I won't order any more of it,' she said. 'It's gone right out of favour.'

As I had suddenly taken a liking to green, a colour that I despised when I was a girl, I decided to give myself a present. It rained all that week and it was the best way of bringing sunshine into my heart. Mme Alin sold me two boxes—eight balls in all— for the equivalent of fifteen shillings. If you have the patience to work with two strands, you can produce a garment of unsurpassed softness, elasticity and elegance. I began this masterpiece that same evening while watching TV. and I finished it at the end of six weeks. I had never before taken so long to make a pullover. On the other hand it was the first time I had knitted anything while watching TV. What is more it proved a perfect fit, which is not always the case with what I make. I have frequent disappointments, and all in all I unpick as much as I make. 'To make or to unpick', my mother would say, 'keeps your hands equally busy.' She couldn't tolerate the idea of a woman doing nothing.

Market day was the most important day of the week. None of the wives in our village would have dreamed of missing it. I thought I would wear the green pullover for the first time but, as by some curious coincidence, I met nobody I knew. I was robbed of the pleasure of creating a sensation. I decided to weigh myself, taking my turn behind two elderly Americans. The man held the woman's handbag while she clambered on to the gently swaying platform, making little frightened sounds at finding the ground so insecure under her feet. Having put a coin in the slot they carefully examined the result. 'There, my dear,' said the man. 'You have put on a little weight. Just what the doctor said you must do. Congratulations, my dear!'

Bread was my own chief enemy. If only it didn't come out of the oven smelling so crisp and good! The baker's wife wore a different nylon overall every day. One never knew if she would be in pink, mauve, canary yellow or sky blue. Her dark eyes flashed you a welcome from behind her narrow marble cash desk. If an English tourist came into the bakery and she was aware of his nationality, she would ask smilingly: 'What can I do for you?' The tourist was sometimes misled by the apparent ease with which the pretty bakeress addressed him in his own tongue. But what would have been the good of telling him that? He generally answered brightly: 'Just one of those long loaves, miss—and

how nice to hear a Frenchwoman speaking such good English.'
He told her that he came from London, Manchester or Hull and
had left his wife and children in the car, and that they planned to
have a picnic on the beach. She did not understand a word, but it
all ended with a great deal of laughter and the sale of a loaf of
bread. Before her marriage she worked in the perfumery department of a big store at Caen and learned this one phrase, 'What can
I do for you?', to capture the hearts of the British and American
male tourists who composed quite a large percentage of customers. 'Once you catch a man's attention with a smile and a few
words of his own language, the rest is easy,' she explained. 'A
good perfume sells itself.'

So does a loaf of crisp French bread just out of the oven. No
wonder the young wives in our village found it so difficult to
slim.

Three doors farther down in this main street, which is so
narrow that two cars have barely room to pass, Mme Legros, the
butcher's wife, sat behind her cash desk on which there was
always a vase of freshly cut flowers. In summer her husband
had a stall in the market-place. She was therefore in charge
of the shop, and nobody could be more efficient. As her
mother used to tell me, at school she was always top of her class.
Before her marriage she worked at the local bank, where she
learned book-keeping and quite a lot about stocks and shares,
and how one buys and sells a bar of gold. She was also a fine cook
and gave excellent culinary advice to her customers.

Since my return from the garden party I had turned my house
upside-down in the hope of finding the key to a safe deposit in the
bank. My husband had asked me casually what I had done with it.
'I expect I put it in the linen cupboard,' I answered. But when I
searched the linen cupboard there was no key. I emptied all the
other cupboards and drawers in the house and finally worked
myself into a sort of frenzy which was out of all proportion to the
importance of the key. One of the two young men who shared the
responsibility of running the bank explained that for obvious
reasons there was no duplicate, and that if I had really lost it he
would have to call a locksmith.

Mme Legros, to whom I recounted my misadventure, remembered that when she had worked at the bank a customer had told
her that he had lost such a key for ten years. She pointed out that

the key was a large one and that I was almost bound to find it. 'It's not nearly so serious', she said, 'as finding the key of a safe deposit and forgetting—as some people do—the whereabouts of the box.'

This stupid business began to affect my health. I was in no immediate need of the key. There was nothing of importance in the box. But the humiliation was extreme. I kept on telling myself that my carelessness proved that I was not a fit person to be entrusted with anything serious. The image I had built up of my reliability was shattered.

I have already said that during the summer months M. Legros had a stall in the market-place. In previous years he had hired some young woman, generally a school-teacher on holiday, to sit at the cash desk, but this year their daughter Régine was in the seat of honour.

While M. Legros attended to one's order he recounted the village news. Watching football on TV. gave him a new awareness of the English. He liked to ask how his rump steak compared with what I could buy in London. On this occasion his mind was running on something different. He put down his knife, pushed aside his blue apron to delve into his trouser pocket and handed me a new silver franc.

'Take this,' he said, 'and be so kind as to buy me some pears from the stall over there. A little girl has picked them in her garden and has come to market to sell them. I have already bought her flowers, but if she sees me buying her pears she may think we want to get rid of her and she would be hurt. The fact of the matter is that there's a cold wind blowing up and she would be better off playing with other little girls of her age.'

I took the silver coin and went in search of the little girl. She was just tall enough for her head to be visible above the boards of a trestle table. A few garden pears, rather stunted and not quite ripe, were grouped pathetically in the centre of her table. A notice read: 'You can have the lot for one franc!'

Seeing me stop and look at her pears, the little girl put on a thoughtful expression.

'Are they sweet?' I asked.

'Oh, yes, madam. Very sweet.'

'Well,' said I, 'it's still a little early for pears and none of mine are ripe yet. I will buy the lot.'

The little girl put the silver franc carefully in her plastic purse, looked round to see if she had forgotten anything and ran off through the crowd. Régine Legros, who had been watching us from her place behind her father's cash desk, came with some paper in which to wrap the pears. M. Legros looked very pleased. We had played out our little drama unnoticed by the crowd of holiday-makers round us. The business of the morning could go on.

3

MADO and Gaston Duprez, hearing that my husband was over for a short visit, invited us to dinner towards the end of that week. Their beautiful house on the main road to Caen stood on high ground and was amongst the most imposing in our village. Mme Lehérissey, Mado's mother, would be there; also Annette Laurent, whose husband had an important post with an American pharmaceutical firm. We were to consider it a very informal occasion, almost a family affair.

For Mme Lehérissey, her own house down by the sea had become both too large and too full of memories. She escaped from it whenever she could. Mother and daughter had been inseparable since the doctor's death. Mado's young daughter Martine was in England, where her parents had sent her to learn English. Both Gaston and Mado were determined that she should have an international outlook. Martine was their only child and there were great plans for her future.

Gaston, whose profession was to buy and sell large country estates—he negotiated the purchase of those horse-breeding establishments where so many Derby winners had been raised—had just acquired a tiny thatched farmhouse, not for a client but as an eventual present for Martine when she was old enough to have a place of her own where she could entertain her friends. He was now busy turning what had originally been a peasant's house into a toy fit for a princess. The thatchers had just redone the roof and a staircase and bedrooms were being put in.

We had been to visit this little gem earlier in the day. About two miles up a quiet and picturesque country road, Gaston had told us, we would come upon an isolated farmhouse. This we were to pass. We must then look out for a tunnel of green leading off to the left, a narrow lane with deep cart ruts, mossy banks and a mass of hazel and wild cherry making a roof above our heads as in a church. This lane, damp but picturesque, meandered along for the best part of a quarter of a mile, at the end of which we would see a gate. If we pushed open the gate and walked in we would find ourselves in the orchard where the doll's house was situated.

The search for half-timbered houses, many of them four centuries old, had increased of late. They could be modernized by craftsmen no less cunning than their ancestors. The thatchers, the carpenters and the tilers took a pride in saving these little museum pieces for future generations. Unfortunately they were no longer so easy to come by. Rich people had discovered that there was no such thing as inaccessibility. Three or four miles from the nearest village was nothing by fast car.

Annette Laurent announced that she was expecting the visit from America of an uncle, her mother's brother, who had gone to Texas forty-five years ago, married an American and had not been back since. She said that when Michel, her husband, first joined the American firm for which he was working they went to Texas to meet the uncle, who had a passion for horses and wild, open spaces. What would he think of France after so many years?

Annette's father had been in the Diplomatic Service. For a long time he was attached to the embassy in Bucharest, and as a little girl she would spend her school holidays with her parents, travelling alone in the Orient Express. 'For a little girl to cross Europe in one of those crack expresses with her own *wagon-lit* was an unforgettable experience,' she said. 'One felt like a grown-up with a drawing-room of one's own, and then there were the meals in the dining-car with different food each time one arrived in a new country.'

These snatches of conversation, unimportant in themselves, contributed to a sense of relaxation which invariably proved one of the nicest aspects of Mado's intimate dinner parties. The last few months had been poignant for all of us—for Mado herself and her mother, for Annette who had lost her mother-in-law and for me. Mme Laurent who had been very ill the previous winter had appeared to make an excellent recovery and we had seen her with her family in her villa. I remembered Annette calling out to me on the beach one afternoon: 'Mother is looking very well. She has just gone off to attend a wedding.' A few days later I met her at what Mme Lehérissey used to call a *Rond de Dames*—a circle of ladies. These very formal afternoon teas were quite Edwardian.

We used to meet, often in Mme Lehérissey's drawing-room, and be invited to sit on those very pretty Louis XV chairs in which one had to keep a straight back, as straight and prim as if one had been laced. As new guests arrived we moved our chairs about until we formed a big circle. That was the moment when gossip really started to fly. In due course doors would be opened and we would be invited to take our places at the dinner table, upon which the food reposed on a tablecloth superbly embroidered by Mme Lehérissey. Chocolate, coffee and tea would be served from silver pots polished to a shine that morning by whatever maid was just then going through her apprenticeship in the doctor's house, for Mme Lehérissey was a perfectionist, and a terror with her maids. Port wine also, chocolate cakes and thick cream made their appearance, and then the gossip would begin all over again, never scandalous or ill-intentioned but delightfully concerned with love, music and dancing, the Paris Bourse, M. le Curé's latest sermon, the price of farm land, the best method of heating a house, the sayings of the fortune-teller and spiritualism. Occasionally the doctor himself would appear at tea time, the only man present. 'Ladies,' he would say, 'I draw the line at spiritualism. Don't try to guess what lies beyond.'

Mme Laurent worked part time with a chemist. She refused to remain idle and used to say that this occupation brought her nearer to her son, who was so clever at pharmaceutical research. She had lost her husband during the war when Michel was in the army. They were without news of him and every day her husband used to go in search of the postman hoping there might be a letter. One morning, waiting too long in a bitter east wind, he caught pneumonia and died. She claimed that it is in the first weeks of widowhood that a woman is most apt to lose her head and act foolishly. 'I would have been wiser to close my house and go away,' she said. 'After a while the pain gets less intense and one becomes sensible again.' Her house at Villers was in a charming square not fifty yards from the sea. There were trees to give shade in summer, and it did not seem to her so very long ago that she could sit out in the evening and watch the people go by. The young bloods came with their bicycles. Now strangers parked their cars three deep and the noise was incessant. That spring in

London, while glancing at the *Figaro* which somebody had given me, I learned of her death. In spite of the fact that Michel was now a grown man with three children he had become an orphan, and I repeated to Mado what I had said to somebody else after my mother's death, that one of the things that I would miss most was no longer being called 'thou' by a woman. In French the 'tu' and the 'toi' have a treasured flavour.

'If that's all that worries you,' said Annette, 'Mado and I will do so forthwith!'

But in spite of their efforts it did not come at all easily. I found those one-syllable words sticking in my throat, and Lili Durville, who has a caustic wit, exclaimed: 'Your good resolutions sound a bit laboured to me!' 'Have patience,' I replied. 'It will come.'

At all events it was past one when we suddenly became aware of the time. Madame Lehérissey had been tempted to talk about the early years of her marriage, with the result that all sadness had momentarily flown out of her eyes. She was with her husband and they were both young again. None of her listeners had been anxious to break the dream and bring her back into the present. But then she suddenly stopped, and in the silence the spell was broken.

Gaston drove his mother-in-law and Annette back to the village. At the top of our home orchard I switched the headlights full on, for the cows were there and their presence near the house calls for caution. What a glorious picture stretched ahead of us! The grass was emerald green and the herd in all its beauty lay across our path—some thirty cows caught in this sudden glare and yet not a single animal showing any sign of fear.

The kitchen was warm; two great elm logs burned brightly in the living-room. The little house seemed modest compared with the grandeur of Gaston's castle. There are moments when one wonders if the present is real·or if one is unconsciously playing a part in some unwritten novel.

The next morning I received an important-looking letter with the Roubaix postmark. I imagined that some firm must be sending me a sample of worsted to make myself an autumn skirt. No, it was not. I was informed that most women miss the joys of having the perfect table on which to iron. Too many of us, for instance (said this long affectionate letter), are apt to clear away a corner of the dining-room table, lay down a folded blanket with a piece of linen or cotton on top, and start a very uncomfortable morning's ironing which is entirely inadequate for a skirt or a girl's dress—or even a slip. But in the good city of Roubaix somebody has been thinking about us. He feels that it is high time that our lives should be made more pleasant and that our virtues should be rewarded. All we have to do is to send him a postcard, and the lightest, prettiest, most cleverly designed ironing-board in the whole of Europe will reach us through the mail.

Brigitte was standing in front of me. She was inspecting a photograph of the ironing-board and asked teasingly if I owned anything half so commodious.

'No,' I answered. 'I do just what the man says. I clear away a corner of the table and iron on that.'

'I know,' she said. 'I've seen you. Mother also irons on a corner of the table. So does Granny. So does that lady we went to see at Douville. Why don't you order one, just to see? After all, it's not very expensive.'

Brigitte's ideas about money were not quite the same as mine, but I was tempted to fill in the postcard. We sat down and did it together. This put Brigitte in the right mood to discuss other plans. Should she learn to swim in the big new fresh-water pool that had been built by the sea front? 'School children will not have to pay,' she said importantly. 'As for the others . . .' She gave a long low whistle and threw up her slender arms to show that the others would doubtless have to pay through the nose, and why not? Her question needed no answer. Her parents would certainly insist that she should take advantage of the scheme. I recalled how, when I had first bought the farm, there was not a peasant who did not fear water, even the muddy water of the cattle ponds which one then saw at the bottom of every orchard. Many a child even managed to get drowned in them while trying to catch frogs. As for going down to the sea to swim, no farmer would have allowed his children to do such a thing. How enlightened they had become! Brigitte suddenly asked:

'Do you believe in fairies?'

'I'm not sure,' I said. 'I have read all of Grimm a hundred times. I wouldn't be surprised to meet a witch, for instance.'

Brigitte turned this over in her mind. Then:

'You remember that piece of tapestry I made mother for her birthday last year?'

'Yes.'

'This year I've made her nothing. I've been too busy. But my money box is nearly full, so I can buy her something. Something she wants dreadfully.'

'Like what?'

'Like your red umbrella with the long gold handle and like mine too. Only mine doesn't unscrew. That is what mother would like—a red umbrella. Only . . .'

She looked at me with her cunning, peasant-like look, and added:

'Only I would have to go to Deauville to buy it, and I can't go alone.'

'Well, that's easy. How about going tomorrow?'

Her face lit up.

'That's exactly what I wanted. Only I didn't dare ask you. So I asked if you believed in fairies.'

She had spent enough time with me now. I watched her running up the orchard.

I went up to my room to make the bed and tidy up. The loss of the key of my safe still worried me. Even Brigitte, who asked me every day if I had found it, gave me one of her pitying looks as if there must be something wrong with me. Her parents kept their keys on a square board by the door of the living-room. Big ones and small ones hung side by side. The biggest was the key to the cider press. Our farmers made a great fuss about their keys. An angry word with a neighbour and they would fasten their gates with a heavy chain and add the key to the board. The next day they would unfasten the chain and let it hang limply to the postern till it became covered with rust. Their quarrels were not of long duration, but to put a padlock on a gate was a big show of authority.

I had taken my woollen dress—the one Anny Blatt made me—to the cleaners but I forgot to give them the belt. Cleaning is such an expensive business in France that I was annoyed and sought out the belt to see how it would look against the clean dress. I had hung it on a rail against my cupboard door, next to a lot of other belts, many of which were too wide or too narrow to be any longer in fashion.

I found the one I was looking for and gave it a sharp tug. Something heavy fell at my feet. It was the key to my safe attached to its wooden label. I must have hung it up amongst my belts. My heart missed a beat as if the world had almost come to an end— and then started off again. The whole thing was utterly absurd, but there I stood with the belt in my hand, looking down at the key and remembering that I had promised ten new francs to St Anthony if ever I found it.

My purse was empty. I would have to go to the bank. Well, that's where I intended to go anyway to tell them that I had found the key. I drove down and walked proudly in. 'I've found the key to the safe,' I said, 'and I need some money to pay St Anthony.'

They made me promise to put it in a safer place next time, and handed me ten silver coins, which I took to church. The coins made a terrible row as they dropped into the box. Had it been cleared lately or did nobody remember to pay St Anthony? A young woman came into the church, looking at me as she passed. She was bare-footed and wore shorts.

'What's the world coming to?' I thought.

Then I felt angry with myself for being intolerant. Surely it was better that she should come like that than not at all.

Having discharged my debt to St Anthony I went back to the farm and once more set about tidying my bedroom. Two freshly washed nylon sheets must be put away in the linen cupboard. They are exasperating to fold, slipping through one's fingers like a live snake, but after much resistance I have brought myself to them. There was a time when I scoffed at the idea of sleeping between nylon sheets or putting them in the beds in the guest rooms. Only Irish linen seemed good enough for the conscientious housewife I tried to be. But the new nylon sheets I bought at Harrods, though expensive, were of the loveliest pastel colours and were dry in less than two hours. In these country villages where laundries are practically unknown the advantage of nylon outweighed prejudice. With their matching flounced pillow-cases they made a delightful splash of colour, and as I passed a hand tenderly over them my only concern was that life is short and I might not live long enough to wear them out.

In the midst of these feminine occupations I became aware of a dreadful din in the great beamed room below. Running down, I discovered a baby bird yelling for its mother. It must have fallen from a nest just above the kitchen door. I remembered that when Georgette brought me the milk at breakfast time we had seen a baby flop down on the path, but it had almost immediately managed to fly away. Could this one be the same or was it another? Georgette had been telling me a long story about one of her cows that at milking time had turned in a nasty mean way on the donkey that had the churns slung across its back. Georgette talked about her cows as if they were her neighbours. She attributed the same sentiments to them that she might have to the women along the street. One was good-hearted and generous, another was a bit mean, yet another was excitable and jealous.

The baby bird continued to screech. From time to time the mother would come to look at it, but one sensed that she had the rest of the family to look after and possibly the housework up in the nest. I therefore picked up the anxious ball of fluff, holding it gently in my hands. I felt its heart beating painfully, but the warmth of my hands and the fact that it was exhausted from crying out for its mother soon made it fall asleep.

This tiny bundle of silky feathers was endearingly pathetic. I put a chiffon scarf in a basket, placed the baby bird in the folds and laid the basket on a corner of the Aga. That was how my mother used to nurse her wounded chicks.

From time to time during the afternoon I would peep into the basket to see how it was getting on. Towards evening it drank a few drops of water, and as it kept on opening its beak I managed with the help of some tweezers to give it a minute quantity of bread and milk. Its appetite left me in no doubt about its general state of health. Every now and again it would yell for more bread and milk. Meanwhile the mother bird kept on flying to the bird table opposite the kitchen, taking up as much bread as she could carry and returning to the nest, where presumably she was feeding the rest of her family in exactly the same way as I was feeding this one.

Later that evening, while the cows were being milked under the walnut tree, Brigitte looked in.

'See what I've found!' I said.

She inspected it carefully.

'You won't save it, you know.'

'One can but try.'

She nodded her little head gravely and said:

'I suppose so—if it amuses you.'

'Don't you feel at all sorry for it?'

'No,' she answered. 'He's so little, and besides, he's going to give you a load of trouble. Now if it was a heifer or a foal, that would be different. Are you going to read me a chapter of *Sans Famille*?'

I was reading aloud to Brigitte this book which generations of French children have loved. Every evening she would draw up a stool and listen attentively. A little boy abandoned by his parents is brought up by a poor but God-fearing couple. While the husband works in Paris, sending back what little he can, the wife remains with the boy in their humble country cottage. She has a cow, and they are happy because the cow gives them milk and butter; the garden provides vegetables. But one day the husband falls from a scaffolding, is injured and taken to hospital. The poor man claims compensation but loses his case. Their savings go— even the cow has to be sold.

When I was little, the part about the woman and the cow made a profound impression on me. At an age when most little girls only play with their dolls, I was already worrying about the complications of grown-up life. I could clearly see that even the better husbands had a hard time paying the rent. But if a woman owned a field, a cottage and a cow, the two main sources of financial worry were swept away. She lived rent free. The cow produced milk to drink, cream and butter to sell. Only some outside calamity like the husband's accident could make things go wrong.

Girlhood dreams occasionally cling. I carried mine along with me till as a young wife I was able to do just that—buy an orchard with a cottage and a cow. Since then I no longer have nightmares about not being able to pay a rent and I am reasonably certain of my glass of milk. Brigitte or her mother would certainly bring it, as they did now, to my door. I even like to think that if I were hard pressed I could exist without money. Fundamentally that is probably every woman's dream.

This evening Brigitte was not showing her usual attention to the book. She even stifled a yawn.

'Are you not sorry for the poor woman who is going to be parted from her cow?' I asked.

Brigitte fidgeted on her stool.

'She only had one,' she said. 'What would you do with one cow?'

Here stretched the great expanse dividing my girlhood from that of Brigitte. Penury was not a word she could understand. In the world of her parents she could count thirty cows, a donkey, a German tractor, a roadster, a scooter and a bicycle. Should I not close the book and put it away beside *John Halifax, Gentleman*? This was my punishment for always wanting to play the role of schoolmarm. I am driven by an insatiable desire to teach. But I teach the wrong things. I feel humiliated. Children nowadays are too clever. They never give the impression of needing one, and not to feel needed is the worst rebuff that a woman can receive.

What a disappointing summer! No sooner had Brigitte gone home than rain fell in torrents and a strong wind blew up from the sea.

But the house was warm and cosy with the Aga giving life to the kitchen, the logs in the great fireplace of the raftered room being devoured by gyrating tongues of yellow flame. Supper was set at one end of the polished table. A reading lamp gave a soft glow to the pictures on the wall and the tall pillars of Caen stone standing like sentinels on either side of the eater of forests. The flick of a switch and the happenings of a busy world would be brought to me from outside. There would be music or the voice of the announcer. These things would appear at my bidding and fly away when I was tired of them. My Rhode Island Reds had given me four brown eggs. A long warm loaf of freshly baked bread lay on the white tablecloth. Beside it lay a jug of milk from the evening milking, warm like the bread, with the froth of its cream on the top.

Thank you, dear God, for giving me an opportunity to appreciate this sweet little house. My desire is to be worthy of it. May I never forget to be grateful.

Delving into his nest of pink chiffon I took up the now sleeping bird, who woke up but made no attempt to escape. I put him gently back. He had assumed importance, for he was a guest enjoying a night's hospitality under my roof.

In the morning his chirping brought joy to the kitchen. I laid breakfast on the table by the window and invited my guest to join me. He looked round with interest, then perched on the edge of the transistor which was disseminating the B.B.C.'s eight o'clock news. The fact that it was in English in no way surprised him. Clearly he was born to be a linguist. But after a time he tired of this position and perched on a geranium in a pot where he proceeded to stretch out his wings and preen himself. He had put away quite a helping of warm bread and milk and his stomach was healthily rounded, but firm in an adolescent way. I thought him extremely good-looking in his pearl grey waistcoat with the darker jacket. From time to time he would stand on one leg. Yesterday his legs were covered in mud. This morning they were clean, so that although I am short sighted I had an excellent opportunity to inspect their marvellous mechanism. He was entirely without fear.

I put him back in his basket and drove down to the village, and as by now my husband had gone back to London I joined the young married women on the sands and bathed. It must have been close on two when I got home. I decided to make myself a quick lunch, but I had no sooner put the frying-pan on the fire than a small anxious head appeared at the window.

'I hope I'm not late!' cried Brigitte.

She skipped into the kitchen and added in one long breath:

'I told mother that you had lots of things to buy at Deauville and that you had said I could come too. Will that be all right?'

It was no good explaining that I had not yet lunched. I would have to wait till tea time. She danced in front of me accusingly, dressed in pink gingham with a long cardigan of nasturtium-coloured wool. She wore a headband and was clutching her purse. Her whole body quivered with impatience. Once or twice she tried to sit demurely like a visitor on the edge of a chair, but almost immediately she was up again questioning me with her eyes.

'Very well,' I said. 'Let's go!'

She was far stronger willed than I was.

We took the country road to Deauville. It's a little longer, but extremely beautiful, and one escapes the heavy traffic of the coast road. There are some fine houses whose owners I am acquainted with, but Brigitte knows the farms. As we approached Tourgeville, for instance, she informed me that this was where they had come to buy a pig to fatten for Christmas. 'We put it in the boot tied up in a sack and it was as good as gold!'

Here also is 'Les Longchamps', owned by a young Englishman whose parents, excellent friends of ours, died in the full vigour of youth. They brought to this Norman estate the green lawns of an English country house, herbaceous borders, tea time conversation and the English charm of that quiet hour before dinner when one drank whisky in tall tumblers with ice. Though her husband was entirely English, Mrs Skepper was half French. Tall, elegant, beautifully proportioned, a fine musician, she spoke both languages without accent. We enjoyed those long intimate talks that are possible only between women. As soon as a man joins in such conversations he dominates them. This is natural and what every woman wants, for she likes the stronger sex always to be victorious.

Now we came in sight of the Golf Hotel, the racecourse, the polo field, and all the trim beauty of Deauville, which remains one of the most sparkling cities in the world. There was just room to park my car between two others in front of the Printemps. 'Ah!' cried Brigitte after I achieved fair success with this manoeuvre, 'I shall tell mother that you've done it at last!' Her compliment pleased me. We hurried laughing into the shop.

The Grand Prix was taking place on Sunday and the sales had already begun. The big race is virtually the end of the season. There were only a few days during which to tempt wealthy visitors. This had been a summer of nautical sweaters embroidered with a compass card. Young girls wore blouses with cheeky messages to boys written on them. The same fashion seldom blooms two summers running. There was a table stacked with these at tempting prices. Garden tables and chairs had been pushed into the background. Exercise books and pencil cases were a reminder that children would soon be going back to school. Summer was almost over.

Brigitte was searching for the longed-for umbrella. She wanted it exactly the same as her own but larger. At first it looked as if there were none left. Then she found one—the very last. What a triumphant moment! Twenty-nine francs. She opened her purse and counted her savings. Alas, there was not enough. We decided to share the cost. She would contribute fourteen and I fifteen. I had half intended to buy myself a bikini, but now that Brigitte had found what she wanted her little hand in mine kept urging me to come away, and so we went back to the car and drove home.

I was to keep the umbrella hidden away in a secret drawer until Sunday, which was her mother's birthday, and then, when she arrived with the milk, I would hand it over to her.

'Oh,' she cried solemnly. 'I do hope it rains on the day of the Grand Prix!'

The birds in the garden welcomed us on our return. They made such a noise that they made me feel like Snow White coming home. I took the baby bird out of his basket, and as he was howling his head off I gave him bread and milk with the aid of the tweezers. Brigitte was obliged to admit that she had seldom seen a young bird more full of life, and she could not hide her wonderment. We made tea, after which she ran home, crying out over her shoulder: 'Remember Sunday!'

The next day after lunch Annette Laurent telephoned to tell me that the American uncle had arrived. She wanted to show him the farmhouse. Would four o'clock be all right for tea?

That gave me an hour and a half to tidy the house up and another half an hour to do my hair and manicure my nails. There was no time to lose. The weather was cold and overcast, and it looked as if Brigitte's heartless wish for rain on the day of the Grand Prix might be granted. I made up a splendid fire and decided to fill the house with flowers. Armed with pruning-scissors I hurried off to the rose beds, caught a foot in a piece of string that I had left taut to trim a grass border, and fell headlong into a lavender bush clutching the pruning-scissors in one hand and a bunch of pinks in the other. For a few seconds I remained stunned, wondering if my guests would arrive in time to drive me to hospital—bringing my own flowers. To my relief I got up shaken but unhurt.

At four o'clock exactly a tall man wearing a cowboy hat and a curious tunic with leather sleeves came walking down the orchard. This was Uncle Pierre, who had gone to America so many years ago and was now seeing the land of his birth for the first time since the 1914–18 war. After a happy marriage his American wife had died. Broken-hearted and disenchanted, he had left his two-thousand-acre ranch in Texas and come back to visit his family in France.

Annette brought him into the kitchen to be introduced. While I had been tidying the house she had been baking us a cake for tea. This she now deposited on the kitchen table. It was her habit to bake a cake every day after lunch while their Spanish maid went off to the beach to meet a sister who was maid to Lily Durville's mother. Annette claimed that this was the only time she had the kitchen to herself. All her young friends were aware of this, with the result that most afternoons, by the time her cake was ready to be taken out of the oven, Martine, Estelle, Sophie, and her own daughter Caroline were seated round the table waiting for it.

We took the tall Texan into the raftered room and toasted French bread in front of the fire. He told us that he had left France in 1915 for New Orleans, where he had relations. He was then sixteen—old enough to note the contrast between the gloom of a country fighting for its existence and the picturesqueness of a youthful America bursting with vigour. This was the America of the films of Charlie Chaplin, Mary Pickford and Tom Mix, the America that all Europe aspired to know. Uncle Pierre fell in love, married, and began a free, open-air life on the ranch in Texas.

Annette said that Uncle Pierre's hat caused surprise in our village but, she added, as she herself had seen when she had gone with her husband two years ago to visit Uncle Pierre in Texas, many townships were still as one saw them on cowboy films. Men rode into town on horseback wearing just those hats, and could be seen dismounting, tying their mounts to a post and going into bar or shop.

While she spoke, Uncle Pierre smiled indulgently. It was not easy to guess his secret thoughts. Doubtless he was vaguely amused by the interest shown in his attire. On the other hand the things that surprised him in his homeland were seldom those that we expected. Annette, for instance, had tried to impress him with our magnificent suspension bridge across the wide Seine at Tancarville. He merely replied that they had larger bridges in America. Even his arrival by liner at Le Havre had lacked the flavour of a sentimental homecoming. The dockers were out on strike and nobody was quite sure whether the passengers would be able to disembark.

Uncle Pierre had a tendency to exclaim about anything that was the opposite of big. My house, that was so small that one had the impression that he could have picked it up and put it in his pocket, delighted him. He was, I think, also surprised to discover that every village and small town still had its market-day. If ever this custom, which must have been handed down from medieval days, were abolished the French way of life would be radically changed, for a busy market encourages people to spend half a day in the open air. The market-place is the forum where people meet to discuss their affairs. Farmers still come in with their produce. One even sees behind her stall the old woman who grows lettuces in her garden. The local market gardener brings his produce, the horticulturist his begonias, rose trees and geraniums in pots. The cutlers and the shoe-vendors, the people who sell porcelain and kitchen utensils, go the round of the markets every week. On Monday they will be at the market town of Dozulé, on Tuesday at St Pierre-sur-Dives, on Wednesday at Beaumont-en-Auge, on Thursday at Deauville, on Friday at Villers-sur-Mer and on Saturday at Trouville, while Sunday may find them at Honfleur. Because our province is to me one of the most picturesque and romantic in the land, I envy them this continual shuffling round, never far away but always on the move. But then what would you say to those more adventurous merchants who, instead of keeping within the confines of one province, methodically travel round and round France, taking so many weeks or months to journey from the Mediterranean to the Pyrenees, from the Basque country to the Vendée, from the tip of Finistère to the Cherbourg peninsula? That might be the most romantic life of all. When I was little I dreamed of living in a caravan and going round and round France in this way. Many such caravans, fitted with every modern appliance and spotlessly clean, spend a few hours with us before moving off to the next village or town. To Uncle Pierre the rich colour of these markets, with wizened peasant women selling their own butter and cream, with a bundle of radishes or a punnet of early peaches artistically set out on their trestle table, was as delightful and strange as his great Texas cowboy's hat was to us. The young woman who sells materials in the market-place (she is one of those who travel round) is very expert at her job, and that same morning I had been watching her trying to convince a customer that thirty new francs was not expensive for three yards of woollen cloth to make a winter dress. The customer, though she thought the material very fine, could not be persuaded to part with her money, and was on the point of turning away when the good-looking and determined owner of the stall exclaimed:

'Come, madam. Do you realize it's only the price of a good bra?'

The customer appeared to be taken by surprise. She thought this over for a moment and answered:

'You are quite right—I'll take it!'

The scissors bit into the material, then flew across it before she could change her mind. The purchase was neatly folded, placed in an elegant carrier bag and handed across the stall.

'You see, Mme Henrey, what it needs to sell three yards of beautiful material! The art of persuasion. Ours is a hard life.'

That it was hard I had no doubt, but I was equally convinced that she would not have changed it for another. She said this was true. She and her husband enjoyed handling all these rolls of cottons, silks, nylons and jerseys. They liked the excitement of this high-speed salesmanship, this battle of wits that lasted from seven in the morning till midday without a break, this determination not to allow a customer to go away without selling her something; then the packing up of the merchandise, the departure to the next village or town.

'But I don't think our children will want to follow in our footsteps,' she said. 'The winters are apt to be hard and they want regular pay envelopes and the certainty of a pension scheme.'

I was up before eight on the Sunday of the Deauville Grand Prix, and perhaps I was wrong not to take the car and go to the big race. The idea of the crowds put me off, but next year if I am on the farm I shall rebel against this tendency never to do the obvious. While my mother lived I so often curbed my impulses for fear of hurting her susceptibilities. It was too hard to leave her

at home and go off and enjoy myself. Now to some extent I had
lost the habit.

Getting up early was also a matter of discipline. A house
without servants, a house that is also a farm, gets going soon
after daybreak whether you like it or not. The farmers come to
milk the cows, the hens need feeding and letting out, the Aga has
to be stoked up unless you are prepared to see it lose its heat
during the day—these are only a few of the things that pull you
out of bed. Whether you go back or not is another question.
There were times when I ran up again, wrapped myself in a
Shetland shawl and wrote letters or read till lunch time.

The hens hated to be kept waiting. They were hungry and
longed to run away across the grass. If the cows were in the home
orchard one could feel certain that the hens would go off in search
of them. Whenever I think of Normandy I see cows and hens
together.

The log that I had left burning the previous night when I went
to bed had burned entirely away, leaving a pile of lovely white
wood ash. I laid some faggots on top of this, meaning to set a
match to them after lunch, but the ash must have been red hot
underneath, for five minutes later I came back into the room and
found a fine blaze. My mother always philosophized about this
ash, that looked so harmless and burned so fiercely underneath.
She had picked up the saying, like most of her pronouncements,
from her mother at Blois. She would say, for instance, of some
demure-looking girl: 'Beware of the fire that smoulders under
the ash!' By which we were to understand that the young lady in
question was not nearly so demure as she seemed to be. For this
reason I learned at an early age to believe that appearances were
deceptive.

You will remember that the Sunday of the Deauville Grand
Prix had a particular significance for my young friend Brigitte. As
I rather expected, I had no sooner finished my morning coffee than
I saw her head bob up behind the panes of the kitchen window.
Bursting into the room, she exclaimed:

'Here you are! I've brought the milk! I couldn't keep still a
moment longer, so I told mother you had asked me to bring the
milk earlier than usual, but while saying it I was careful to keep
my fingers crossed as you told me to when I was saying a white
lie. You don't think I did anything wrong, do you?'

We fetched the red umbrella from its hiding-place and inspected the wrapping. Then we went into the garden to pick a bunch of roses, which we fastened to one end. Without waiting to say thank you, Brigitte hurried off holding her gift in front of her, like the soldiers of 1914 who went off to the trenches with bunches of wild flowers tied to the muzzles of their rifles.

I am never quite sure what I feel about Sunday in the country. After Mass the holiday crowds throng the streets and the *plage*. The fathers have arrived from Paris to join their wives and children. The wives are happy but a little self-conscious. For five days a week during the summer months they run their seaside establishment without marital criticism; on Saturday and Sunday a stronger will takes over.

I was tempted to spend the morning in my quiet orchards, but I couldn't resist jumping into the car and having a quick look round. On the way I met Daniel Gaudin and his father, M. Gaudin, a former opera singer of some fame. They were walking down to the village where M. Gaudin was going to take the bus to Deauville. As I had absolutely nothing to do I offered to drive them there, but I had bargained without the stubborn character of the singer.

'No,' he said. 'I prefer the country bus. I like to travel with a host of people. Their conversation amuses me.'

I thought it might be polite to drive them to the bus station, which was quite a long way off, so I asked:

'What time is your bus?'

'I haven't the slightest idea,' said M. Gaudin *père*. 'No, really, not any more than I know what the time is. I own neither watch nor radio. And even if we had a sundial it wouldn't be much good this summer. Look at the weather!'

I guessed that father and son were anxious to talk about theatrical matters as they walked slowly down to the sea, so I left them and went down to the beach, where I found Daniel's wife, Nathalie, and the children. Nathalie was talking to a friend with whom she had been at school at Caen during the war. They made a place for me between them on the sands, for though the sky was overcast the weather was tolerably warm. The two young women took turns to tell me how their friendship had begun.

'My father was soldiering at Metz,' said Nathalie. 'You remember the Maginot Line. Everybody thought that the war would turn out to be a replica of the earlier one. My father was anxious to send his family as far away as possible. Somewhere safe where I could go to school. Caen with its schools and university seemed the ideal choice. So mother and I settled there. I went to school, and loved every moment. Then during the allied bombardments my friend here and I spent wonderful hours in shelters talking and dreaming. Looking back it may seem strange that while one of the greatest battles in history was going on, two girls were having a wonderful time in air-raid shelters dreaming of dancing and theatres. But that's just what does happen in real life. For some people it's never quite like historians think it must have been.'

'Well it's quite true that I dreamed too,' said her friend, 'but perhaps less about the theatre. I dreamed of having the comfortable married life that my parents had, with a house at Caen, a summer villa at some seaside resort like Luc-sur-Mer, children . . . all that sort of thing. Perfect married happiness, if you understand me. The wonderful thing is that we both got what we dreamed of —or perhaps I should say that this is how it appears so far. One must never count one's happiness too soon. All the same, Nathalie has been both dancer and actress, while I married a doctor who works extremely hard and loves his calling. I have beautiful children just as I wanted them, a villa by the sea at Courseulles and a car of my own. Today, for instance, I drove with my children from my *plage* to Nathalie's.'

I looked at this happy young woman. Not only was she a picture of contentment, but she was pretty. Some girls really have everything, I thought, but few are ever satisfied with their own lot. Her knitting-needles were clicking away at a fine speed, but her gaze was always turning to where her children were playing. A real mother hen, I thought. But a boy of fifteen had been drowned here at the beginning of the week and one cannot be too careful. These young mothers are aware of that. If you were to ask them what frightens them most in their pleasant lives, they would say: 'Motor-car accidents and children who get out of their depth while swimming.'

After a while Daniel arrived in search of Nathalie.

'Father missed the bus,' he said. 'He was asking for it,

wasn't he? He refused to know the time of day or the time of the bus, but felt quite certain it would be there waiting for him.'

Just before lunch time the sun condescended to come out. went into Patsy's bathing-machine, put on a swim suit and ran down to the sea. It was low tide but the water was pleasant, and I had got into the habit of swimming every day. On my return to our magic circle in front of the bathing-machines I found that the younger Dr Durville had arrived. He was the son of the famous Dr Durville who owned the nudist colony on the Île du Levant in the Mediterranean, the father of the four girls we used to call the Little Women—France, Martine, Sophie and Nathalie. In spite of the doctor's youthful appearance he was already a grandfather. France and Martine were married and he had two grand-daughters and a grandson. I told him the water was warmer than it looked and suggested that he should follow my example and have a swim, but he said no, he was bored. He was terribly bored. As soon as he stopped working he got so bored that he read Dostoyevsky, and that made him even more depressed. The holidays seemed interminable. The fact was that he was never happy doing nothing. Women were made differently. They were quite satisfied to live at half speed. They gossiped and knitted or sewed, but men of action needed exercise for their brains. They felt the urge to solve problems, overcome difficulties. Medicine was something that never stopped, and a doctor could not forget it, even for a short holiday by the sea.

At this point his wife Lily arrived, sat down, and then sprang up as quickly, exclaiming: 'That reminds me, I clean forgot to buy wool for Sophie's pullover.' She turned to me and added 'Mother wants you to come and have coffee with us at "La Pastourelle". Would two o'clock suit you?' As I had no appointments any hour was suitable for me. Like M. Gaudin, I could have done without a watch.

Lily Durville's mother, Mme Charollois, was a widow. She had turned her villa, 'La Pastourelle', into a luxurious guest house. She and her husband had come to the seaside for the sake of Lily when she was little and had decided that it would be much nicer to build a villa of their own than to stay in an hotel. After her husband's death 'La Pastourelle' was too large for her alone and yet too beautiful to sell, and so she turned it into a guest house.

every apartment having its own balcony and private bathroom. She claimed that it was a replica of the Paris Ritz.

At two o'clock I found Mme Charollois embroidering a flounce of black lace on a sky-blue nightdress. She could never stay still for a moment. Her hands had to be occupied. She did the marketing and cooking for her guests, and even as she worked at her nightdress she told me how she planned the food.

'I have a plan of the dining-room in my mind's eye,' she said. 'Every table represents either a family or a couple. So I arrange my menus separately as if I were planning each family's menu personally. It's more fun for me, and it gives my guests the feeling that I think of them individually.'

She once told me that the work her villa entailed was just enough to burn up her surplus energy, so that she had found the ideal solution to the particular problem of her life. But one must not suppose that her interests were limited to running a super boarding house by the sea. Paris remained her great love. At Easter, when it was time to leave the capital, she could hardly tear herself away. 'The shops, the theatres, the cinemas, even the Métro, I love them all!' she exclaimed as her embroidery needle flew in and out of the sky-blue nightdress. 'I am in love with crowds, and the more I am pushed and jostled the happier I am. For, between ourselves, I hate being alone. I am terrified of shadows or an empty street.

'When I was in Paris I used to visit my daughter Lily. The road used to lead me past big private houses with gardens. Tall trees stretched their branches over the pavement and I used to hurry along with a beating heart. By the time I arrived at Lily's place I was thoroughly frightened. One tries to be brave, but it is not always a matter of merely being able to keep a tight grip on one's nerves. Some people succeed, others find it physically impossible, or else they have too much imagination. Perhaps I have read too much about what can happen in lonely parts of a city at night. Lily used to see that I was all upset. She would take pity on me, and when it was time to go she would come with me. The parts of Paris I like best are those filled with light and noise. The Place Clichy, for instance. It would be like living in Times Square in New York or in Piccadilly Circus in London. Theatres and cinemas, shops and restaurants, people milling about till the small hours of the morning. I once lived in that part of Paris and if I

C

happened to find myself alone one evening, instead of moping about waiting for somebody to telephone me, I would go out and lose myself in the crowds going into the theatres and music halls or going to the restaurants. Their gaiety was infectious. Their laughter made me laugh. I just followed the crowd.

'My family once prevailed on me to spend a winter at Nice. They told me about the sunshine and the flowers, the carnations, the mimosa, the casino and the blue sea. I didn't believe a word of it, but I did not like to hurt their feelings, and so in the end I gave way. When they came to say goodbye to me at the Gare de Lyon they found me in tears. They could not understand what I felt. "Mother," they said, "are you out of your senses, weeping because you are going to spend a wonderful holiday on the Riviera?"

'I arrived in the middle of the Carnival. I had not bargained for that. The hotels were all full. As soon as I asked the reception clerk for a room, he replied by asking me: "For how many persons, madame?" The first time this happened I got cross and answered: "For one, of course, you silly man." Afterwards I realized that a woman on her own was of small interest to them, so they would tell me that they were very sorry but the hotel was full. After some trouble I found an hotel near the station that gave me a room as if they were doing me some enormous favour.

'I walked along the fine streets at Nice but I never met anybody I knew. That made me want to cry. Every hour seemed a day. I went to the theatre one evening. You will think me very foolish, but in order to get to it I had to pass through a district where girls waited for men, and I didn't know where to look. They realized, of course, how stupid I was. Their cynical laughter made me blush. I did not enjoy the play. During the whole of the last act I was wondering how I would get back to my hotel. This experience made think about other ways to spend my time. As my family had told me so much about the beauties of the Riviera, I would take a number of excursions. The Riviera is indeed one of the marvels of the world. I went to Genoa. We had to leave at seven in the morning. I don't like getting up so early, and if agreed to do so it was less to admire the scenery than because hoped I might meet somebody interesting in the course of the trip. One day I travelled beside a charming girl with whom could have got along very well. She was leaving Nice that same night. Then I met a woman of my own age. She was very nice too, and we exchanged quite a lot of confidences, but she went on her way and I never saw her again.

'Then there was the day I took a trip to Eze.

'I lunched at the famous Chèvre d'Or and went for a walk in the village. The sky was deep blue. The sea looked just as it does on picture postcards. It was as blue as the sky and there was not a ripple on it. The houses were blindingly white with roofs of bright colours, and the air was heavy with the scent of mimosa, camellias, gardenias and carnations. There were tiered gardens with exotic plants. It was all so beautiful that I burst into tears. My loneliness choked me and I said to myself: "What's the good of all this beauty if I can't share it with anybody? What's the point of discovering the Garden of Eden if Adam has flown?" I went back to Nice, packed my bags and booked my passage home. I never wanted to see the Promenade des Anglais again, with those elderly gentlemen in black overcoats strolling along the sea front, their dimmed eyes hidden behind dark spectacles, their scraggy necks muffled up in case they should catch cold. What a dreary sight! Oh, the joy of being back in Paris to smell the ozone of the Métro, the exhaust fumes of traffic in the Champs Elysées, the mud of the Seine at low tide. And the wonderful sense of security and excitement in being jostled and smiled at, or merely ignored, by the crowds in the Place Clichy. You can keep your gardenias and mimosa.

'When Easter comes round I am obliged, of course, to come to Villers. But that is a set thing, a rendezvous with the villa that my husband and I designed and built. I need hardly tell you that the weather is seldom warm at that time of year, but I plant my petunias and paint the fences and part of the house. I also clean the cement with a wire brush, an exhausting, messy job which uses up my surplus energy. During my spare time I mow the lawn and change the earth in my window-boxes.'

This amazing woman laid down her nightdress, looked up at me with her big blue eyes, patted her blond curls and then re-threaded her needle. One had only to touch on a subject for Mme Charollois to enthuse upon it. Had I seen the pastries she had made for tea? And the open fruit tarts? She liked to prepare them early in the morning. Pastry should rest, but not remain too long in the oven. There was a knock at the door and three little girls came in—Sophie Durville, Mme Charollois's grand-daughter, Estelle Mathieu, one of Mme Lehérissey's grand-daughters, and Caroline Laurent, Annette Laurent's daughter. Tea was made ready, chairs were drawn up by the fire and the TV. switched on. Sophie cut slices of what is known as *pain brié*, a very close-textured bread, which we spread with butter and then sprinkled with coarse salt from an olive wood salt mill. Mme Charollois's pastries followed. Meanwhile we watched a film.

At seven o'clock we bade farewell to our hostess, the three little girls climbed into my car, and I drove them to their respective homes, after which I went for a moment to look at the sea.

The sea was grey and angry and I thought of Nice with its blue sky and mimosa. Was Mme Charollois right? Did most people fail to notice the beauty of our northern coast?

4

HARDLY a dozen hot days had graced this extraordinary summer, and yet the fruit was ripening. I took advantage of a fine September morning to cut the tall grass under a peach tree. The branches were laden, and I filled a basket with large Rouen peaches which I stoned and cut into quarters for jam.

In the garden weeds grew up overnight amongst the rose trees, so that the beds were beginning to look like the jungle of a Kipling story. Weeding was something I would have to do; I ought also to bring into the house two days' supply of coke for the Aga, for if it rained I would be glad to have it under my roof. I was beginning to feel like Noah's wife. However, before breakfast I saw a rat in the stables. I had no desire to find his companion to invite two into my Ark.

As most of my geraniums had died in the frost of the previous winter, I bought new ones whenever I went to nearby markets. They all flourished. Their leaves were dark green, their flowers bright with the night's rain. As for the hydrangeas, those thirsty drinkers of water, one might say that this summer they had never had it so good.

Philippe, the youngest of the Poirot children, had just celebrated his third birthday, and this afternoon he and his sister Anne were coming to tea with their *au pair* girl. Nathalie Durville was coming too with hers. The first was a German from Ludwigshaven; the second a Dutch girl from Hilversum.

Nathalie's *au pair* girl had been something of a sensation this summer on the *pluge*. Her predecessor, also Dutch, who had looked after Nathalie the previous year, though beautiful, had never been surrounded by admirers. I think she withered them with her aloofness, and I was tempted to say that perhaps beauty in itself was not enough to prove an irresistible magnet. The *au pair* girl from Hilversum had turned men's heads as seldom a girl had done. They all came under her spell—the old, the middle-aged, the young husbands who should have known better, even little boys. This well-built creature of exactly twenty was just the right shape for a bikini. Her features were so perfect that she needed no make-up, and her body, in spite of the fact that there had been so little sun, was burned to the colour of a ripe apricot. I had watched her progress with the amused detachment of an impartial witness, but I might have thought twice about bringing such a blinding ray of sunshine for any length of time into my home.

Now that we were in September, husbands were back at work in Paris or elsewhere; the older, more important ones looking grave and wise (or so one supposed) behind executive desks, and the younger ones struggling for advancement. The boys were at school or college. The girl from Hilversum, spreading jam on buttered toast, murmured nostalgically: 'The beautiful summer is over. How sad can the seaside become when all the men have gone!'

Gone too were the young wives who, in their warm city apartments, shook the moth balls from their mutation mink coats and telephoned their friends to arrange dinner and theatre parties. Autumn is the time to be in Paris. The tiny cloud hovering over the Dutch girl's smile made me feel, strangely enough, tenderly protective. I might have been right about her predecessor. Beauty needs an illusive something else to help it capture the fairy prince. One occasionally wonders (but that is downright silly) if beauty in itself is such a staggering advantage. The fact remains that, like the rich man's fortune, it must quickly be turned to account.

The *au pair* girl from Ludwigshaven gave me the impression of having her fair share of German common sense. She had her shapely feet firmly on the ground. One guessed that Inge (for that was her name) was too matter-of-fact to want the unobtainable or, as the French say, to try to capture the moon. But my little Dutch friend was like Hans Andersen's match-girl. She gave the impression of being innocent and dream-like, and one felt afraid that she might get hurt.

We were sitting in the raftered room and she said:

'I love the big open fire. When I was little, mother used to tell me that Granny once owned a farm and a windmill. The farmhouse had a fireplace like this one, and whenever mother smelt burning logs she started telling me stories about Granny's farm.

'Didn't she ever take you there?' asked Inge.

'No,' answered the Dutch girl; 'how could she?'

Presumably forgetting the nationality of her companion, she went on:

'The Germans blew it up—all Granny's lovely farm and the windmill too—to build one of their V1 launching sites.'

Whether Inge had missed the slight lowering of the voice, its undertone of sadness or bitterness, I could not tell, but she showed no embarrassment. A summer in France must have conditioned her to the occasional blunder, intentional or not. She was well aware of the great drama that, just about the time of her birth, had been enacted on this coast, and she had purposely visited Caen and the landing beaches. Her German thoroughness demanded that. But who can tell what goes on in the mind of a young girl when it comes to a question of war and its responsibilities? Did she sympathize with the Dutch girl because her Granny's farm and windmill had been destroyed? Was there this much understanding between girls of the same age? Or did she consider that the German cause had demanded the cruel blowing-up of an old woman's home? At what point did femininity and patriotism part company?

There was silence as my guests tasted the newly made peach jam, which had scarcely had time to cool.

The children kept on running in and out of the garden. Occasionally they came in with tight hot bunches of lavender which they offered to the Dutch girl as if they were already aware that beauty must receive its due. Their shoes brought mud all over the house. Fifille, my Pekinese, was furious at this invasion, but greedy enough to beg for pieces of bread and butter from any sticky childish hand. The house became full of noise and laughter, and when it was time to go home we all piled into the tiny car and shook and bounced up the orchard. The two *au pair* girls conversed in French. At Montauzan, the Poirot home, we deposited Anne, Philippe and Inge, and then went on to the Durville villa to put down Nathalie and the Dutch girl.

Before leaving home I had picked the prettiest of the roses to put on my mother's grave at Auberville. Alone in the car I drove along the top of the cliffs, my bouquet on the seat beside me. I felt the need of this moment of withdrawal, this opportunity to recall my own girlhood when, on my return from school, dirty, dishevelled, out of breath, I hurried towards her smile and her embrace, anxious to recount the happenings of the day, the successes, the injustices, the friendships and quarrels—and perhaps to show her a scratched leg or a bleeding knee if I had fallen down during the recreation hour.

The roses from my garden—her garden—now lay on her grave. The plot beside hers which my husband and I had reserved for ourselves was overgrown with tall coarse grass, so thick that the notice, *Reserved*, was no longer visible. Puddles of rainwater reflected the evening sky and the big white clouds floating softly across it.

Peaceful was the evening in this country churchyard—calm, sad and beautiful.

Life must go on, thought Mme Lehérissey, and decided to send out invitations for one of her *Ronds de Dames*, the first since the doctor's death. Mme de Lusigny, who regularly attended these exclusive social functions, having ascertained that I also had been invited, stressed the general opinion that we should strike a happy note. 'We must try to cheer her up,' she said when I arrived at our accustomed place on the sands some mornings later. 'You, for instance, could wear something special. Rumour has it that in London you are, on occasion, extremely elegant.'

Rumour, I fear, was ill-informed. Fashion is the essence of femininity and when the time comes round for the Paris collections I feel the old excitement rising up in me. A pretty dress, a piece of fur, a new material, can make my heart miss a beat. But even in London my dreams nowadays far outstrip what in the end I consider reasonable. On the point of buying something fabulous I invariably think of a hundred better ways of spending the money, and in the end I do nothing at all. As for the country, unless one is rich enough to have servants, to dress well can put one in fetters. Many times I have put on something nice, only to find myself obliged a moment later to chase away a fox, to feed the hens, to relight the Aga which has mysteriously gone out, to fetch in a log or to save a baby bird. And what happens then to that little outfit which had to be worn with care? So in truth it would never occur to me to call myself elegant, and as one always believes that others manage better it is my opinion that almost any of the young marrieds, who nearly all have foreign girls *au pair* to help them out, are ten times more carefully turned out.

I am at least in a position to be my own hairdresser. My hair, which retains its lustre, only requires long and vigorous brushing to make it spring to life and shine. This, I decided, would be the occasion to inaugurate a most up-to-date blouse-tunic made on my expensive sewing-machine from a superb piece of Liberty material. The almond green jersey skirt cost £1 in a Susan Small sale to which she invited the girls of a fashion magazine. White shoes would complete this moderately successful ensemble, for which nobody could accuse me of extravagance.

I slid my feet into the shoes and walked the length of the room to get re-accustomed to very high heels, one of the joys of city life. Something seemed to stab my right foot—once, twice, and then again. Could it be a thorn? A nail? A tiny sharp stone? In taking the shoe off and shaking it, a wasp fell out. As the unfortunate insect had been imprisoned in the pointed part of the shoe, it must have experienced the same fright, or worse than I did, when it stung me three times in quick succession. Freedom is something that even a wasp does not want to lose.

There was no longer any question of wearing the white shoes. The pain was acute and soon my foot began to swell. I searched for the places where I had been stung but without success. By this time I was frantically late.

When finally I rang at Mme Lehérissey's door, it was she who came to open it. Her maid was on holiday. Mme de Lusigny, whose remarks had goaded me into this show of elegance, doubtless felt that I deserved encouragement, for she looked me up and down and exclaimed joyfully: 'I knew it! I knew that you could be smarter than any of us if you set your mind to it. You should spoil us more often!' 'The cost would be too great,' I answered. 'I'm likely to pay for it by having to stay in bed for ten days. Three wasp stings to gain your approval. Admit that's a high price.'

They listened to my story and Mme Charollois said:

'I pity you, for only yesterday I was stung by a wasp on my wrist. Fortunately my doctor son-in-law, Jacques Durville, was able to neutralize the sting and put something on the place.'

The circle of ladies was not willing, however, to waste too much of its sympathy on minor ailments. Mme Durville, senior, had just arrived back from Paris, where she had buried her husband's brother. She lamented especially how sudden it had been, because only a few days earlier he had written to her to say that he felt quite rejuvenated after a long sunny holiday in the Île du Levant, her husband's nudist island. 'Oh dear,' she said, and began to enumerate all the people we knew who had died since the beginning of the year. This was too much for us, and we tried to veer the conversation round to more cheerful matters. A young woman was wearing a very pretty amber two-piece, so one of us asked her where she had bought it.

'The cleverest little dressmaker,' she answered, 'but, alas, I have lost her.'

'Not dead?'

'Virtually. She has retired.'

We must have shown our relief.

'She was quite extraordinary,' she went on, using the past tense. 'She must have made a fortune. Yes, indeed, she had an apartment in town, a country house and her own car. But she didn't want anybody to know she worked as a dressmaker. We were absolutely forbidden to write to her. She would not even allow us to telephone. If she needed some material for lining, buttons or trimming, the shop must on no account deliver. We had to buy anything we wanted and bring it personally.'

This also seemed dangerous ground, and so I said to Mme Lehérissey:

'Won't you talk to us about the dear doctor?'

'Yes,' said the other ladies, 'tell us about the good doctor?'

'What sort of things?' she asked, looking round the circle with obvious pleasure. 'What shall I tell you about him?'

'About your honeymoon?'

'About my honeymoon!' she exclaimed, and it was good to see the radiant smile that lit up her face. 'I scarcely remember where we went. I had eyes for nobody and nothing but him. Yes, even when we walked along the street. To think that this clever, good-looking man had chosen me! I couldn't believe it!'

None of us said anything, but one or two of the ladies drew their chairs up to narrow the circle while waiting for more.

'Of course, when he first began to practise here he wore the regulation dress of morning coat, cravat and striped trousers. He carried a malacca cane with great dignity. As he walked so grandly down the street he struck terror into the hearts of those who feared they might fall ill. For a little while I accompanied him on his rounds. There was so little for me to do at home. We employed a married couple to run the house. The husband waxed the parquet floors, brought up the coals and made the fires, cleaned the windows, looked after the garden and put on white cotton gloves to serve at table; the wife made the beds, did the housework, the washing and the ironing and cooked three meals a day. From time to time she had a baby but I do not remember her staying in bed for more than a day and, as she would immediately dispatch the child to a relation on a farm, her household duties were not affected. That was the pattern of things.

'I worked on and off at my tapestry and planned receptions and dinner parties. It was during the first years of my marriage that I covered most of the chairs you are sitting on, also the settee and much of the other furniture in the house.

'When I went with my husband on a visit I would talk to the family while he attended the patient. We received a note one day to call on a farmer who had injured a foot. The farmer's wife took us to the bedroom, where the farmer was propped up in an old-fashioned Norman bed with a tester. My husband, having examined the injured foot, asked to see the other, which was hidden under a mountain of sheets and blankets. The farmer looked embarrassed and made no effort to comply. "What's the matter?" asked my husband. "Why won't you let me see it?" "The thing is, doctor," the farmer's wife explained. "I didn't expect you would want to see his other foot, as there's nothing wrong with it—so I only washed the injured one!"

'Before long my husband abandoned the pompous medical garb of his time, morning coat and satin cravat, which was still thought necessary in cities, and accordingly ceased to be a figure of fear. The telephone was still rarely used. The front-door bell was what used to wake us up at night. If somebody was ill on a farm, a man would be sent—and sometimes, if it was a dark night and evil spirits were thought to be about, two men to keep each other company. Thus one winter's evening two men rang at our door, and it was clear that they had been afraid of meeting the devil on the way, for in order to bolster up their courage they had called at every inn on the road, and were now scarcely able to stand up. My husband's gig was at the smithy. He had therefore no alternative but to accept the two men's invitation to drive him to the woman who was on the point of having a baby in a lonely farmhouse. The two brave men clambered on the driving seat of the light, high-wheeled cart, the Norman *carriole* you must have seen a hundred times, and my husband, sleepy and far from reassured, took his place behind, tightly gripping both sides. "Eh, cocotte!" A crack of the whip and off they went, out of the village, up the hill and along narrow country lanes so full of pot-holes that the three men danced up and down like corks. The night was impenetrably dark and the oil lamp did little more than cast eerie shadows on the trees. Those bumpy, grassy tracks between orchards, bordered by hazel and tall cherry trees and elms, have no right to be called lanes. They are hardly wide enough for a hay cart to pass comfortably along. The cold was bitter, and soon the man who was driving, groggy with too much drink, fell asleep, his head beating rhythmically against his wide chest like the pendulum of a great clock. All might have gone well, for the horse knew its way and there's an old dictum that God looks after drunkards, had it not been for a big stone that sent the whole equipage tumbling into the ditch head first. The two drunkards were brought to their senses by the icy water of a rivulet which meandered across the track at this point. Doubtless this stream was responsible for the stone which had upset the cart. Probably somebody had used it as a stepping stone. They began to beat and insult the horse which, as it turned out, was not theirs. So the horse, not knowing them, refused to respond. They had been in such a hurry to call the doctor that seeing it grazing in a nearby orchard they had borrowed it from a neighbour.

'Fortunately my husband, who could not have been more sober, had fully expected the spill. He pushed his two companions into the ditch, righted the *carriole*, put back the stolen horse in the shafts and drove off by himself to the farm, where all the women were anxiously waiting for him. It proved to be a long business. The midwife had been there for hours, and when a midwife sends for a doctor you can be sure there is something wrong. The baby is not likely to pass as easily, as the saying goes, as a letter through the post. The sun was up before it was delivered. My husband then went out into the garden damp with dew, lit a cigarette and thought about breakfast and home. Alas, there was no horse. The light cart was nowhere to be seen. The neighbouring farmer had taken back his property in a towering rage and my husband had a six-mile walk home.'

She looked anxiously round.

'Who will have more tea? More of my chocolate cake? Of course, when I couldn't go with him, I was too anxious to sleep. I knew what our roads were like. I imagined him unconscious in a ditch. But there were times when I wasn't fit to go. I also had moments when a baby was on the way.'

She gave us one of those rather touching smiles which may have suggested that she was sorry to think it could not happen again. Even pain has its joys. One of the ladies, putting down her cup and saucer, said:

'He was so loved.'

'No,' said Mme Lehérissey decisively, who was not afraid to call a stone a stone. 'He provoked hatred, suspicion and jealousy. A doctor saves this one but is accused of killing that one. He does his best and the patient who is destined to recover will recover, but the one whose hour has come will die.'

'True,' said Mme Durville senior, whose husband and son were doctors, 'but if you see a lot of death you also see a lot of life.'

'Exactly,' said Mme Lehérissey, 'and just now I am going through the doctor's papers and correspondence, all his old note-books and diaries. Yes, his daily visits since we were first in practice.' She walked over to a table on which were some papers. 'See here! "Mme Lebouteillier safely delivered today. . . ." All these babies who have had time to grow up and get married and have children of their own, even grandchildren. A country doctor sees life flow past him like a swift river, but nothing is ever as one expects. Those we thought strongest to fight against the current were brushed aside and wrecked; others starting from nothing (I have a certain orphan girl in mind) became wealthy and important. Then again some men one thought of as being with us always, the dear doctor, for instance . . .' Her eyes became damp and she exclaimed: 'If only they could talk to us from where they are! Does that sound so wrong? But my husband was adamant. Time and again he said to me: "If I go before you, see to it that you leave me in peace. Don't try to get in touch with me."'

Dr Lehérissey had died in Nice.

He went there, as I think I have mentioned before, during most of the winters since his retirement. They owned an apartment which his wife may well have bought originally as an investment. She had bought one also in a very fashionable part of Paris. Buying apartments was good business. They invariably increased considerably in value within two or three years of purchase. Mme Lehérissey was always one for diversifying her interests.

As we saw that there was no keeping her away from the subject of her husband, and as we were by no means averse to hearing about the last days of his life, one of us asked her to tell us how his death occurred.

'One afternoon I had some business to attend to,' she said, 'and he went out alone. On his return I asked him if he had been to the cinema. There are a good many small cinemas in Nice and we often used to look in at one of them for an hour. "No," he answered, very gently, "I went to confession." This surprised me, though I'm not sure why it should have done. He was, as you know, an excellent Catholic, but during the last few weeks he was pretty tired—so tired, in fact, that on one or two occasions I had noticed that it had been almost too much for him to stoop down and tie his shoelaces. When he told me about going to confession I had a picture of him having to kneel down in the confessional box and that, I knew, would have been a considerable effort. Then too he was apt to get short of breath, and that might well have happened, especially with a priest who would have been an utter stranger, whereas the priests here in our village are all our friends.

'Because of this I started to look at him with different eyes. Was it possible that after living together for so long (we were about to celebrate our golden wedding anniversary), there were still compartments in his mind that were closed to me? Could it be that he had moments of shyness? I thought that perhaps I ought to suggest that we pray together, for is not prayer a conversation in which three can take part as easily as two?

'I did not broach the subject. One never does. The next morning at breakfast he said he would take nothing because he was going to communion. There was a nasty cold wind blowing down from the mountains, and as the idea of his going out without eating anything worried me, I decided to go with him. In fact this rather suited my state of mind.

'As we were coming out of church he was taken ill. All day he had difficulty in breathing, but at night he seemed better. I even got some sleep myself, but I woke suddenly at six o'clock, and when I put out a hand to touch him he was dead. Half demented I ran to my daughter Monique, who said to me: "I was in the middle of a dream. Father was quite well again. It was wonderful!" "Alas," I said, "your father died while I slept beside him."

'People swarmed round me saying all the things I have said to others without it really affecting me. Sympathy, politeness, indifference—or should I say aloofness? But this was my husband, the companion of my life, and *clichés* were an insult. He was my love, my existence, my man whom I had come to believe immortal. Had he not always found the right word to calm me when I lost control of myself? He was the little corner of blue sky when things looked darkest.'

She had touched on what was perhaps one of the most striking aspects of their marriage. Mme Lehérissey had always endeared herself to us by her bouts of delightful inconsequence, explosions of femininity—against the income tax demands; the plumber's bill. 'Why don't you *do* something?' she would ask the doctor, who looked at her with such indulgent affection and then found just the right word to restore reasonableness. 'What does money matter', he would say, 'as long as they leave us our freedom to be together?' And she would look at him with great melting eyes and say: 'You are too good, my love!'

'Now', she said, 'I am alone when the letters come in the morning. I have to open them and read them without his help. What will be the good of ranting against the income tax or the tradesmen any more? He won't be there to listen to me. We only shout when there is an audience—an audience of whose love we are certain.'

5

MORE of our friends left us over the week-end: Annette Laurent and her children for the Midi; Lily Durville for Paris with her two younger daughters, Sophie and Nathalie, and her grandson, Landry, France's baby. This unbelievably young grandmother was overjoyed to have Landry under her wing while France was at the Île du Levant in the Mediterranean introducing her husband to the delights of the family nudist island. What entertaining now took place in our village was likely to revolve round Montauzan, home of Jacques and Patsy Poirot and their children; and 'Le Plein Air', the stately house of Gaston and Mado Duprez, who had just come back with their daughter Martine from a holiday in Italy.

Italy for our village notables had much the same attraction as it had for the English aristocracy in Byron's day. Martine was in raptures over Murano, where her father had bought a chandelier of Venetian glass for his bathroom. They had also gone to the Danieli to pay homage to the ghosts of George Sand and Alfred de Musset.

Martine, prettier than ever since her journeys to England and to Italy and of the age when girls begin to dream romantically, found an unexpectedly enthusiastic listener in her cousin Didier Mathieu, whose mother Monique was Mme Lehérissey's second daughter. Didier had caused some surprise at the beginning of the summer by announcing his intention of going into the hotel business. Instead of sunbathing on the beach he had signed on as waiter at the Grand Hotel at Blonville, and was now wondering what his next step should be to become one of those legendary figures like Caesar Ritz or Ricardo Zucchi. I had half a mind to talk to him about the great Cigolini who, when he was director of the Hotel du Palais at Biarritz, enjoyed the confidence of crowned heads and millionaires. Sir Malcolm MacAlpine brought him to

England to open the Dorchester where, venerable and white-haired, he could be prevailed on by his friends (amongst whom he counted Queen Ena and King Alfonso of Spain) to reminisce most interestingly about his various experiences. I would also have liked to tell him about M. Schwenter, of the Meurice in Paris, who was unwilling host to the German military governors of Paris during the war, and whose wife was one of the last of the great Swiss housekeepers of these fabulous establishments that will never again know the glory of an age that was just disappearing when I was in my twenties. On reflection I said nothing. Better for him to collect his sister Estelle and their cousin Martine Duprez, and pick greengages on the farm.

Estelle and Martine had been gathering winkles on the rocks. They now came running towards us in their bikinis, the sun shining on their wet hair, for miraculously the Indian summer had begun and the two girls wanted to make the best of it before they went back to school.

We all piled into my car and drove to Mme Lehérissey's house to unload the winkles. The doctor's widow stood on a first floor balcony vigorously shaking blankets.

'Heavens!' she cried. 'All those winkles! I do hope we don't catch typhoid.'

Without interrupting her blanket-shaking she told us how one of her husband's patients had died in a Deauville nursing home after eating a dish of winkles. Her information had the effect of cooling our ardour considerably, but in order to comfort us and bring back smiles on the faces of her grand-daughters she exclaimed: 'Well, never mind. We may as well risk it. Aren't we always in God's hands?'

On the farm Didier, being the only man, climbed to the top of the ladder. The girls and I remained at the foot of the tree. Before long we filled three baskets of fruit. A mile or two to the south the beautiful turreted façade of the Louis XIII *château* was caught up by the afternoon sun. I remembered Mme Lehérissey telling me that she had been invited by its chatelaine, Mme de Carpentier, to have tea there. At the end of the summer this excellent and pious woman used to bring together the notables of the region in her tall rooms and tapestried halls. There were some fine Lancrets to admire. The courtyard was vast, while from the terrace one could look over deeply wooded slopes to the rich farms on our plateau above the sea. From the castle one could make out the silvery slates of my house which, though more modest, was older by nearly a century.

Raiteault the woodcutter had been well acquainted with the trees in the castle woods. To see him, axe in hand, amongst oak and giant beech in some historic part of the seigneur's land was enough to make one dream of a régime long since past, for he had both the rugged likeness and the cunning, where wood was concerned, of woodsmen in seventeenth-century tales. He spoke too, as did many Normans of his generation, in the half-forgotten tongue of his ancestors. When his body was brought back from Caen to lie in our village church, Mme de Carpentier came down from her castle to pray beside the coffin for, though in some ways she was withdrawn and not easy of approach, in others she was simplicity itself and not afraid to let it be known that she believed in God and set high store by patriotism, duty and the sanctity of family life. A young heir to the castle, Lieutenant d'Hérouville, had been killed in 1914. A street in the village bore his name and he was buried in the cemetery above our toy railway station that is open only in summer. Beside him now lie Raiteault and Dr Lehérissey.

'By the way,' I asked Estelle, 'I thought your grandmother was to have tea at the castle this afternoon—and there she was shaking blankets on her balcony.'

'Granny is expecting relations,' said Estelle, 'so she couldn't go to the party.'

'Good for your grandmother,' I said, 'putting her relations before an invitation to the castle. That does not surprise me, knowing her as I do.'

We loaded the heavy baskets of fruit into the car which, having so recently smelt of winkles and seaweed, now smelt deliciously of ripe greengages. Our arrival at Montauzan was greeted with cries of pleasure. There would be jam-making soon.

Yolande Huet telephoned me that evening. I have described her before. She is a tall slim blonde. In the street men turn round to take a second look at her. She has that indefinable quality known as sex appeal.

The previous year just after my mother's death she had come to console me. I recalled her as she stood by the kitchen door, the wind in the orchard blowing her hair about, but she had put it back in place expertly. She knew all the best hairdressers in Paris and London, and changed her hair styles so often that I could not keep up with them. Everything about her was volatile. Her laughter changed to tears without warning, a tragic narration would be brusquely held up to allow her to lament the inadequacies of a new lipstick. She was never without an enormous handbag in which amongst a thousand other things she carried a large mirror of a kind that according to her did not lie. Every time she looked into it she invariably exclaimed 'Oh, what a face!' though countless women would have given much to possess features half as attractive.

On that occasion she had implored me to find her a tiny house facing the sea, but I was too preoccupied with the loss I had just sustained. Yolande now told me that he had discovered a small half-timbered cottage in bad repair near Quillebœuf on the estuary of the Seine, and that she was modernizing it. Would I come and look at it?

So Yolande, like Gaston Duprez and so many others, was turning one of these old Norman houses into her particular dream house. How much wiser than pulling them down and building anew! The important thing was to allow these crumbling peasant houses, so typical of their period with their thatched roofs and oak beams, to be furbished up and have another long stretch of life. So many sixteenth-century and medieval houses were destroyed during the battles for Falaise and Caen that one felt grateful for this modern hankering after what was small, beautiful and old. Careful restorations never hurt an architectural gem.

I liked particularly the estuary of the Seine from Honfleur to Quillebœuf, much of which remains both wild and romantic. I found Yolande looking rather like a cover girl from a woman's magazine directing her workmen in front of the half-timbered cottage, whose new thatched roof gave it the prettiest appearance. Though she was happily married and had a son she was proud of, there had been times when I feared she would become neurotic. I perceived in her a new serenity. She it was whose tenacity was rewarded by at last finding this house. She put down the first payment, arranged for a mortgage, engaged the workmen, drew up the plans and organized the entire operation. She had dreamed a dream and now stood erect, blond hair touched by the wind, giving orders as to how the dream was to be carried out. One felt that she had discovered the secret of how a young married woman was to retain a personality of her own. No woman I know gave a greater impression of being entirely frivolous. None had a greater determination or a stronger will.

There must have been a moment when as the children's demands lessened, frustration was likely to attack her. Does not this happen to so many of us? Is that not the dangerous time for a woman?

'Two things saved me,' she said as we stood side by side in what would soon be her garden. 'My small car, which for the first time gave me independence, and the purchase of this cottage. My car was an eye-opener. It allowed me to go where I liked when I liked. Power was delivered into my hands. There was no longer anything that others did that I could not do myself. A child is a fine thing to have. No woman can be counted a failure who has produced one, but she only keeps it to herself for a short time. Then others take it from her. This cottage gives me a fresh chance to create something—something that may last for another hundred years.'

I had brought a luncheon basket with cider and cream buns, and we ate in the open air. There was a pond with ducks who came to beg for crumbs. I remembered the fun we had modernizing our own house. Did I regret that it now seemed so long ago?

But that evening on my return I regretted nothing. I was glad to live in the middle of an orchard, and to be so near the sea that I could bathe every day.

In the morning Jacques Déliquaire, my young farmer, arrived on his German tractor to mow down the tufts of sour grass. As soon as they heard him the cows converged from all sides to be near him, and one could almost hear their cries of joy. I pointed this out to him, and he said:

'Your home orchard has the best grass of any and yet the cows don't particularly like being here. They are happiest in the orchard we call "La Cour du Cerf" [The Field of the Stag]. That is heaven for them. Next they like best to be at Berlequet, the orchard where we live, and that in spite of the fact that we invariably have far too many animals on it. It was the same on my father's farm. As soon as my parents moved their cows from their home field to another orchard the cows, in spite of the new grass, gave less milk. With Farmer Poulin, your neighbour, it's the same story. His cows don't particularly like their home orchard. The one they like best is the one on the other side of your hedge yonder. That one is their heaven. Cows are extraordinary, Mme Henrey. I was born on my father's farm. I thought I knew about cows, but I had to have a farm of my own to discover how little I knew.'

Whether the cows liked my home orchard or not, they certainly came as near the house as they could when the weather turned stormy or cold. A coastal fog thickened that evening and the fog-horn blew all night. It was like being on a liner in the middle of the Atlantic. Morning found the orchard still enveloped in this eerie blanket. One stumbled against apple trees groaning under the weight of fruit. Sometimes a great branch, unable to take the strain, would break with a long, pitiful, rending sound. The pear trees full of hard little pears pointed up into the mist. There was not a breath of wind and the orchard seemed poised on giant scales. On autumn days such as this when my mother was alive I used to feel broken-hearted at the thought that soon I would have to leave her. I used to wish every day would last twice as long. All winter she would remain alone in the farmhouse enjoying this solitude, following with painful steps a routine of her own design. Our goodbyes were strained, she hating such scenes, far too proud for tears.

Now it was time for Didier and Estelle to go to Paris. Brother and sister announced that they would take the two o'clock train. Didier would stay with father and his new wife, Estelle with mother and her new husband. The station was a quarter of a mile away at the top of a long avenue bordered by Italian poplars. It was a white, powdery road. A hundred yards above the station, which was painted bright as a toy and only opened in summer, was the cemetery. Thus the avenue served a double purpose, to take people to and from the station and to their eternal rest. Most of us had walked in slow procession more times than we cared to remember along this avenue to follow some village notable from church to grave.

'Who is driving you to the station?' I asked.

'It will be the lunch hour. We dare not ask anybody.'

'Then I will take you,' I said.

They were waiting for me in front of their grandmother's house. Estelle was a bundle of nerves because, being a true woman, she hated to go but was terrified of missing the train. She had a fine new case covered in black, white and green tartan, as heavy as the Pont Neuf, as the saying runs, and too large for her to lift easily into the car. I can't think how she expected to carry it unaided to the station.

We put it on the back seat, very carefully so as not to scratch or harm it, for I could see that it was precious. Indeed, she explained of her own volition that it was a present to celebrate her first communion and, having chosen it herself, the more she looked at it the more she liked it. She had also received a mandolin, a less desirable instrument than an electric guitar, but still calculated to bring her a good deal of prestige amongst her friends in Paris. Suddenly anxious again, she exclaimed: 'Do tell Didier to hurry. He always makes me late.'

Her brother, as strong as a young ox, moved with the calculated slowness of a snail. His bag was small, but felt as if it contained bricks. As we drove between the poplar trees, the sun suddenly came out strongly as if to shame the fog of the previous day. 'We could have bathed', said Didier, 'and gone shrimping. Why did it have to do this to us?'

At the station he jumped out first to buy the tickets. Suddenly Estelle's eyes, blue as periwinkles, filled with tears. 'I hate going!' she whispered. But I knew that in Paris she would forget. There would be so much to do and to talk about. Most of all there was her own young life to plan. Last autumn she had wanted to be a model. This year she dreamed of being an interpreter. She thought it would be glamorous to stand under the arc-lamps between the Russians and the French.

The village as I drove back along the avenue was beginning to have its sleepy autumn look. The cider factory smelt of bruised apples. The leaves of the maples were turning red. Maître

Vincent's clerk swung through the notary's white gate, and was about to cross the street when he stopped to talk to the good-looking young chemist who had just built himself a fine house on the hill half way between the sea and the plateau. M. Barbe, the painter, sauntered out of his house, suddenly saw the notary's clerk and the chemist, and went over to join them. There was hand-shaking all round. M. Barbe lived on the opposite side of the street to the notary. He had a garden with gravel paths and had lately built a top storey with a wide balcony to attract summer visitors. In August one saw their bikinis drying on a line.

I stopped for a moment in front of the new State school in which children could be heard reciting their afternoon lessons, their voices monotonous like the droning of bees. Half a dozen young mothers had brought their perambulators under the plane trees and were gently rocking them with one hand while they waited for their children of school age to come running out. This was the mothers' meeting-place, and very pleasant it was. From snatches of conversation that came my way I gathered that the one great topic was the summer season. Had it been profitable? Summer was the time when the entire village tried to make enough money out of the visitors to live in comparative idleness through winter and early spring. In summer everybody who could do so moved into outhouse or attic to let their best rooms. Children were sent to Granny so that mother could hire out her services to the highest bidder. But now the visitors had gone and the natives once again occupied the best bedroom and the front parlour, and the question was: How did it compare with last summer—or the summer before? How much money had the visitors left behind?

Mme Lehérissey once told me that when she was newly married she also came here with her children in the pram. Eventually she had four—two girls and two boys. I asked her who was her best friend in those days. Well, she answered, there was Claire Vincent, the notary's wife—who was also to have four children. Jean and Jackie, the two eldest boys, were now gradually taking the practice over from their father who, during his long life, had proved himself one of the most astute men in this part of Normandy. The land he gradually accumulated as a young man had now become fabulously valuable. He was a character who might have delighted Balzac. Nobody knew how rich he was. Those who did business with him feared and respected him. He was said to be able to shrivel up an adversary with a smile. He was, however, a striking example of the popular saying that great riches do not necessarily bring happiness. What had happened to his wife Claire? And to the two younger children, a girl Marie-Claire, and a little boy? Towards the end of the war, in order to be nearer the university, they had gone to Caen. The allied bombardment which preceded the battle took them by surprise. Nobody ever heard of them again. Presumably they were pulverized under the house in which they were living.

The first of September marks the beginning of the season for 'la chasse'. In our Pays D'Auge there is little to shoot except an occasional rabbit, but the farmers unhook their guns from the oak beam that is to be found in every old farmhouse and go off with their dogs into coppice and wood. Unfortunately I own two woods which tempt them in spite of my entreaties to them to forbear. I have a horror of guns, and every year I fear they will mistake my Pekinese for a red squirrel or perhaps a young vixen. Afternoon is the most dangerous time, for the opening of 'la chasse' is celebrated with picnics and libations.

This year it was on this particular day, given over to shooting and merriment, that I saw my first robin. He looked into kitchen and bedroom as if reconnoitring before flying back into the woods—where I hope he kept at a safe distance from the guns.

Half way between the village and my farm, at the top of a steep hill, stands a villa, 'La Feuillée', from which, in spite of the profusion of tall trees, there are magnificent views of the sea. Here during the summer months those close friends Denise Besnus and Simone Marchand spend their holidays. Mlle Besnus, who is so short-sighted that she peers at you through thick lenses, was left the villa by her father, who was killed in the 1914–18 war. She also owns a house in the Square des Batignolles in Paris. Her friend, Mlle Marchand, teaches mathematics at the school in Clichy where I went as a girl, and by a strange coincidence she was born near the house in Montmartre where my mother made lace blouses when I was a baby.

Mlle Besnus has so many cats that her household is run for them rather than for herself. The furniture is sparse and rather strange. Some of her rooms look like theatrical sets designed to make your flesh creep. Cats jump down at you from the top of cupboards. Hay is sometimes strewn on the floor to make beds. All the cats have their own little dishes and you must not be surprised to find them set on tables or sideboards. At the villa by the sea there is still some writing on the walls left there by German troops who were quartered there during the occupation. Mlle Besnus does not worry about such things. She moves silently amongst her cats and, aware of their various idiosyncrasies, talks to them in choice and beautiful French so that one has the impression of listening to an actress at the *Comédie Française* reciting her role in a play by Racine.

Unable after my mother's death to bring Fifille, my Pekinese, back to London because of the quarantine laws, I gratefully accepted an offer by Mlle Besnus to keep her for me in Paris. Fifille, after sulking for three weeks, greatly enjoyed her stay in the Square des Batignolles. She was now as much at home at 'La Feuillée' as at the farm, and would make her own way from one place to the other.

Hearing that Mlle Marchand was returning to Paris this first of September to be ready for the new school term, I said I would drive her to the station. Mlle Besnus would, of course, come with us to see her off.

A narrow gate leads into an overgrown shrubbery and the villa, which is tall and castellated, rises from all this like the castle of the Sleeping Princess. Indeed until a short time ago this appellation was appropriate, for there lived on the top floor Simone's grandmother, who was born when Worth, the dressmaker, was making crinolines for Empress Eugénie, and who went on summer after summer being brought from the house in Paris until she died at the age of one hundred and five!

'Mademoiselle Besnus!' I called, and the cats, who had learned to recognize my voice, preceded her along the passage. We had taken them one after the other to a veterinary surgeon at Deauville to be treated for a mysterious malady. Mlle Besnus would emerge with a wicker basket and seat herself beside me in the car. The vet gave them all injections, adding that of course one never knew with cats, they might not live. They were now all back in arrogantly good health, all seven of them. The vet's own chow on the other hand caught influenza and died. This year Mlle Besnus had added a poodle to her *ménagerie*. Just before she came on holiday she had found him wandering disconsolately in a Paris street. 'Simone and I call him Karim,' she said.

I thought it appropriate to say something about the grand-mother, whose death must have left a curious emptiness in their lives. I never quite got over the sight of her sitting up in bed, so frail that you could have blown her out of the window and across the sea.

'Yes,' said Mlle Besnus and Mlle Marchand together. 'She has left a void. One hundred and five is after all a great age. But this winter when we are both back in Paris we plan to have—in addition to the seven cats, Karim and your Pekinese—a baby.'

'A baby!' I exclaimed. 'To replace the old lady of one hundred and five?'

'Why not?' asked Mlle Besnus, peering at me through her thick spectacles. 'The grandmother was a baby in her way, and the house in Paris is so large. The cats will love to have a baby.'

'And whose baby is it?'

'The young mother is a career girl who wants to go back to work. We admit, Simone and I, that it is an experiment but we are going to risk it.'

'The time!' cried Simone. 'The time! We must not be late for the Paris train.'

The school reopened the following day. Mlle Besnus would remain by the sea a fortnight longer. Then she also would return to Paris, taking Fifille.

We drove by the path across the fields to the station. We met nobody but Mme Javeault, my mother's friend, pushing her wheelbarrow. The sun painted the fields golden and the sea deep blue. Distantly one heard shots from the intrepid sportsmen —doubtless in my woods.

Our station would be closing down soon for the winter, but just now it glistened with new paint. It was so clean and toylike that one could imagine a child receiving it as a present in a Christmas stocking. Three old cronies sat on a bench waiting to see the train go by. The train, which was an old-fashioned one, ran backwards and forwards in summer between Deauville, Trouville and Cabourg. Proust had watched it. We heard it

morning and evening on the farm and when the weather was fine
we could see little wisps of white smoke bobbing up behind the
hayricks.

Simone bade us goodbye. She looked sad. I had not realized
before that, if little girls are sometimes sorry to be sent back to
school, the maths mistress is just as sad when the summer holidays
come to an end.

That evening I went to see Titine Bayard. Georges, her
husband, used to work for M. Barbe, the painter. He built a house
to live in when he retired. Titine earned the money to furnish it.
When the house was finished Georges, who had overworked
himself, nearly died. Titine nursed him slowly back to health.
Every summer they let the house and lived in an attic over the
garage. Titine's old mother, Mother Blanchard, was a real terror
as they say. But she was brimming with character. She lived in a
curious edifice at the back of the house which she refused, like the
mother of the five Rothschilds at Frankfort, ever to exchange for
something more comfortable.

Titine and Georges were back in their best sitting-room. The
summer residents had gone. 'The damage they do!' cried Titine,
whose sister Charlotte came up the garden path. 'The damage
they do!' But Charlotte kissed her sister and said: 'Lucky when
they don't go off without paying. I've known that to happen.'

The season, it transpired, had not been at all bad, but July was
so cold that the Bayards had to lend the tenants some of their own
blankets to keep them warm. 'Well, they paid,' Titine agreed
comfortably. 'They paid. That was the main thing, and that will
help us to keep warm this winter.'

For Titine, renting the house her Georges built meant more
than just disappearing into the attic. She looked after them every
day, Sundays included, and helped at other villas too, so that she
averaged eleven hours' work a day. Now with her sister Henrietta
she would begin her winter work of making mattresses stuffed
with the wool of Caen sheep. Her carding machine stood like
some prehistoric monster in the garage, which was otherwise
empty, as she had no car. Every winter also she re-made the wool
mattresses of the village notables, beginning with those of Mme
Lehérissey in the doctor's house. She spent her evenings with her

husband by the fire in the living-room, with iron shutters over doors and windows for fear of burglars.

Titine's mother had been ill. She was breathing rather heavily. A real peasant woman, she spoke in the beautiful language of three centuries ago, putting the personal pronoun into the plural verb thus: 'J'sommes fatiguée!' or 'J'sommes point contente!' Her brown cape hid mountains of woollies which ranged in colour from brown to black. Her cheeks were the colour of a ripe apple, glowing pink, and when she passed along the street, proud and haughty like a Chouanne, an insurgent Breton royalist, she was followed by enormous dogs of unknown origin which she cared for as if they were children, and nobody would have dared cross her. She was over eighty now and her breathing was heavy.

Her three daughters, all grandmothers themselves, took turns to watch at her bedside.

Charlotte Masure, the eldest, had a husband who was partly paralysed.

'How is Masure?' I asked.

'He has trouble in climbing the stairs at night,' she said.

'Perhaps he could sleep on a sofa in the living-room?'

'My good lady!' Charlotte exclaimed, shocked. 'The very thought of it!'

'If he didn't sleep in the same bed as Charlotte,' Titine explained, 'Masure would be the most unhappy man in the village. Next to his wife in the same bed, he is afraid of nothing. Single beds or twin beds may suit the young marrieds, but for us they would herald the separation of death. We are too accustomed, Georges and I, for instance, to see each other and to hear each other breathing all through the long day, not to lie close together at night.'

One of Mother Blanchard's animals, a large black dog, went fretfully from sister to sister. There were also four cats which Titine had found abandoned by summer residents who must have adopted them at Easter when they were kittens. 'One has not the heart to refuse them a home,' she said. 'We suffered too much ourselves when we were young.' She looked shyly at Georges, and said lovingly: 'We still fear, Georges and I, that something could happen and we would find ourselves without a roof over our heads, that we might starve or be in the position of having to ask a favour. Our children don't know what that means. Nothing frightens them. They are not haunted by the thought of unemployment or poverty. We envy them, but we can't change. As with our double beds and our need to feel each other's warmth at night, it's too late to change.'

Now that the holiday-makers had all gone, we reverted to being a rather sleepy agricultural community living by the sea. This was not without charm. The wide expanse of sands with hardly a soul in sight for miles was both wild and romantic. We still had our Friday markets, though they became smaller, more personal affairs and the shops were all open on Sundays to catch the people who went to Mass, and to sell them meat and cakes and hot bread. But on Mondays the village slept. The butchers and the bakers were closed. I decided to drive over to Patsy's place to ask her how she made a particularly good cake which was one of her specialities.

Those of us who have farms often boil the milk as soon as we get it, for we leave it to the farmers' wives to make cream and butter. The milk they bring us is merely for our daily need. We therefore boil it, allow it to cool and then put it in stone jars in the refrigerator. The thick cream that settles on the top of this lightly pasteurized milk can be put to a number of uses. Patsy made it the basis of this cake.

When I arrived at Montauzan I found her reading Elia Kazan's book which I had just received from London. Philippe, her youngest child, was playing on the floor. When I sat beside his mother he ran from chair to chair offering us his toys. It was a delightful way of spending a Monday morning.

'Ah, the cake?' said Patsy, taking a pencil and a piece of paper. 'It's very simple. The whole secret is in the baking of it. Your oven must be just right. Now for the recipe. You take a bowl of cream, a bowl of sugar, a bowl of flour, the yolks of three eggs, three egg-whites whipped to a firm snowy whiteness, a stick of vanilla, a tablespoon of rum, some baking powder—and an hour in a slow oven. See?'

'Yes, I see,' I said. 'Sounds simple enough.'

She looked at me quizzically:

'How is the projected trip to Russia?'

'I'm waiting for a visa.'

'I hope you won't be disappointed,' she said. 'As a matter of fact I also have a trip in mind—to visit my friend Thérèse in the new Algeria. I want to see how it's all working out. The wind of change is blowing even faster than anyone expected.'

She leaned back in her chair dreaming of the coming journey. It was now two (or was it three?) years ago that I had met her friend Thérèse and her husband during one of their short holidays in France. I remembered her coming in from the garden, a tall slim young woman with very dark hair and light blue eyes; she wore jeans, and told us that the situation in Algiers at that time was almost worse for the women than for the men, especially for young mothers.

The sky had clouded over and it was beginning to rain; soon it was falling quite fast, making a curtain between the bottom of Patsy's lawn with its tall Scottish firs and the bay of Le Havre. The house, since Jacques had installed oil-fired central heating, was greatly improved, and I liked the grey walls which Patsy had painted herself the previous winter. Eduardo Malta, the great Portuguese portrait painter, once told me that whenever he rented a house in which he intended to work, he first painted the walls grey because that was the colour that inspired him. Philippe, sucking his thumb, was looking up at us with large wondering eyes. We were all unconsciously enjoying the particular flavour of autumn, the warmth of well-heated homes, a good book, something to knit, a child playing on the floor, the companionship of friends.

As soon as it stopped raining I left Patsy to return to my comparative loneliness. The hens were waiting for me by the garden gate. For the last four days I had been unable to discover where they were laying, though they must have done so for I heard their cries of triumph. Tomorrow if the weather was finer I would go searching secret places for eggs. I had been less brave since seeing the rat in the stables. I boasted that I was not afraid to be alone in the country—though there were moments when fear sent shivers down my spine. The other night, for instance, I heard youths shouting at the top of the orchard. It was dark. I turned out the lights and stood by the telephone. Fortunately the cows were round the house, and they gave me that little extra feeling of being protected. When Georgette and the milking-woman arrived the next day they found that although the cows were all there the gates were open. Had the youths planned to frighten the cows, or had they merely been thoughtless? I would never know, but I spent a bad night and this stupid fright stressed what I was all too aware of: that none of us sleeps safe in bed, that there is always illness, poverty, a thief, or death lurking round the corner.

When before breakfast I went to let the hens out the sun was already hot, and the sky so blue that it was almost dazzling. The great expanse of grass across the orchard shone with a thousand fires, the trees were beginning to turn colour, and from time to time a ripe pear would fall from the tree growing against the front of the house.

This crisp autumn weather is ideal for the Aga stove, causing it to burn almost too fiercely. The kettle freshly filled with rain-water boils within a few minutes. After breakfast, coming upon an old pack of playing-cards belonging to my mother which she kept at the back of a drawer, I shuffled them and started a game of patience which would not come out. The one I was trying to do is known as the Marie Antoinette. When just before my marriage I went with my mother to Pau I used to resort to this game in the hope that it would tell me if I had any chance of regaining my health, for I had gone there to cure a lung trouble that could well have proved fatal. My preoccupation with the cards used to infuriate my mother, who was only too aware of what I was asking. She thought rightly that the situation was too desperate for me to base my calculations on anything so contrary to good sense. Presumably this particular game was never solved by Marie Antoinette, who would not otherwise have lost her lovely head on the scaffold. It turned out better for me, as I have already lived thirty years beyond the moment of peril. Be that as it may I never handle a pack of cards without thinking of my mother, with whom I played countless games of bezique. Nobody in my family will any longer play bezique with me, and I quickly tire of patience. I now turned my attention to washing the linen and tidying the house, and while passing from room to room I amused myself by changing all the furniture round in my imagination. I made the fire in the low room, dusted the table and sideboard, filled the place with roses and then went upstairs to make the bed—which is perhaps the thing I would most like to find done by magic every morning.

It was while making the bed and reflecting on the usefulness of nylon sheets that my mind jumped to market day at Dozulé, where earlier in the summer I had bought some particularly fine geraniums from which I could now take a few cuttings and pot them. I hurried down, spent half an hour in this agreeable occupation and then decided to look up *Everyman's Encyclopaedia of Gardening* to see what they had to say about it. Perversely they informed me that I would have been wiser to wait till spring. I should of course have consulted the book first, but that would have been against my nature, and how could I be sure that I would have followed their advice?

The grandfather clock in the low room struck ten. I must collect my alarm clock from the village watchmaker who had told me to call this morning. I usually kept it by my bedside not to waken me in the morning but because it made such a noise at night that it prevented me from feeling alone. It had not been ready last week. 'Come on Tuesday,' said M. Berbet, the watchmaker.

'Alas,' I answered, 'I promised to lend it to Mlle Besnus, who must take a bus to Courseulles. The only way she has of telling the time is by listening to the church bells which practically scream into her windows. It is because her house and the church tower are on much the same level. At seven in the morning the bell rings for first Mass, midday is announced by the angelus, seven in the evening by vespers. Normally these reminders that the day has begun, is half consumed and is coming to an end suffice her, but to go to Courseulles and be back by nightfall she must take a bus that leaves before the first Mass. So how will she know the time?'

'I understand', said the watchmaker, 'that the case is exceptional, and I would be churlish to refuse to lend you another which you may then hand to your friend Mlle Besnus. With my compliments, of course.'

With this he called to his wife at the back of the shop to bring him an ancient but trustworthy alarm clock that went by the name of Vedette. When his young wife appeared with it, I could not take my eyes off her pullover. I thought the design quite sensational, and forgetting all about alarm clocks I decided on the spur of the moment to make myself a pullover just like the one that the watchmaker's wife was wearing. I wondered for a moment if I should go to Mme Alin's shop and buy some wool for it, but on second thoughts I resolved to unpick what I termed my Roman sweater because I had begun it at Milan with some wool that I had bought in the cathedral close and finished it in the Eternal City. On the whole I should have found a more comprehensive appellation for it, for though I had finished it in Rome I had knitted considerable portions of it not only in Milan but also at Verona, in Venice and in Florence. Perhaps it was because it kept on reminding me of the *Divine Comedy*, I am not sure, but I never felt at ease in it. My shoulders are too frail for so much learning. The past weighed too heavily. I decided by the warmth of the log fire in the low room to unpick my Roman sweater and make a pullover to bear the name of Mme Berbet.

Now I would have time to make that cake for which Patsy had so generously given me the recipe. I hurriedly set out the ingredients on the kitchen table. Everything augured well. The mixer, a new toy, beat the whites of the eggs to perfection, the transistor played a 'twist', the cream smelt delicious. How could anything go wrong? Except, of course, that the Aga which on sultry airless days had an infuriating way of going out was now almost red hot owing to the crisp, dry autumn weather. I had an electric cooker as a stand-by, and also to grill on, but it was not in my nature to waste electricity when I had two ovens, the hot one and the cool one, in the Aga doing nothing. Nevertheless Patsy had warned me that the secret of the cake was in the baking of it, and that my oven must be just right. But what was just right? Hot, but not too hot. Well, it seemed that I had no choice. Crossing my fingers, I put the cake in the hot oven.

Nervousness proved my undoing. After a while, convinced that the hot oven was too hot, I took out the cake, which had risen much too quickly, and put it in the cool oven—but this one was not hot enough. The result was that the cake collapsed and the inside showed no sign of reaching the proper consistency. I had no choice but to put it back in the hot oven. A moment later Mlle Besnus rang up to know if I would drive her to market at Deauville. Before leaving I removed from the hot oven a piece of charcoal that was all that was left of my cake. Sadly I enumerated the ingredients: three eggs from my own hens—hence the best eggs

D

in the world—a bowl of cream from the milk of our own cows, a bowl of sugar, a bowl of flour, some baking powder, a tablespoon of rum, a stick of vanilla, a carton of glacé cherries brought from London; for though glacé cherries are made in France I could never find them in my village. I had also lost an hour of my time and, what was worse, my good name as a cook. When I was a little girl my history book told me that King François I, though often defeated, never lost his honour. Alas, he did better than I. I would have to fall back on the story of Alfred the Great.

When I stopped the car in front of 'La Feuillée' and sounded my horn, Denise emerged like a witch in a fairy story from behind an unclipped hedge. In her right hand she held a bunch of wilting yellow wild flowers. 'They are not much to look at,' she said, 'and I'm afraid they won't last, but they are what the Bible calls flowers of the field.'

A steep winding road leads down to the village past San Carlos, which once belonged to a Comtesse de Béarn. The beautiful house stands in a park in which cows still graze amongst splendid oak and chestnut trees. We were about to witness the transformation of this house from its former magnificence into a streamlined, modernized, expensive block of individually owned apartments. Denise Besnus told me that when she was little her parents used to take her to the country fêtes which the countess used to give every summer in her park.

'The countess, who was very much the great lady, was in fact the daughter of a wealthy textile manufacturer from Roubaix,' said Denise. 'Her husband, of course, could trace his aristocratic descent back to the earliest times. The Béarn, of which Pau is the capital, had a distinguished history long before it was united to France in the reign of Louis XIII. But the young countess, née Démachy, had made a tragic marriage. Her husband and her son were killed in an accident. The young woman for whom life no longer had any interest pined away. It was then that her father built her this beautiful house in Normandy in the hope that it would give her a new interest. This did indeed prove the case. The countess by her generosity and sweet disposition became a legend all along the coast from Trouville to Cabourg. There is, as you know, a street named after her in Villers.'

We had left the car by the iron gates and now we walked through the deserted park.

'The story you have told me could be turned into the first chapters of a novel,' I said.

'People don't write that sort of novel any longer,' sighed Mlle Besnus. 'It would have to be an Edwardian novel, what I call 'Le Temps Joli', the period when Georges de Porto Riche, Robert de Flers and Francis de Croisset were writing their plays. Soon these fine trees will be cut down to make a swimming pool and a car park, but today they are still with us in all their beauty, and as I walk under them I can indulge in the luxury of feeling romantic. Behind the thick lenses of my spectacles, somewhere inside this curiously shaped box which is my head, I harbour inexhaustible reserves of love. I feel at peace under these trees. Look! The chestnuts are already falling on the ground. They are breaking out of their spiked green cases and shimmering, light brown speckled with white, amongst the damp leaves. Once or twice in every day love and affection spill out of me. On waking up in the morning, for instance, after a good night's sleep, that exquisite moment when I go down into the kitchen to make the breakfast and my cats run towards me to arch their backs against my legs. Don't laugh! Love takes many forms. The affection of these mysterious, intelligent animals supplies a need. Their love conjures up some greater romantic love in a private world of my own making. Love is a thing too beautiful to soil or tarnish. Some people call love the relations between woman and man in a broken-down marriage. I have too many friends whose marriages are like that. I don't envy them. Better not to have been married at all.'

My mother said the contrary. She claimed that for a woman any marriage was better than barrenness.

Now we were approaching the house. There was a balcony with climbing rose bushes entwining their sweet scented arms round the pillars of damp, crumbling stone. Moss-covered steps led up to it.

'What would we do', asked Denise, 'if somebody were to leave us a place like this? To sell it would be a crime. To try to keep it would be to face ruin. How do I know that one day some-body will not leave me just such a place? I am the sort of person who believes that her dreams will come true. Nothing has ever seemed too difficult or too unlikely. I have what you might call a confident heart.'

She smiled, but I felt that it was part of her private world. It seemed impertinent to question her. After a while she said:

'Simone is the contrary of me. She is distrustful. She has known and enjoyed great affection but she can't forget past resentment. In short, she lacks the capacity to forgive.'

'Whereas you——?'

'Oh, it's such a bore to chew over old insults. Why should I tire myself? I'm for opening the tap as wide as it will go and letting love rush out like a torrent. I couldn't get to the end of all I have, you know.'

With her quiet, almost apologetic voice and her gentle, short-sighted movements she was much more daring than I was. This was the first time that I had penetrated this ghost-ridden park which I had walked or driven past a hundred times, never daring to enter. The railings had hemmed it in like the wall round the gardens of Buckingham Palace. Then one day there is no longer a railing, no longer a wall. One just walks in.

We went back to the car and drove to the bottom of the road which is called the Chemin de San Carlos. Here there is a STOP sign, for we were about to enter the main Caen highway. There is a white statue of the Holy Virgin of Boulogne-sur-Mer which was brought to us by sea from this port, which English people know because of the Channel crossing. The legend says that the statue at Boulogne (Caligula named it thus after Bologna) arrived in the seventh century in a fishing boat with two angels:

> Comme la Vierge à Boulogne arriva
>   Dans un bateau que la mer apporta
> Et l'an de grâce ainsi que l'on comptoit
>   Pour lors, au vrai, six cents et trente-trois.

By the thirteenth century the most distinguished pilgrims were visiting the statue, amongst whom were Winchester-born King Henry III, Louis IX, or St Louis of France and Cardinal Foucaud who, when he became Pope, took the sanctuary of Notre Dame under his protection; and it was here that Edward II of England married his French wife Isabella, daughter of Philip the Fair, in a ceremony which grouped five kings or future kings, four queens and fourteen sons of kings round the statue.

While waiting patiently by the STOP sign, Mlle Besnus and I

were intrigued by the antics of a large black dog crossing and re-crossing the highway in peril of its life.

'Oh dear!' cried Mlle Besnus, 'I can't stand it any longer. Did you see how that poor animal was nearly run over by the lorry? Now it's done it again. Follow it and see where it goes.'

Carefully I crossed the highway and followed the dog that had disappeared down a narrow road on the other side which leads to the village. The dog had not gone far. We saw it standing uncertainly in front of a villa, in the garden of which a man was potting geraniums.

'Stop the car,' said Mlle Besnus. 'I want to find out if it's wearing a collar. The owner's name and address may be written on it.'

She had turned on the tap of her boundless pity. Stealthily she approached the dog, but it was clearly afraid of her. Every time she got near it the dog raced a few yards away, then stopped to look at her with large, frightened eyes. They made an absurd picture as I slowly followed them in the car, Mlle Besnus stalking the dog, the dog giving increasing signs of being lost. Then it began to rain. Mlle Besnus, realizing that her tactics were getting her nowhere, decided to sit on a stone at the side of the road and try calling the dog. Somebody is going to think that she is asking for alms, I thought. They are more than likely to offer her a franc—she who has a house in Paris and a house by the seaside. How can I put a stop to this? Perhaps I could make my Pekinese act as decoy?

The animal was not unfriendly, but whatever had happened to it during the last few hours or days had made it nervous and suspicious. Suddenly it turned and fled. By this time Mlle Besnus was in a sorry state, and so was I, for the rain was heavy and I had felt it my duty to go out and join her.

Back in the dry warmth of the car, Mlle Besnus said plaintively, more for her own satisfaction than for mine, 'Didn't it see that I wanted to help it? How does one get the message across?'

'Perhaps it wasn't lost.'

'Oh yes, it was,' she answered sharply. 'Anybody could read that in its eyes. It was the same with Karim.'

'I don't really know about Karim. You never told me.'

'There's a station on the Paris Métro called Brochant, the one before you get to Porte de Clichy. A neighbour on her way to work noticed the poodle sitting at the top of the steps. On her way home eight hours later the poodle was still there. A shop-keeper told her it hadn't moved all day. She's a good woman. She imagined the animal sitting there all night. Her conscience would have troubled her. She borrowed a piece of string and brought it to us. Mlle Marchand took it in and locked it in the kitchen because of the cats. It howled so much that when she went to bed she took it with her. It jumped up on the eiderdown and made as if to doze off but every time a car stopped in the street it jumped down and whined at the door. Poor Denise got no sleep at all.'

'In spite of that you decided to keep it?'

'We went to the police station. We did all we could to find the owners, but they must have gone away and left it. Gradually it became fond of us. It returned our love.'

These last four words were spoken in Mlle Besnus's quiet, dreamy voice. They made a curious impression on me. But there was always an element of strength about her for she added: 'He has a new name, new owners, a house in town and another in the country.'

'Yes, Karim was lucky.'

'That's why I'm so worried about the black dog.'

'Isn't Karim enough?'

She looked at me sharply.

'You are wrong,' she said. 'Do you put a limit to human kindness?'

The children were coming out of school by the time we were back from Deauville and, after depositing Mlle Besnus and her provisions at 'La Feuillée' and bidding her a successful journey to Courseulles, I met Brigitte cycling home in the rain. She dis-mounted and put her smiling face through the window of the car.

'Mother is going to invite you to lunch on Thursday,' she announced importantly. 'Father shot a hare at the bottom of your orchard on Sunday and it's going to be delicious.'

Even on this wet misty evening my little house looked so lovely as I glimpsed it through the trees that I became sad at the idea of having to leave it so soon. The four hens were perched as usual on the long green bench in front of the pear tree. The Aga, which had burned so fiercely all the morning, was now nearly out. A few pieces of charcoal and some Russian anthracite would soon bring it to life again, but what was this charred object on the

table? Alas, it was the cake on which in my enthusiasm I had set
such store. Before deciding to throw it away it would be wise to
see if there was anything worth saving inside. With a sharp knife
I cut away the exterior, and to my surprise found that there was
more than enough for my supper. It only remained for me to set
the Aga going again, light a log fire in the low room, put the hens
to bed and make tea. Fifille and I would share the kernel of the
cake.

Was it that I had a troubled conscience about Mlle Besnus's
absurd stalking of the black dog, or was I preoccupied in some
way with vague thoughts about my inability to achieve even some
of the things I wanted to do? Whatever the cause, my solitary
evening proved a dull repetition of futilities. Earlier in the year I
had found in a drawer a piece of woollen material holed by moths.
I then undertook a task which a saner person would have dismissed out of hand. I began to embroider round every hole so
that the object which most women would have thrown away was
now becoming worthy of nuns in a convent. Now I was worried
lest I would not have time to finish it before leaving Normandy.
Every hole was embroidered in a different colour. I admired it but
I was tired of it. A play was being shown on French TV. and, as
most of the actors were members of the *Comédie Française*, the
acting was beyond criticism, but the chief character had an un-
rewarding task, for the author used him to enunciate many
admirable truths that only served to underline the fact that a good
play (like a good dish) needs to be spiced. I took the English
papers up to bed. Judging by their front pages the civilized world
was poised in space waiting for a learned judge's report on the
amorous adventures of a girl of twenty-one. At least it tended to
show that the English remain a virile race. Long may the Phrynés
of the world continue to shake empires and governments. One
wonders what future generations will make of that other girl who,
in comparing herself to Lady Hamilton, at least had an eye on
history.

Though I had been up early I found sleep impossible. I put out
the light and did a tour of Europe on the radio by way of Oslo,
Prague, Vienna, Budapest, Rome and Madrid. Subconsciously it
must have been the idea of having to leave the house that troubled
me. I switched off the music from Spain and then into my room
through the open window came the hooting of an owl. This was

a sound I particularly loved. I re-lit the smaller of my bedside lamps and tried to read. The moths that until only a few nights ago danced round my light were absent. Was summer gone so soon? But autumn was lovelier. The noises of the countryside at night are peaceful. Then suddenly Mme Gille's sheep, two orchards away, started to bleat. They grazed on a green hill that rose on the other side of the stream, and when I passed by they reminded me of a picture I had, when I was a little girl, of Joan of Arc tending her sheep. She was supposed to be hearing voices, which were pictorially represented by angels floating in a blue sky. Our saints were fortunate in having visions which, like ghosts, witches, spirits and hobgoblins, no longer form the subject of a winter night's tales.

When two o'clock struck I decided I was hungry.

The refrigerator in the kitchen contained nothing to tempt me. I then remembered the words of Lucie Delarue Mardrus, to the effect that all the beauty of Normandy is contained in the bite of an apple. I had put on the house coat that Jenny Bell sent me from New York, and I wondered if I would have the courage to go into that part of the orchard where I would find the Reinettes de Bretagne and the Cox's Orange Pippins. My son had arranged powerful lamps both in front and behind the house. I floodlit the front garden. The geraniums looked surprised to be invited to a ball. They were superbly dressed, and it hurt me to think that I was to leave them so soon. The strong light picked out the white railings beyond which the grass glittered like an ocean of green. I passed through one of the garden gates into the orchard. For a few moments I was guided by the light, then suddenly I could see the house no more. I waited for my eyes to accustom themselves to the change. How beautiful it was! How quiet and peaceful! The grass was tall enough to reach above my ankles and softly caress them as I moved forward. The ground was a succession of hills and vales and I knew that I must be careful not to trip. There were tufts of sour grass left by the cows and broken branches and cow dung. I could see the great walnut tree heavy with walnuts, a giant with powerful outstretched arms. From time to time an apple would fall from one of the hundreds of eating-apple trees, gently flopping down on the damp ground. Every morning when I came here I would find a dozen or more in a circle at the foot of each tree, some bruised, some pecked by birds, others undamaged

but torn away by a sudden gust of wind from the mother branch.
Mme Gille's sheep began to bleat again, and now the moon shone
over her little house on the brow of the hill. Why were her sheep
bleating? What was on their minds? I put up a hand, picked an
apple and dug my teeth into it. I felt brave and adventurous as if I
had done something daring. Perhaps I had. Perhaps I had crossed
the invisible line between the present and the past, the age of
radio and TV. and the centuries-old eeriness of a moonlit orchard
when one is all alone. Had I been braver I would have waded
across the tumbling waters of the stream, explored the woods and
hayfields, sought out the vixen in her lair and tried to catch a
glimpse of the owl. But I turned homewards and was suddenly
glad to return to the fairyland that was my illuminated garden
with the house behind.

Sleep, however, still eluded me. I now tried to understand a
few words of what the Russians were saying in Moscow. Four
o'clock. Fifille snored in her basket. On my return from the
orchard she had waited anxiously for me at the top of the stairs.
Her existence, which on the surface appears so uncomplicated,
must on the contrary be full of fears and premonitions.

I came down to breakfast feeling extraordinarily refreshed.
Good country air is doubtless more necessary to me than long
hours of sleep. I made fresh coffee, Fifille ate a bowl of bread and
milk, the tits were squabbling in front of the coconut in the
garden. My robin had not come back, and while cleaning out a
little house I had made for the birds I found a dead baby sparrow,
which might well have been the one that fell from its nest and
which I had tended so carefully.

I was no longer oppressed by the slight malaise which I had
experienced the previous evening. I could if I so wished prolong
my stay until mid October, and already my mind was trying to
decide what improvements could be made in the low room, and
these plans brought new delight to the autumn evenings. The
things I needed most were a new carpet, a large comfortable
settee and a host of intelligent friends. On the other hand I felt
increasingly that my mother's personality had merged into mine,
and that might well explain my indifference to solitude. With her,
of course, it had been a passion; with me it was a question of

waiting. I suffered my loneliness and had learned by experience what use I could make of it. Besides, I never was alone. Many of my evenings were passed in communion with her and I could now tell myself that we were at peace. She on her side must love me with a tranquil love; otherwise I could not feel for her as I did. I liked to think of her talking things over with her husband Milou, my father, with her sister Marie-Thérèse and with Rolande, her niece—with all those forceful characters who peopled the girlhood of *The Little Madeleine*. I wanted to imagine them happy and reunited: my father, whose work in the building trade had been so uncertain and ill paid; Matilda and her sister, who never had a franc to spend on themselves; Rolande, whose gaiety was cut short by tuberculosis. I just had to believe in their ultimate reward. Without that belief the years left to me would be intolerable.

Madame Lehérissey, in a black pleated silk blouse and a black cardigan, was cleaning her windows.

'The blouse belonged to my mother,' she said when I admired the fine quality of the sewing. 'I love wearing her blouses. They make me feel unworried. It is as if she were protecting me.'

'I have noticed the same thing,' I said. 'Every time this summer I wore a shantung blouse belonging to Matilda I was struck by the soothing effect it had on me. Its influence was beneficent.'

Mme Lehérissey put aside her chamois leather and took me into the doctor's consulting-room, where his sporting guns were laid out on a table. She had been reaching certain decisions. She would give the guns to her eldest son. That piece of furniture over there would be for her daughter Madeleine; the inkstand and the pens for her second son. As for his instruments, well, they didn't amount to much—a stethoscope, a speculum, forceps. 'Oh, the forceps,' I said, shuddering. 'I shall not forget them easily. They tore me cruelly. So these are they! These are the instruments of torture.' Mme Lehérissey looked at me over her spectacles. 'Yes,' she said. 'They would be the ones. You had a bad time, didn't you?—and so did he.' 'It ended well,' I said. 'They look like sugar tongs.' 'Oh, no,' said Mme Lehérissey. 'That would not describe them at all. They are so much bigger. More like the tongs they give you in certain restaurants to eat asparagus with.' 'What will you do with them?' I asked. 'They are unsaleable!' she cried with real regret. 'The man who bought his medical books and a whole lot of other things wouldn't make me an offer for the instruments. He said he couldn't. The only people who would buy them were what he called *les faiseuses d'anges*—the makers of angels, and you don't suppose I would allow them to get into their hands. So I'll just leave them where they are, in their cases.'

She looked round the room, checking the various objects. There was a pile of medical journals and other technical literature.

'A doctor is like a housewife,' said Mme Lehérissey thoughtfully. 'His work is never done. In the evening, while I embroidered or sewed, he would read all about the new inventions and the latest drugs to keep himself up to date. Many people claim that doctors are cynics. That's not true, but they often become enthusiastic about a new drug only to find that their high hopes end in disappointment. They oscillate between enthusiasm and despair.'

I picked up a handful of pamphlets. There was a treatise on syphilis, another on diseases of the kidney, another on the pancreas. 'If you can't sleep at night,' said Mme Lehérissey, 'try reading those. I shall throw them all away. I don't want to see them any more, as I shan't see my loved one reading them again.'

'No,' I said, 'I wouldn't understand them.'

'I'm getting ready to close the house up and go back to Nice,' said Mme Lehérissey. 'I'm almost ashamed to realize how life goes on in the same way. What's worse, my head is full of new ideas. Just as it always was. The truth is that my husband always agreed with anything I wanted to do, and when I asked him for money he would hand me his wallet and say: "Take it all and if you want more let me know." The members of his family were generous by nature, whereas mine cut every centime in four. My mother once told me that my father had never in all their married life taken her to a restaurant. As we lived in the Boulevard Saint-Germain, just imagine what that meant! On the opposite side of the road, for instance, was *Les Deux Magots* which, when we were children, was one of the most famous restaurants in Paris. We used to look out of the nursery window at all the fine people driving up in their carriages. It was not that my mother blamed my father. I remember the respect with which she touched her golden louis. My yellow bits, she called them—*mes jaunets*. She had the same feeling about warm yellow gold as Père Grandet. She kept her gold pieces in different boxes, some for the running expenses of the house, some for clothes, some for holidays, some for the bad days, some for old age, some for a funeral. On the other hand, most families like ours who had their roots in the country with, as likely as not, peasant ancestry, were always coming into small legacies; perhaps a farmhouse, a field or an orchard, none of it very valuable, but nice to have. Land was worth very little fifty years ago and it did not fluctuate much.

'The dowry my parents gave me was small enough, but I didn't even get the capital. They only gave me the interest. Quite a lot of parents followed this practice. The excuse was that any girl with a known dowry was potential bait for unscrupulous fortune hunters. So the family kept back the capital till the husband proved that he was not going to steal it from his young inexperienced wife and squander it. It never entered my head to blame my parents, for I had been brought up in such a spartan way that I took it all for granted. Besides, I was far too busy being happy with my doctor husband to worry about such things.

'What did surprise me was the difference in behaviour and outlook between my family and his. The members of his family were always arranging long, charming, gay dinner-parties just for fun and because they liked to eat and drink and teli one another amusing stories. Also they really did enjoy spending money and giving one another presents. The presents they gave one another were often quite large cheques. My husband himself was princely in his gestures. Many doctors in those days did not worry much about putting money aside. Their patients often paid them in gold coin, or at least in silver, so that by the end of the day the money jingled pleasantly in their pockets. But I was careful never to squander it and, as my husband approved of everything I did, we made an ideal partnership.

'Sometimes, as I have already told you, I would accompany him on his drives into the country, and it might happen that when we passed a tiny house for sale or perhaps a cottage with a flower garden that was derelict, I would exclaim: "Oh, isn't that lovely! I would love to own a little house like that!" "It's yours," my husband would answer, and as soon as he had finished his rounds he would go and buy it. A cottage, of course, or a field cost next to nothing. One needed very little money to buy one's dream house. And yet there was more poverty. Today when there is none, or practically none, the cottage costs millions of francs. My husband never changed his attitude about money. Each visit brought some in and it was his profession that mattered. "Why should I bother about money?" he said. "Aren't you my Minister of Finance?"'

The contents of the doctor's filing cabinets were now stacked in their folders, on the couch on which so many of his patients had obediently lain. These case-histories compiled in his own hand were often yellowed with age, and if one turned them over, looking at the names of the families they concerned, it needed no great imagination to see the doctor and his young wife driving from farm to farm along the narrow lanes with their tall hedges of hazel and wild cherry. A similar idea had often occurred to me on occasions when I had waited for Maître Vincent, in his outer office where his clerks drew up title deeds and where the walls were stacked high with faded green boxes containing the history of countless farms bought or sold since he had first come to Villers as a young man and married the daughter of the then notary. Was there anything that he also did not know about the countryside? The doctor, the notary and the priest—what a mass of human material they must have collected between them! How would the doctor's files dovetail into those of the notary? Cupidity and riches, they concerned the notary; so did forced sales of land when a farmer could not curtail his drinking or when he hanged himself from a beam in his cider press. The doctor came out to write the death certificate, the notary put the land up for sale. Then there were quarrels over hedges and right of way, midnight distillation of apple-jack so that the revenue men would not catch them. There were babies born on winter nights or in the middle of a storm with no telephone to call the doctor—cruel accidents, attempts at murder, jealousies, rich farms taken over from old people for annuities, acts of witches and sorcerers—no wonder Flaubert had a wealth of material to draw upon.

Here was Mme Lehérissey, the widow in black, smiling softly. 'Tell me what you've found,' I said, seeing that she was reading something from the doctor's files. 'This case-history,' she said.

'How my husband used to amuse us! All those distinguished men and their pretty wives at the fabulous medical dinners of lobsters and champagne at the dawn of the century—he used to have them rocking with laughter!' I waited expectantly. She went on: 'The Père Beaumont had been a terror with the girls. One might even say that he had enjoyed virility beyond the normal. At an advanced age he fractured a thigh-bone, became bed-ridden and was dying of congestion. While my husband was on his way to the shack in which he lived, a kindly old ruffian with whom the old man had emptied many a bottle was trying to make him sit up in bed, but the genitals kept on getting in the way, not easily following the elephantine movements of the body. Then the Père Beaumont (he was already very near death) pronounced these last words: "Ces saletés là—elles m'auront embêté jusqu'au bout!"'

'My husband used to say that, when he was a young doctor, what exhausted him most was having to repeat the simplest instructions a dozen times and then knowing that they would be wrongly carried out. The peasants had the queerest notions about caring for their bodies. Their lack of comprehension caused them to panic very easily. Illness of course could disrupt a farm with insufficient people to milk the cows, feed the animals, cut wood and tend fires. A peasant woman who complained to him of headaches was given several aspirins, but instead of swallowing them she stuck them on her forehead with adhesive plaster.'

Raiteault, when he had last come to the farm, had said with his wonderful big smile and husky voice: 'I'll come with my men and do your garden for you in the autumn, Mme Henrey, that I promise you. Just as soon as the Michaelmas daisies come out, I'll be here. We'll bring new earth to put between the rose trees and pull up the weeds in the kitchen garden. And after the apples have been gathered in I'll cut and stack you ten cords of wood. Count on me, Mme Henrey, count on me. Raiteault never goes back on his word.'

But Raiteault, the giant, had himself been felled in a night and I could think of nobody to replace him. The Michaelmas daisies were out (in France they are called 'Vendangeuses' because they bloom when the grapes are being crushed), and here I was inspecting my ailing rose trees like a matron walking through the wards of her hospital. Why did some of them look so unwell? I questioned them aloud. I implored them to answer me. Were they in need of a holiday or a change of air? I could at least give them a change of earth. I had a white rose tree called Virgo that would need urgent attention if I did not want to find it dead when I returned in the spring. I would dig it up and plant it elsewhere. Drastic action alone could save it. I soon discovered what was wrong with it. My spade dug into an enormous ant hill. Poor white rose tree that was being eaten away at the roots without knowing how to call out for help! I plunged it into a bucket of rain-water to drown any ants I had dug up with it, and turned my attention to the others. Altogether I dug up six, which I determined to plant in the kitchen garden in the hope that I could re-create the miracle of the red rose tree which, after ailing in the front garden, had prospered exceedingly when I replanted it over the grave of a favourite Pekinese in front of a curtain of fir trees

The kitchen garden, which until only a short time ago was a model of neatness, had now become a jungle. Infuriated by the tenacity of the couch-grass that was stealing the goodness from my precious earth, I went to fetch a sickle and attacked the insidious enemy. Many generations back farmers had a great fondness for perry, sometimes mixing it with cider to produce an extra-potent Calvados. It must have been such a one who planted some of our pear trees. In one very tall old tree a great commotion was going on. The swallows were getting ready to fly away. The weather was ideal for gardening, crisp and grey, restful to the eyes, invigorating to the lungs. The fruit trees were heavy with fruit. One of Ernest Poulin's mares put her head between the branches of hazel in the hedge that divided my orchard from his and watched me working. From time to time one heard a distant gun shot. From the village came the church bell for vespers.

I would need to buy a suitcase, I thought, as I planted my third rose tree, pricking myself cruelly on the thorns as I did so. Nothing is quite so dangerous as thorns on a rose tree, for certain birds use them as larders to hide insects they want to eat later, spiking the insects on the thorns; and when one pricks oneself— or so the dear doctor used to tell me—serious complications may arise. But one can't always be dabbing iodine on one's fingers while replanting rose trees.

I needed the suitcase because my family had more or less emptied the attic of our store of them. We had innumerable suitcases and hold-alls, but they would often be in London or in Paris when we needed them in Normandy, and the other way round. It was not that I had much to take back with me to England this time, but clothes that seemed important to take had a habit of piling up at the last moment.

I had never been very fussy about suitcases. I bought one when I had to without giving the matter much thought. But a few days ago a woman had called to see me, and because of what she told me I was beginning to hate the idea of going into a shop to buy one.

She had written me a letter the previous winter to say that she knew Villers. What a coincidence, wasn't it? She had come here every summer with her parents, who owned a jeweller's shop in Paris and another at Villers where they came during the season. Now she had read a book in English and well, it wasn't often that one knew a place and then discovered that somebody had written about it. If ever she came back—one could never tell—she would look me up.

She arrived one summer evening and introduced herself. Did I remember the letter? The memory of Villers had become so important to her. It was here that she had been young, pretty and very spoiled. And it was not so very long ago, just before the war.

'Daddy and Mummy gave me everything I wanted. Daddy was such fun. He had worked as a young man in Hatton Garden and knew everything about precious stones. We all loved our summers by the seaside. Every day there were parties, fancy dress balls, games on the sands, tennis tournaments, excursions, and we danced—heavens, how we danced!'

We were in the low room, and she looked up at me wistfully:

'Do you remember?'

'Yes, I remember.'

'The war upset everything. Daddy closed his shop here and we went back to Paris. A year went by and then the Germans came. A day came, a terrible day, when they came to fetch Daddy. We had implored him to hide, but he always said: "What difference would it make? They are everywhere. I don't want to go on living if it means being frightened all the time, never knowing from one moment till the next, always expecting their ring at the door, the sound of their jackboots in the hall." They came just as he had expected them to come, and they gave him three minutes to pack a suitcase and follow them. I can still see him looking lost as he tried to decide what to put in the suitcase, and since then I can't see a suitcase without it all coming back to me, and I feel sick and faint. They took him to Drancy. Mummy and I went to see him there, or rather we stood outside and made signs to him and he made signs to us. Then they closed the camp and sent him elsewhere. We didn't know at that time about the gas chambers. We just went on hoping till it wasn't possible to hope any more.

'Mummy tried to be both father and mother to me. She was strict, but one summer after the war she allowed me to go camping with friends on the Riviera. It was there I met the young Englishman who was to become my husband. Eventually Mummy sold the shop in Paris. We had found her a little house in England near ours, and she might at last have known a moment of happiness, but it was as if Fate did not want her to enjoy anything without Daddy. She was asphyxiated by a leak in a gas-pipe. When we found her she was dead.'

'You have become English? You have begun to live a second life?'

She nodded, opened her handbag and produced a faded photograph.

'That was the shop. Harrison. Can you read the name? I was Deborah Harrison.'

It was getting dark. I had planted the last of my rose trees. I must put the hens to bed. More and more I hated the idea of buying a suitcase.

6

ON THURSDAY Brigitte came to fetch me for lunch.

'There is no catechism class this afternoon,' she said, handing me the milk can. 'M. le Curé said that as it's the first Thursday of term we can have the afternoon free to make brown-paper covers for our school books and put our affairs in order.'

This announcement was made very seriously, as if her school satchel had been a cabinet minister's briefcase. She went on:

'As I am nearly nine and in a higher form, I've been given a whole lot of new books. You can have no idea how wonderful it is. My new geography book is much larger.'

'Yet the world is the same size,' I teased.

'Yes,' she answered slyly, 'but there'll be the moon when they reach it. Now hurry. Put the milk in the refrigerator and wash out the can so that we can take it back. Mother says that Fifille is invited too. By the way, I am going to let you in on a secret. Mother has put pimento into the jugged hare—but don't tell her I told you.'

'It sounds delicious.'

'She's afraid you may think it too spiced, because we all know what your cooking is like.'

Her peals of laughter danced round the kitchen. She was alluding to a certain lunch to which I had invited her years ago when she was four or five. Her parents had gone to a wedding, or perhaps to a funeral, and I had told Georgette to bring her over for the day. We ate in the English way, very simply. I remember the menu exactly—rump steak and tender French beans, blackberry and apple tart. As soon as Brigitte tasted the French beans she pulled a face. 'I don't like your beans,' she said. 'Mother makes hers with lots of pepper and salt and fresh cream!' Matilda and I looked guiltily at each other. This infant's stinging criticism hurt, though we pretended to laugh it off. The simplicity of our cooking was not only from taste; it was designed to meet Matilda's strict regime and must indeed have appeared insipid to the little girl accustomed to her mother's rich food and sauces. What pained me was that Matilda had grown the beans lovingly in the kitchen garden, and they were of the tenderest. Jacques and Georgette, back from their day's outing, had been told in great detail about my culinary imperfections, with the result that they had become legendary.

Brigitte, whose eyes were still bright with laughter, went on: 'There'll be fried potatoes. Mother makes them wonderfully.'

'I can't wait to taste them!' I said. 'Take the milk can and jump into the car.'

We drove there, though their place was only two orchards away. There was a nice warm sun, and enough blue in the sky to make, as the English say, a sailor's coat, or, as the French say—or said in the days of my grandmother in Blois—a cape for the Holy Virgin. In the courtyard of the Déliquaire farm we were noisily greeted by the latest arrival, a young pig that according to Brigitte had a fondness for the sound of a car engine. 'It brings him happy memories,' she said, skipping round me. 'Father went to fetch him in the roadster from a farm beyond Beaumont-en-Auge where he was shut up with his brothers and sisters in a horrible black hole. As soon as he came out of the car we allowed him to run about free as air, and so he has never stopped being grateful. He follows us like a puppy!'

The smell of the jugged hare reached us across the beds of chrysanthemums and Michaelmas daisies.

The table was laid in front of a log fire.

We started with tomatoes stuffed the Polish way, for Georgette, like Chopin, was born of a French father and a Polish mother. My heart sank a little when I saw Brigitte, the apple of my eye, attack her tomatoes with a knife firmly grasped in a clenched fist like a real little peasant girl. She held it vertically while she solemnly munched away. Was it possible that she was the same little girl whose behaviour was so perfect in my house? How adaptable to their surroundings are little women!

We were served on the well-scrubbed table on which there was no cloth. The hot plates were now brought and Jacques undid the wired corks of the champagne cider, which came out with a roar like a gun, spreading foam. The hare proved a dish I shall never forget. I doubt if I shall ever eat anything half as succulent again, and the fried potatoes (which are a French national dish) were done to perfection.

Georgette answered my compliments with great simplicity. What she was really looking out for were signs of approval on her husband's face. If he found her hare to his liking, then her day was made. To what lengths will some women in France go to give daily satisfaction culinarywise to their men! But the pleasure they derive from this constant straining is not far removed from slavery. Brigitte also gazes at her father with unbelievable tenderness. He proclaims that the hare is good. Brigitte's young face breaks into a relieved smile. He has said that the hare is good; mother will be happy, and when mother is happy Brigitte is filled with joy. When mother cries Brigitte is heartbroken. Mother and daughter are as one. Their love is a wondrous thing.

Now that Jacques has shown his approval, the two women are free to pay more attention to what I have to say about the meal. Brigitte is leaving nothing to chance. She wants to hear me say it all over again. '*Hein!*' she cries triumphantly, 'Didn't I tell you that mother makes fried potatoes wonderfully?'

'She does indeed,' I said, remembering suddenly what Dr Véron, that erudite gourmet who lived in Paris during the Second Empire, had written in his memoirs about them, that they must be as succulently soft within as crisp without. It is in this that the art of making them resides, he wrote. To make them perfectly you must make them every day, and preferably for a smallish company of people. For this reason it was his experience that one found them at their best in the smaller restaurants and in those private homes where the family was a large one. But this was in a Paris where cooking had taken on a poetic quality.

Georgette now served an endive salad—firm, white, curly and lightly perfumed with garlic—in a large china bowl. This caused Jacques to say that in his opinion there was no tastier salad, not even the first lettuces of the year. For a sweet Georgette produced a rice cake covered with an English custard (it was she who used the appellation) into which she had poured half a tumbler of her husband's most potent brew of Calvados, whose fumes alone were enough to make one feel tipsy. Coffee, neat Calvados for Jacques, but not for the women. Brigitte ran out to stretch her legs and to discover what had happened to Fifille, who in spite of the smell of hare had refused to come into the house. On a chair beside us slept a big white cat, whose apparent lack of appetite surprised me till Georgette admitted that before our arrival it had eaten a generous portion of hare.

Jacques was pleased with the lunch. His face was as red and as shiny as an apple, and he told us that he intended to finish this day —which had begun so well—by taking his gun and going through the woods with a friend. We watched him get up and fetch his double-barrelled gun, stroke it affectionately and then buckle on a belt full of cartridges, so that one had the impression of watching a Western on TV. The gun terrified me, but with great self-control I said nothing. Brigitte, who had come back into the room, read in my eyes the fear that I had hoped to keep secret within me, and her expression was quizzing and tinged with scorn. There might have passed through her wicked little mind the words of the great Marshal Turenne about to go into battle: 'You tremble with fear, carcass, but you would quake a deal more if you knew where I'm leading you!' The spectacle of Jacques with his gun and his cartridges cannot separate itself in my mind from those pathetic paragraphs that appear regularly from the first of September onwards in the *Bonhomme Normand*, recounting the fatal accidents of *la chasse*. May they not drink too much before nightfall!

Brigitte longs to accompany her father and his gay companions. 'When you are older', he tells her, 'I will buy you a gun and we'll go and shoot rabbits together!'

'How wonderful!' cries the child, whose eyes sparkle in anticipation.

Yet, when Jacques had gone, leaving the three women together, it was Brigitte who asked her mother to show me the animals. In a pen carpeted with sweet-smelling hay a foot deep—God's carpet, Brigitte called it—was a family of rabbits, or rather the result of a cross between a rabbit and a hare. Eight soft, intelligent creatures, slightly russet in tint, with pointed ears and large wondering eyes, were grouped round the mother. She had also taken under her protection a bantam hen, who herself had mothered several large families and was now so friendly that when picked up she pecked your cheek and then remained quietly on your arm. They smelt of clover hay and they waited for Georgette to lift the lid of the grain bin. When she filled their trough the bantam took her own place resolutely amongst them. From here we visited the young pheasants that Georgette was rearing for the first time, and I recalled a late summer afternoon in Ireland. Gretta Mahoney and I were picnicking in a field near Dublin when a male bird, frightened by the sound of a distant truck, rose suddenly a few yards away from us into the air.

I took leave of my farmer's wife and daughter and the little Paradise which beyond doubt gave them for the moment a feeling of solid achievement. They were young and the world stretched before them. I tried not to feel anything more than qualified happiness, for there must have been lots of women far more intelligent and worldly wise than I who in the past had counted too much on ties of affection between themselves and their tenant farmers before great eruptions changed the concept of things.

Driving back to my house I saw Fifille seated by the garden gate waiting for me, a small statue of fidelity. I had scarcely taken her up in my arms to return her kisses when I heard grunting behind us. The little pig must have followed me from Berlequet, trotting as fast as he could, and now gave every sign of also wanting to embrace me. This indeed was disinterested affection. A moment later Georgette and Brigitte came down the orchard.

'Whatever shall we do with him!' cried Georgette. 'He simply can't resist the noise of a car. We saw him running after you, so we followed!'

The little pig was at my feet, a picture of rosy contentment.

'You must stroke him under the snout,' said Georgette. 'He wants to be loved.'

I caressed the soft part she indicated and the little pig's eyes narrowed with satisfaction. I once saw a magnificent film the Russians made from a book by Gorki, in which the master passed through his house and his yard dressed only in a shirt, caressing his pigs and talking affectionately to them in the admirable soft tones of the Russian language. But I think Georgette's pig realized that he was only on a visit, for soon he got up, and at the sound of Georgette's word of command followed her home.

Brigitte had stayed behind to help me light the fire in the low room. She said that now the summer residents had gone, taking their little girls with them, the gardens in which they had played together were deserted, but that didn't matter because on half holidays she went there and played by herself. Deserted gardens were more exciting than inhabited ones, and she didn't have to wait till the other children had finished with the swings. The swings were all hers, and she could stay on them for as long as she pleased. Next Thursday the catechism class would start again, and that would be fun, and had I noticed that the Chemin de San Carlos was strewn with horse chestnuts—and then we would soon be in winter, and she hoped there might be snow like last year because mother had bought her ski-ing shoes.

'Well, goodbye!' she said, and kissed me fervently as if I had been a member of the family. In Normandy we kiss a lot. She darted up the orchard after her mother and the little pig. I remembered when Jacques, her father, was her age—nine exactly —and how every evening he crossed the bottom of my orchard on the way to his father's house on the other side of the stream. He would whistle a rumba as now his daughter hums a 'twist'.

7

THE following evening Jean Cocteau appeared on French television. He had been a legend in Paris for as long as I could remember. I had just come back from the village, where wisps of white smoke curled up from chimneys. A smell of burning logs sweetened the crisp autumn air. Trees had started to shed their leaves and apples were ripening. Now that I was back in the house preparing supper by my own log fire, here was this curiously complex septuagenarian, a near genius, introducing us to a new production of his best known play *The Infernal Machine*, based on the Greek legend which inspired Sophocles to write *Oedipus Rex*.

My husband, who had known Marie-Laure de Noailles at Oxford, had early aroused my interest in the brilliant set of musicians, painters and writers of which both she and Jean Cocteau were prominent members. Cocteau was, of course, senior in age. Before the First World War he had played a part with Diaghilev in creating the Russian ballets which revolutionized traditional choreography. They were an audacious band and included musicians like Stravinsky and De Falla, painters such as Bakst, Picasso, Matisse, Derain and De Chirico. Cocteau's imaginative talent had through a long life found expression in novels, poems, dramas and films, and he had a gift of identifying himself with any new genius or movement in the arts. For this reason, though he was bizarre and in the eyes of the uninitiated often ridiculous, he held the secret of eternal youth. He was exactly what is meant by *avant-garde*. His amazing sensitivity picked out the talent of the morrow before the crowd recognized it.

On this particular evening I thought he looked very old, rather like an elegant monkey, skin tightly drawn over bones, and only his admirable hands and sharp eyes gave him life. But he had a sense of the dramatic. He knew how to stand and how to comport himself in front of the camera, and when he spoke his command of

language—words cascading, limpid, simple to the point of decep-
tion—put him amongst the few whose erudition and talents set
them apart.

In these days of psychological complexes and cheap travel to
Greece even those who have not read the plays of Sophocles know
something about Laius, King of Thebes. He was warned by an
oracle that he would be killed by his own son, and so when
Oedipus was born he had him suspended by his feet from a tree on
Mount Clitheron. The baby, rescued by shepherds, was taken to
the King of Corinth, who brought him up in a princely manner.
While wandering through the country of his birth Oedipus met
his father but, not knowing who he was, killed him after a
quarrel. The Sphinx was then in the land devouring travellers who
could not answer its riddles correctly. Creon, now tyrant o
Thebes, promised both the throne and the hand of his sister
Jocaste, Laius's widow, to anybody who could get rid of the
Sphinx. Oedipus solved the riddle that the Sphinx put to him,
whereupon the creature threw itself into the sea. Reaping the
rewards, Oedipus mounted the throne and married his own
mother. When, much later, Jocaste learned the horrible truth she
hanged herself. Oedipus gouged out his eyes. An old man now,
he left Thebes guided by his daughter Antigone. He went to
Colon in Attica and finally entered the woods of the Eumenides,
where he was lost for ever.

The title of Cocteau's play strikes me in a new way. How
greatly we err through ignorance! World politics with their tragic
moments of blindness and misunderstanding too often appear like
the slow grinding of an infernal machine. If only we could be
warned! There is a scene in the play where Jocaste, after hanging
herself, emerges from the sombre kingdom of the dead, to talk to
her blind son and husband. Tears moistened my cheeks. I take the
oft repeated but ineffective lessons of the ancients too seriously.
But the Greeks were right occasionally to bring their dead from
the outer regions to console and warn the living. A log burned
lazily in the big fireplace of the low room and I wondered for a
moment whether to add a piece of ash to make a bright flame or
go up to bed. I decided to take a book and go upstairs. My room
was cold, but from the orchard came a brittle rustling sound, and
opening the window I saw by the light of the moon the poplars
my husband planted down by the stream ten years earlier now

dancing a fantastic ballet, and suddenly I recalled the words of a song that my mother used to sing when as a young woman she sewed her lace blouses:

Le vent souffle dans les ramures;
Entendez vous ce doux murmure?
C'est la chanson des peupliers.

I worked at high speed during the next few days getting ready for my departure, but unconsciously I was, I think, making the house ready for my return. Nor could I forget altogether those former autumns when I made the house snug for my mother, who would be remaining there alone till the following spring. I used to arrange heaps of coal in places easily within her reach and fill cupboards and sideboards with provisions. Indeed I would have brought her the world if it had been within my power, for she was not only my mother but in some respects my baby, my daughter, my sister, my other self. Time had fused our personalities so that when we were obliged to bid each other farewell our throats were parched. Her great age was leading her inexorably into the unknown. I for a time was going back to my family and the lights of the city.

This autumn I followed the example of the summer residents who closed up their villas for the winter. They bolted windows and put up wooden shutters to keep out light, sand and sun. Mme Lehérissey, Mme Durville and Mme de Lusigny even stuck old newspapers against their window panes. 'My dear,' they said to me, 'in truth we put them there against the moon. The moon does more harm to curtains and pictures than the sun. Learn to beware of the moon. The poets were misinformed.' Fortunately I had no need to take such precautions. Georgette would come every day to air the rooms.

Half way to the village I came upon tall, spectacled Mlle Besnus in deep conversation with little Mme Javeault, who firmly grasped the handles of her wheelbarrow as if she were afraid it would run away. Though Mme Javeault could not console herself over the loss of her husband, she had a gentle philosophy and a serene nature that endeared her to all of us. In addition she had boundless energy and robust good health. Every morning she pushed her wheelbarrow down the steep hill to the village to do the shopping for her daughter, Mme Salesse, and her grand-daughter, Michèle, both schoolmistresses married to schoolmasters. There were two great-grandchildren, both baby girls. When she reached Mme Baudon's self-service grocery store opposite the post office, Mme Javeault would park her wheelbarrow against the kerb, cover it with a piece of weather-beaten material and go off on her rounds. She started off as the church clock struck twelve, pushing her wheelbarrow home again; it was now filled with treasures. These were the provisions she had bought for her daughter and grand-daughter, various small things for the neighbours, and a bone for her dog. She was so punctual that I could set my watch by her progress up the hill. Every afternoon she went back to the village to her grand-daughter's house where, transforming her wheelbarrow into a pram, she took her great-grandchildren out for an airing.

Mme Javeault proceeded on her way and Mlle Besnus came to sit beside me in the car. As we passed my butcher's shop she put a hand on my arm and asked me to draw up by the kerb. It was nearly half past twelve and M. and Mme Legros and their grown-up son and daughter were having lunch in the back room. She had caught sight on the other side of the street of a little old lady dressed in black—black shoes and stockings, an overall of black satinette, a black woollen cardigan and a black scarf over her head. Nothing could have been more sombre than the manner of her dressing, and yet her features shone and her cheeks were wrinkled but ruddy like apples in December. Denise Besnus jumped out of the car and proceeded to embrace her.

This was Françoise Colemiche, whose poetic name seemed to fit her admirably. For many years this Norman peasant woman had worked on the large farm belonging to our neighbour, Mme Anger, who had died less than six months earlier. It was she who delivered the milk from Mme Anger's cows to customers in the village. Since there were no children the great farm had to be sold to meet death duties and as it was now in the process of changing hands Françoise Colemiche had retired into a little house beyond the station. There was no water laid on, so she had to take a bucket to the stream. There was no electricity, so the house was still lit by oil lamps, but this made it all the more romantic. Everything in the house shone like a new pin, and the neighbours helped her whenever they could. Today, she said, she had been 'portered' into the village in a friend's car, for she needed to buy a few things.

I had not heard this expression before. Mlle Besnus enlightened me. She claimed that the older peasantry used the word which in the eighteenth century had described the act of being carried in a sedan chair by porters. Things had changed, but Françoise Colemiche, she said, was not the sort of person to modernize the language of her ancestors.

Françoise Colemiche smiled as she peered into the car. Her shoulders ached a little because, she said, she had carried so many milk cans suspended from the yoke that her shoulders had become hollowed out like a country lane along which too many haycarts and wagons had passed. To see this old peasant woman, so clean, so dignified, so 'appetizing' as they say in French, made one reflect on the hard work of the farm, which often deforms a person but does not kill so quickly as the factory or the mine.

When she had gone Mlle Besnus said to me, jumping back into the car:

'I have a confession to make.'

She coloured a little, then broke into laughter and her features were illuminated.

'I am in the process of saving the life of another cat.'

I must have looked horrified, but she went on, her voice charged with emotion:

'A kitten deserted in an abandoned villa. Maria saw it. I spent hours calling it but got no response. Somebody suggested that it must have sought refuge in another villa on the opposite side of the road.'

'Perhaps they are looking after it?'

'The second villa is doubtless as deserted as the first. Nearly all the summer residents have gone home.'

'What is this villa? Do I know it?'

'The "Villa Germaine". The Countess of Béarn was called Germaine. She once owned it. I'm not quite sure who owns it now, but a charming woman, Mlle Mouton, lives there. What troubles me is that I think she must have gone back to Paris. The kitten may be starving. Shall we go and see?'

So once again I became involved.

The villa was typically Edwardian French, with a little iron door opening on to the garden, an autumnal garden with dahlias and late roses, and paths strewn with yellow leaves. Exploring the gardens of other people, especially when they are away, fascinates me. It might even be possible to take some cuttings from these mauve geraniums, and if I looked carefully I might discover some rare and unknown plants that I could introduce into my own garden. Mlle Besnus was running along the garden paths, very light on her feet, her anxious, spectacled eyes peering this way and that, calling out: 'Puss! Puss!' A pile of magazines had been left by the gate, doubtless for the dustman to take away, but they were in such good condition that they could only have been there for a day or two. Mlle Besnus had momentarily broken off her search for the kitten to stare thoughtfully at the colourful pile and say in a tremulous voice:

'If it rains—and it's sure to rain—these magazine will all be spoiled, and they seem to be such nice ones. My friend Simone is always asking me for magazines with pictures in them to look at on summer afternoons when she's resting. She doesn't mind a bit if they're old. If these are really to be thrown away, do you think I could take some of them?'

'Take them all,' I said. 'We'll put them in the back of the car and drop them at your place on the way home.'

She smiled at the idea of this daring theft, and answered:

'Splendid! There are more than enough to provide holiday reading for Simone next summer.'

Having put our plan into execution we went back to the garden and once again began to look for the kitten. Our calls and laughter had an unexpected result. The door of the villa opened and out walked Mlle Mouton, dressed all in black with the rosette of the Legion of Honour in the lapel of her jacket. Just behind her, tail held high, was the kitten we were looking for. It remained cautiously at her heels, bright eyes shining inquisitively.

Mlle Besnus explained what we were doing.

'Then you have been sent by Providence!' exclaimed Mlle Mouton. 'This charming animal turned up two days ago and just won't leave me. Unfortunately I am busy closing the house up before returning to Paris in the morning—but won't you both come in?'

The villa was furnished in a strangely old-fashioned way, and the kitten, frightened by our eruption into its adopted home, ran from room to room. Mlle Besnus and I tried to catch it; Mlle Mouton encouraged us and to my surprise addressed Mlle Besnus as Madame and me as Mademoiselle. It took me a moment to solve the riddle. That morning I had taken off my rings to work in the garden whereas Mlle Besnus wears her mother's wedding ring on her left hand.

The kitten finally allowed itself to be caught, though it sensed that once again something important was about to take place in its life. Mlle Mouton saw us into the car and we drove off in the direction of 'La Feuillée'.

We had not gone many yards before we came upon a donkey in the middle of the road.

'Oh dear,' sighed Mlle Besnus who had tucked the kitten inside her coat, 'here is Charmante prowling the countryside again all by herself. You had better hold the kitten while I try to tether her to a post.'

Charmante belonged to Rapide, who employed her during the summer months to carry children in a governess cart along the sands. In the winter he and his wife and a large black dog could occasionally be seen seated in the governess cart behind Charmante as she ambled slowly along a country lane. The governess cart was slowly falling to bits but was basically well built. Like so many other old-fashioned possessions round here it probably once belonged to the Countess of Béarn, whose now ruined stables stood in the Chemin de San Carlos hidden from 'La Feuillée' by a twist in the road and a curtain of tall trees.

Rapide's family lived in a German blockhouse very prettily situated amongst brambles and foliage, and so cunningly hidden away that, though I was aware of its general situation, I had never in fact set eyes on it. But there was a rustic green lane off the Rue Pasteur, leading to the blockhouse, which during the occupation was very comfortably furnished by the enemy—so comfortably in fact that, after the Germans fled, rumour had it that the blockhouse became for a time a place of assignation for lovers. After that it must have become vacant for a while. Eventually Rapide and his family moved in and Charmante and the black dog kept watch outside. There were many of these blockhouses on the wild windswept top of Mount Canisy some three miles farther along the coast, relics of the Atlantic Wall.

From time to time Charmante broke her tether and went off fo a walk by herself, grazing by the sides of the lanes, and on these occasions she gave every sign of being contented. Freedom and solitude suited her. Denise claimed that she and the donkey were good friends, because they so often found themselves walking together along the Chemin de San Carlos; but the donkey always turned back before they reached the village. There was also the time that Charmante and Rapide were found by Mlle Besnus half engulfed by the soft sand that runs treacherously down to the sea by the cliffs known as the Vaches Noires. The episode recounted by Mlle Besnus used to divert me greatly. Mlle Besnus, so quiet and unassuming, had several surprising sides to her character.

Having deposited Mlle Besnus, the kitten and the magazines at 'La Feuillée' I hurried home, anxious to see my house again, to be reassured about the fires, to lock up the hens for the night and to begin my own lonely evening with my TV., my sewing, my thoughts and my plans for the future.

The next morning the sun came out after a night of rain, and the sky was blue as if it had been washed clean. I would pick the best of the roses to put on my mother's grave at Auberville, pot the last geraniums and wash the sheets. For the last two nights I would roll myself up in a blanket like an Arab woman so as not to leave any dirty linen for Georgette.

I worked quickly and soon the sheets were hanging on the line with a fair wind making them billow like a ship with pink sails— a ship of happy dreams. Then I took my transistor into the kitchen garden where I wanted to prepare a strawberry patch. The plants were being sent to me by a specialist at Caen to whom I had telephoned the previous day. I had asked him for some Royal Sovereign. 'An excellent idea,' he answered, 'but I suggest that you plant other varieties with them,' and he had named two— La Fertilité and La Belle et Bonne.

My transistor relayed an excellent lecture on Verdi, a peasant's son who himself loved the land, and as I listened to the speaker I felt as if I were being warmed by Verdi's genius. I saw myself walking along that street near the Scala in Milan which bears his name. Into my kitchen garden came an aria from *Aïda* and I remembered a certain evening when my husband and I, both absurdly young, sat in the gods at the Monnaie in Brussels listening to the opera for the first time, excited to find ourselves in this famous opera house.

By the time I had dug my patch the sheets were dry, and I was able to fold them and put them away. Blankets must be made safe against moth and wrapped in plastic bags. These things took rather less time than the previous year. Habit, alas, was creeping upon me. My mother's absence was now a thing I had steeled myself to accept. In two days' time the house would start its second winter of solitude. What surprised me was my growing resemblance to my mother, and when on occasion I found myself staring into a mirror it was she whom I saw in myself, and myself in a faint reflection of her.

When Brigitte came in with the evening milk she said to me in a confidential manner:

'Did you know that Granny Déliquaire is going to have a kitten?'

'I knew that Mlle Besnus was trying to find a home for one. I didn't know that her choice had fallen on your granny.'

Granny Déliquaire and her husband René, Jacques Déliquaire's parents, had been our farmers till they retired. They now lived in the lodge of a big house in the Rue Pasteur. Brigitte looked at me slyly as she gave me the information. She knew that I had been mixed up in that kitten business with Mlle Besnus.

My strawberry plants arrived in excellent condition and I immediately took down the *Everyman's Encyclopaedia of Gardening* to refresh my memory about how best to plant them. You will find in it that very old saying to the effect that God could doubtless have made a better berry, but doubtless God never did. Indeed no fruit is more beautiful or easier to pick. Like so many other of the best things in life one merely needs to stretch out a hand to acquire them.

Towards evening I went down to the village to bid farewell to Madame Lehérissey, whom I found in her dining-room in front of a pile of curtains that she had just washed and ironed and was preparing to put away in readiness for the following summer. She was leaving for Nice at the same time as Patsy was flying to Agliers and I was returning to London.

Though the evening had turned cold she had no fire, partly because she was moving so busily about her house and partly because her daughter, Mado, was coming to take her to a family dinner at 'Le Plein Air'. She complained of feeling lonely now that her grandchildren had gone back to Paris. She was sleeping badly too, alone in her big bed, and she was not the sort of person to recite poetry or count imaginary sheep, though she sometimes tried to sort out her business affairs which, since the death of her husband, had become complicated.

'Then last night', she said, 'I heard a terrible crash on the stairs. There was a sound of broken glass. I lay chilled by fear. This was not like me, for when my husband was alive I was seldom daunted by anything. I would have jumped out of bed to reconnoitre, knowing that whatever happened he was not far away. When at last I summoned up courage to peep out on the landing, I saw that a picture had fallen from the wall. I felt terribly ashamed.

'When the doctor was alive my fears were always for him. People would call him out in the middle of the night, for instance, sometimes for an *accouchement* on the dunes in the rain. My biggest fears for him were during the war, for one never knew, when a man went out, if he would come back. The maternity cases were the worst, because sometimes when he was called out early in the evening to some lonely farm the baby might not arrive till daybreak or even later, and as he could not get a message back to me I would become increasingly anxious. My worst vigils sometimes ended in comic relief. He was sent for urgently by a woman who was said to be in great pain but when he arrived he found that she was merely in travail. The woman received the news with indignation, her friends with disbelief. "But it can't be," they cried. "Her husband has been a prisoner of war for over a year." When an hour later she gave birth to a fine boy the neighbours could not doubt the evidence, but in order to preserve her good name my husband proclaimed learnedly that hers had doubtless been a protracted pregnancy. Nobody questioned him. The doctor had spoken.

'So much of the past keeps coming back into my mind. Now that he has gone I live less in the present than in the years we spent

E

together. Most of my memories are happy ones, but there is always, I suppose, the one stupid misunderstanding that one would give anything to efface. The occasion was my birthday. I don't think I was even aware of it. I have already told you how undemonstrative my family was. We never bothered much about birthdays or anniversaries, but all the members of my husband's family were solicitous, affectionate and open-hearted.

'My husband went for a walk that day and on his return brought me a present. Alas, it was to prove the last present he ever gave me. I opened the package and saw that it was a scarf. I am quick-tongued—my thoughts spring out of my mouth before I can stop them. "Oh, I'm not going to wear that!" I cried. "It would make me look like one of those dear old ladies who toddle up and down the Promenade des Anglais!" I forgot to tell you that we were at Nice. As if this wasn't enough, I added: "I'll go and change it for something else. Do you remember where you bought it?"

'My husband gave me a wistful look, very gentle and sad, and said in a low voice:

'"I'm unlucky!"

'These two words should have burned me up, but I was unaware of their poignancy and let them pass. I took the scarf back to the shop, and as nothing else pleased me there I decided to buy something practical, so I bought—a bra!

'Now I think I would give all the rest of my days to retrieve that moment of childish bad temper.'

Night had fallen and we were still seated on either side of the table on which she had put out the curtains she had washed and ironed. She had not wanted to switch on the light that banishes sombre thoughts. I felt very cold.

I drove back to the farm to make ready for my departure. My bags were already packed. I would allow the Aga stove to go out during the night. The refrigerator must be emptied and turned off. I found myself wandering from room to room, miserable and full of regrets.

With my Pekinese beside me in the car I drove to the top of the orchard where Jacques and Georgette were picking the first cider apples, their transistor hanging from the bough of a pear tree. Brigitte kissed me goodbye. 'Have no fear,' she said bravely. 'I'll look after your hens!'

At the entrance to 'La Feuillée' I sounded my horn and Mlle Besnus came out. My throat was parched as I handed her Fifille. This was the moment I had feared most. Now I drove alone down the Chemin de San Carlos and as far as my garage overlooking the sea where I handed over my car.

A few minutes later the bus for Le Havre came thundering down the hill. Tomorrow at breakfast time I would be back in London.

8

THE idea of trying to recapture my own past would never have entered my head. I had come to think of travelling as lacking spice unless there was a reason to spur me on. I wanted, for instance, more than anything else to go to Russia. I considered that my life would not be complete unless I could see with my own eyes what that vast country looked like. I had for some time been learning Russian, partly by following the lessons on the B.B.C., partly by keeping a grammar in my handbag and consulting it whenever I had a moment.

Earlier in the year I had asked the editor of a women's magazine to send me to Moscow and Leningrad. I needed this incentive for the journey. I wanted to tell young women in Britain about their sisters in Russia.

Meanwhile I was asked if it would amuse me to look into the experiment by a South African, Max Wilson, to make cruising more popular. The *Empress of Britain*, which was on charter to him, was to make a short trip to the Mediterranean with some eight hundred tourist passengers, most of whom had been saving week by week for the journey and few of whom had ever been on a big ship before. Experts seemed to think that this young man—he was only thirty-five—might revolutionize sea travel. Three companies, the Canadian Pacific, the Royal Mail and the Union Castle, had a stake in the venture.

The idea appealed to me and I would not be sorry to revisit some of the places where the ship would call—Corunna, Tangier, Monte Carlo and Valencia. I had not worn a real evening dress for a long time. I had become unpardonably stay-at-home. What precisely would I be expected to wear on board ship on gala occasions? I proceeded to review the contents of a much attenuated London wardrobe. From past favourites I chose a strapless midnight blue sheath which Elsa Schiaparelli once gave me at her

Paris home in the Rue de Berri and which, in its cunning simplicity, I always thought of as one of her most sensational creations; a vaporous blue chiffon from which I would cut the sleeves; and a flowered blouse, fresh as a garden bouquet, with which I would wear a tight black moiré skirt. I also took, much against my better judgment, a full-length brocade.

The journey to Liverpool confirmed my suspicions that with this cruise Max Wilson was staking his future. There is something exciting in watching a man play for high stakes. If he is young the excitement is all the greater. I have met many men who have amassed great fortunes. Some are now legendary figures. But upon meeting them I invariably found myself regretting that I had not known them during the vital months or years during which their future was balanced on a knife-edge.

This cruise would possess an atmosphere of drama. One felt it the moment one boarded the train. Most of the national press had sent senior representatives, and because Max Wilson was born in Johannesburg, South African newspapers, both Afrikaans and English, had sent correspondents. There were also writers from the New York shipping journals. A film unit was to make a film of the cruise and a number of model girls were to figure in the scenes. This first lunch on the train therefore had something of the atmosphere of a film studio, a theatrical first night and a newspaper office.

I had never travelled on the post-war *Empress of Britain* which, like her much larger predecessor, was built for the Canadian run. My husband and I had known the first one well. We had played on her games deck as she steamed slowly up the St Lawrence River from Quebec to Montreal. We had watched the giant forests roll by, had filled our lungs with the clear smell of maple and pine. We had glided past Three Rivers and looked with tenderness at the spires of the little wooden churches and rejoiced to be young and alive.

The smaller ship was reminiscent of the first. I felt curiously at home, though a little disappointed not to be going to Canada. By coincidence the first person we met on board was the Belgian steward of the first-class bar of the old *Empress* who, greeting us in French with that delightful Antwerp accent, bridged the gulf between present and past. He could at least say: 'Do you remember this man or that? And the trip when there were only thirty on board and you went to see that Shirley Temple film with Sir James Dunn?'

We drew away from Liverpool under a grey October sky. A great sea bird looked down on us from the top of the Liver Building. There were soldiers in kilts piping away on the quay-side, a few people waving, a shining police car, a forest of coloured paper streamers which as soon as they were broken were kicked into the water by unromantic stevedores.

Our cabin had twin beds, a very pretty dressing-table, a large interior-lit wardrobe, a porthole and a bathroom decorated in pink. The cabin walls were lined with light Canadian wood and the carpets were thick and soft. The names of our stewardess and steward appeared in the form of visiting cards in the miniature hall, and on the dressing-table there was a little stack of envelopes with cards inside inviting us to forthcoming parties.

Night had fallen. I arranged the cabin so that it had a lived-in look and imprinted enough of myself to make it seem our home —my make-up on the dressing-table, the smell of my soap in the bathroom, my typewriter on a table, my dresses lined up with the shoes underneath, my nightdress on the bed that would be mine, books under the reading-lamp, a string bag and a piece of sewing. There was a cocktail party in what I think they called the Sun Lounge. Max Wilson was giving it for the press. I was surprised and rather pleased to discover that he was on board, but I didn't look at him very much on this occasion. I am not at my happiest at cocktail parties. I dislike smoke and noise and trivialities annoy me. My emotions to be worth anything have to be tempestuous. When I cry with people I empty my whole soul, but their surface politeness is apt to make me sneer, and then I hate myself for my bad manners. I remember Max Wilson saying to me: 'Won't you have a champagne cocktail?' and answering curtly: 'No, thank you!' before I could snatch the words back. Yet there was nobody at that moment I wanted to meet more—but not like that, no impersonally in a crowd. I sensed that a time would come when I could have all his attention.

In the restaurant the *maître d'hôtel* led us rather dramatically, as most restaurant directors do, with a great wave of the right arm to our places. We found ourselves in the middle of the room. Two young women joined us. We eyed one another suspiciously then introduced ourselves. We learned they were South African newspaper columnists. One, Aida Parker, had flown over specially from Durban to London to join the cruise; the other, Mrs Ward-Jackson, herself a writer, was the wife of the London correspondent of a group of South African morning newspapers. Aida Parker was slim, shy and had a small voice and dark wavy hair. She had recently been sent by her paper to Hong Kong and to Russia. We did not talk much that first evening. The sudden change from spring to autumn, all within a matter of hours, had given her a cold but I was avid to listen, to try to understand, and my mind was receptive to the different conflicting waves beating about the ship.

Technically there was the tourist and first class, but I have never seen a ship more democratically run. The first class was smaller and the public rooms gave me the impression of being cold; in truth most of the first class passengers, being invited guests and inquisitive, spent their time seeking the noisy friendliness of the tourists, who in any case were probably much better off financially than they were. But on this first evening at sea nobody, I fancy, stayed up very late.

I woke to the faint throbbing of engines, the high-pitched whir of the air conditioning ventilator above the dressing-table and the sound of a man's heavy footsteps on the deck above. Pale sunshine came through the thick glass of the copper-rimmed porthole and I supposed rather sleepily that we must be emerging from the Irish Sea or perhaps nosing our way into the Channel. I had slept well and took note of the device that had kept the pink eiderdown from slipping off during the night. I felt rather pleased with myself and began to wonder vaguely about breakfast. Did one go down to the restaurant or have it in bed?

We were fortunate in having such a large porthole and that it should be situated on the side of the ship from which in a few hours we might hope to catch sight of the French coast. Later on we would see Spain. Which was port and which was starboard? I never could remember. A knowledgeable shipping man once took pains to explain to me that, in the days of British rule in India, passengers by P. & O. ships, anxious to get the morning sun, asked for cabins on the port side for the outward journey and the starboard side for the homeward journey. He said that this was the origin of the expression 'posh'.

I made a happy little noise designed to rouse my husband, who had the gift of invariably waking up in a good temper. He could be asleep one moment and wide awake the next. There was never any tiresome period of adjustment. I wanted him to tell me if there was anything to be seen out of the window.

He obediently looked out to sea.

'No ships, no birds,' he said. 'Just lots of grey waves.'

My chief concern during the day was to be in the open air. At night there would be dancing, but until it was time to change for dinner I intended to fill my lungs with sea air.

By early afternoon we were presumably ten to twenty miles off the French coast. The sky was overcast, the sea a mixture of greys, blues and greens, the wind strong enough to blow one's hair about and come unexpectedly at one at corners, but the ship proceeded unconcernedly along, and one sensed that it had been built for just this sort of weather and that it rather liked it. I still could not persuade myself that we were heading for the Mediterranean. She was so traditionally bound up with the Canadian run that it did not seem right for her to be going out of her course. This was absurd, because she had gone cruising before, but I think it is true to say that there was a current of sadness somewhere along the decks that she had been removed so drastically from her cold climate run, and a whispering fear that this might in some way foreshadow an eventual abandonment of regular passenger services between England and Canada. Perhaps I was exaggeratedly receptive on this score in the same way that a person in a particular mood seems to capture a message from the atmosphere. Not till our return did we hear that the Canadian Pacific was selling this fine British ship to the Greek Line, who planned to use it for a Mediterranean–New York service. So perhaps I had been gifted with a sixth sense after all.

On some ships one can walk right round the deck, and when I went cruising on the *Arandora Star* my escorts used to tell me how many times round the deck went to a mile. The *Empress of Britain*'s deck space was nearly all aft, and it was in three tiers—

a games deck with two tennis courts, the boat deck, and another, the lowest of the three, overlooking the stern. At times as the weather became warmer they looked like the beach at Brighton on a Saturday afternoon, and that in a way was when they were nicest. Strangers lent one another binoculars to look at anything interesting on the horizon and then, after asking a few questions, they began to unfold the story of their lives. Most of the stories were rather sad. A still relatively young man said: '. . . and then my wife died and there seemed nothing left to live for. So I came on a cruise.'

The little games deck reserved for the first class was sheltered by the superstructure round the base of the funnel, which, painted C.P.R. yellow, gave a great impression of reliability and power, and emitted a terrible shriek every midday. My husband and I played endless games of deck tennis, but the rules were our own. The idea was merely to see how long we could go on swiftly throwing the rubber quoit backwards and forwards over the net before one of us missed a catch—a warming exercise on a cold day, for we became so expert that we could often keep it up for five minutes without a break. There was not a great run on the court. The girl models, when they were not working, relaxed under rugs on deck chairs surrounded by film men and photographers. A veranda lounge opened on to this piece of deck, and so did the nursery, where I occasionally helped the nurse pour out imaginary tea from a miniature teapot to amuse the babies.

I enjoyed changing for dinner. This English habit, though not as universal as it was in the days of the Raj, is flattering to women. At seven-thirty a page boy walked slowly along the corridors playing a little tune on a gong. This was the signal.

The captain's table was at the far end of the dining-room, under the clock. The purser had his table, quite a large one, not far from ours in the middle of the room. Max Wilson sat alone or with one of his senior executives at a modest table for two by the entrance. Often when I looked up our eyes would meet, for my chair was in a line with his. He ate little, smoked continually and never stayed for long. He gave the impression of being always under pressure and wanting to resolve his problems alone, and from time to

time I would see him passing a hand quickly across his forehead.
Amongst the tourist passengers his name had become a symbol.
They spoke of him with admiration, as troops will speak of a
general they love and believe in. I think he was aware of this and
was determined that nothing should thwart his desire to give
them more and more for their money. He was ready even to
change the itinerary of the cruise if he thought that by doing so
he could add to their enjoyment.

Our two companions could not have been more charming, but
Aida Parker's cough was getting worse and she had spent the
afternoon in bed. I found her manner of speaking increasingly
delightful. She spoke very softly, almost jerkily at first, sometimes cutting a sentence short with a little laugh and at the same
time with the swiftness and lightness of a bird she would extend
two fingers of a beautifully shaped hand and make as if to pinch
one on the arm—which, of course, she never did. Later, when she
overcame a natural shyness, these mannerisms were replaced by
long periods of beautiful English.

The South African contingent, as I have already said, was
strong. There passed us on the way to their table two Afrikaner
journalists, J. A. de Beer of *Die Vaderland* and T. Boshoff of *Die
Burger*, with their lovely young wives. When together they spoke
Afrikaans. All this gave our corner of the dining-room a slightly
cosmopolitan air.

We were to have a different film almost every night and there
was some rather sedate dancing in the first class lounge but, just
as the tourists had the most deck space, so they stole the show in
the evening. Their enormous lounge and ballroom were warmly
crowded, vital with laughter, dancing and music, as merry as anything at Blackpool in the height of the season.

The tourists danced with unbelievable energy, so that some
would come back to their tables in a state close to exhaustion, but
a moment later one would see them on the floor again shouting,
singing, tapping, jiving, yodelling, holding hands, linking arms
or frenetically 'twisting' till the sweat poured from their foreheads.
Northern accents predominated, and though there was seldom a
seat left at any of the tables that fringed the dance floor you
could be reasonably certain that anyone passing by at all wistfully

would be welcomed by half a dozen hands stretched out to offer a seat and a drink.

Beyond the ballroom four hundred people were playing Bingo. Beyond that again could be heard the sound of sixpences falling into fruit machines. Soon supper would be served—hot roast beef between thick slices of bread.

Tomorrow would be Sunday. On waking up we should see the coast of Spain, and by lunch time we should be at anchor in the bay of Corunna.

9

THE Spanish coast looked enchanting that Sunday morning. Gulls circled the ship for the first time since we left England. With binoculars one could see little white villages running down to sands. I longed to be amongst new people, hear bells ringing for Mass, smell fir twigs and charcoal fires.

There was a small deck beyond the navigating bridge which nobody used very much. Gusts of wind blew across it and it was the sort of place where men who like to face the bows stand doggedly, feet apart, contentedly telling themselves how much they love the sea.

Somebody prevailed on me that Sunday morning to pass the heavy doors leading to this deck, which technically was part of the first class promenade. I had not been there many moments when a young thrush fell at my feet in a state of collapse. As I bent down to pick him up he tried to hop away, but I had no great difficulty in cornering him against a piece of machinery and I soon felt his tiny body relaxing in my hands. He had a long pointed beak and there was a stain on his throat which was not blood but might possibly have been oil. Very soon he abandoned himself completely to the softness and warmth of my hands and fell asleep.

I took him down to the cabin. At this hour of the day the long corridors were invariably lined with breakfast trays that had not yet been cleared away by the stewards. As I passed I took a small jug of milk and a roll of bread from one of these trays.

My Spanish messenger remained asleep for the best part of half an hour. Seated in an armchair by the porthole I held him close to me and thought him the prettiest thing. My husband prepared a dish of bread and milk and as soon as the thrush opened his eyes I offered him some, which to my surprise he swallowed. A second piece disappeared in the same way. Soon he had eaten a considerable meal. I washed the stain from his throat and put him on the bed. He looked at me with intelligent interest and in a succession of hops travelled its full length.

Through the porthole we could see the Spanish coast growing more distinct. When the bird collapsed on the deck we must have been at least eight miles from land. Why had he embarked on such a strange journey? Was it to emulate the gulls that were now flying round the ship in increasing numbers?

Suddenly from the end of the bed he took wing. I was afraid he would dash himself against a mirror, but he seemed to understand and came back to me. I offered him more bread and milk. His appetite was prodigious and he became so friendly that I think he would gladly have stayed with us, but within an hour we would be anchored in the bay of Corunna and I thought it important to give him his freedom quickly so that he could fly straight to his habitat.

Making my way back to an upper deck I kissed him on the forehead, thanked him for coming and opened my cupped hands. To my surprise he merely looked up at me with bright, confident eyes. My sweater must have represented warmth and safety for he flew against it and clung there. We were already late for lunch and passengers were to disembark at two o'clock. Some people came to see what I was doing. Their voices must have disturbed him for suddenly, while my eyes were diverted, he decided to leave me. There was a slight flutter against my breast. Then he was gone and I saw him speeding away in the direction of land.

Aida Parker's cough was no better, but she had been to the hairdresser's and now looked very nice with a wave across the forehead. Her eyes were full of expression and I noticed again the way she had of accompanying her words with a slight pressure of her hand on one's arm as if the things she was saying were unusually important and confidential.

The engines stopped. Now here we were, our great white vessel riding at anchor in the bay in which the invincible Spanish Armada assembled in 1588 to conquer England.

We were to be taken ashore in small Spanish craft, the first of which now bobbed up and down beside us. Though it was warm enough to wear a cotton dress I had in deference to the Spanish regard for Sunday given myself a more sombre appearance, prepared if the occasion presented itself to attend vespers. As we knew nothing about this Galician city except that its *miradores*, or window balconies, give its houses immense character, we decided merely to take a quiet stroll.

One was quickly in beautiful squares and narrow picturesque streets, and these curiously shaped windows were indeed of rare beauty. The city had a dignified quietness about it, the streets half empty, the shops closed. A woman dressed severely in black was leading her tiny donkey by a string, and her expression as she passed me had something disdainful about it as if she resented the foreigner in her land. A very old woman was seated under a tree, making lace, and I would have liked to be rich enough to buy up all the fairylike produce of her gnarled but agile fingers. I felt humbled by a sense of inadequacy in this city so lovely to look at, so rich in proud history. My imagination tried to picture Philip II passing through these streets in 1554 on his way to England to marry Mary Tudor, in whose reign my half-timbered house in Normandy was built. Does it not have the year 1555 engraved upon its front?

The narrower the streets the more I liked them. There was a smell of fish fried in olive oil, strange fish whose names I did not know. I saw them displayed in the windows of small eating-houses which tempted and yet frightened me. We passed from one narrow street to another and finally came upon another bay not unlike the one we had left behind, except that there was no liner anchored in it. We could not make out how, having turned our backs on the sea, we had suddenly come upon it again. There were beautiful sands, much coarser and more golden in colour than I have ever seen, and full of curiously shaped pebbles that looked like polished glass. Having bruised an ankle against a kerb-stone in the town I thought it would be soothing to paddle, and while I was doing so my husband found a piece of coloured stone shaped like a heart buried in the sand. It shone like a jewel and I decided to keep it.

We tried to return by the same streets but lost the way and eventually found ourselves in what appeared to be a new residential area with large white villas, palm trees and gardens. There was a school, a sanatorium and at the end of a little promontory a church with a row of olive trees in front of it. The fact that we had come upon the sea again added to our confusion. As soon as we turned our backs on it it reappeared. Had we been wise enough to buy a map we would have discovered that the city was built on a tongue of land. At the time I wished we had hired some form of transport, but afterwards I was grateful for certain memories which we would have missed if we had not been on foot.

There was a piece of waste land where two lean cows were trying to graze the almost non-existent grass. They were tethered to stakes like goats. The land was obviously waiting for bull-dozers to prepare it for new building. Somebody was trying to grow vegetables on a piece of it and there was a foul-smelling dump of broken bottles and refuse. From a rickety shanty with a tin roof and window frames boarded up with cardboard came the sound of angry voices—first a woman's, then a man's, then children's. Finally the door, which did not even stand straight, was thrown open and out came a girl of such breathtaking beauty that I thought I had never seen her equal. Her jet-black hair was tied tightly in a pony tail which sailed behind her as she came running towards us. Her eyes were so deep and limpid and her features so perfect that it was as if something celestial had come streaking out of this hovel.

We ended by finding our way back to the centre of the town. We even found a pastrycook's open, and bought two pieces of chocolate cake which we ate in a public garden where young children were playing under the eyes of their mothers and grannies. We stayed watching them until it began to grow dark and then waited at the quayside to be ferried back to the ship.

We passed Cadiz in the night. The next morning after breakfast the sun became really hot, and there in front of us shimmering in all the beauty of this African day was Cape Spartel.

Our call at Tangier meant something more to me than just a colourful hour in the gardens of the Sultan's palace or in the narrow streets of the Grand Soko, where the snake-charmer and the professional story-teller plied their trades. I thought of Patsy in Algiers and of her friend Thérèse who had written to her so pathetically: 'If you want to spend a week with us come now or it will be too late. We are being driven out of the land which we had hoped to make our own.' She had scarcely said this when a decree went out dispossessing the few French farmers left in Algeria;

and now to make the tension greater a fierce frontier dispute was embittering relations with Morocco. What would we find on landing?

A few small cargo ships were rounding Cape Spartel presumably bound for West African ports. From the direction of Tarifa came the elegant white Spanish ferry boat that plies between Algeciras and Tangier, the link between Gibraltar and Morocco. From the speed she was making she would doubtless berth before us.

A gangway led directly to the quayside, so that from lunchtime till three in the morning we could go and come as we pleased. The quay was broad and spacious and all along it were Arab vendors wearing burnous and fez, standing or squatting by their colourful wares. There were also huge wicker baskets of freshly cut flowers—roses, red and white camellias, tuberose lilies of pungent smell, carnations. And all the notices on customs sheds and warehouses were written in Arabic and in French. Here I could freely speak my own tongue.

The excitement that I felt on once again setting foot on African soil was heightened by something which really had nothing to do with it. Next to us lay at her berth the ferry boat from Algeciras. Her name was the *Victoria* and she flew the Spanish flag from her stern. Next to her was a much larger ship, not as large as the *Empress of Britain*, but a fine sea-going vessel of graceful design. She was called the *Transilvania* and came from Constantza in the Black Sea, flew the blue, yellow and red flag of Rumania and had brought Russians on a cruise like ours. I think I must have read into the presence of this ship something of an omen. I still thought of my projected trip to Moscow as vitally important to my future, but I was aware of how much could come between myself and my ambition. This dockside at Tangier took on the appearance of a link, just as during the war this same Tangier brought together people of different countries who, in the normal course of events, would have been completely cut off from one another.

We decided to walk to the Place de France. There had been great changes, but at the Place de France all would come back to me. The idea was also to reach our destination slowly, to accustom our eyes once more to the bougainvillaea and hibiscus and our noses to the aromatic smells of Africa. There were Arab cafés, a fair with coconut shies, merry-go-rounds and fortune-tellers, radios blaring out the news in Arabic, a long avenue with palm trees and the low ochre railway station with bananas and vines growing in the stationmaster's garden. *Gare de chemin de fer de Tanger à Fez*, it said, and here in the station all ready to leave was the long cream and red diesel train that—when the engine driver had stopped arguing with the guard—would start on its romantic journey to Fez. The quarrel was about some luggage that the guard wanted to put in the luggage van, and when the driver of the diesel train felt he was not making his point sufficiently clear he blew the shrill whistle of the train to show that he was about to start and that no guard could stop him. Down the avenue came four donkeys and an elderly Arab wearing a huge straw hat. The railway line followed the bay for a little while then turned inland. Soon we would come to the *plage* where holiday-makers disport themselves in summer. From behind us came a shriller, longer whistle than before and now the diesel train sped past. I wondered what had prevented my buying a ticket and setting forth on the journey. Nothing really, except that we are not nearly so adventurous as we like to think. Things have to be planned ahead as if one were the mistress of one's destiny. Now here, facing the beach, was the Rif Hotel, which the Germans favoured during the war, whereas the English used the Bristol.

We climbed up the steep hill to the Boulevard Pasteur. Most of the shops and the Grande Poste retained a French air, but there was a small café called the Bar Gagarin. At the Place de France everything, as I had hoped, came back to me. Below us stretched the bay, with the three white ships gleaming in the afternoon sun. We went to drink green tea in the gardens of El Minzah which were heavy with the scent of early mimosa. In the Soko we bought tangerines with their leaves still clinging to them and pome-granates which, when you ate them, made you think of rubies. Soon the city became a city of dazzling light. Arab women, looking like classical statues, sat on stone benches under trees, their children playing near them. In a modern office a young woman employee, her day's work finished, expertly wrapped her caftan round her and a few moments later passed us swiftly, her features veiled.

Several times during the night we left the ship to wander along the quay, which the Arab merchants had turned into a fabulous Eastern market. Their lamps turned the place into something out of a fairly tale. Some sat gravely on the floor surrounded by copper or leather work. Others had pulled the hoods of their burnous over their heads and were asleep. In the warm night air the liles and the roses smelt more pungently than before. Two gendarmes stood beside the gangway to the Rumanian ship. The Russians, they said, had gone off in coaches. The ship was to sail for the Black Sea at midnight. They talked about their king— King Hassan II—who had gone to a conference about the frontier troubles. They made deprecating gestures about the Algerians. Behind them was a great consignment of fresh cork bark waiting for shipment. The cork, much of it still with moss growing on it, added its peculiar smell to that of tangerines and roses and charcoal and herbs and warm wool and leather. This is what I dreamed of when I was a little girl and read the *Arabian Nights*. The wonder was that time had not destroyed it.

Our ship now turned into the Mediterranean with Monte Carlo as our next port of call. Betty Ward-Jackson was to leave us there in order to fly back to London. Aida Parker, as we steamed past the Balearic Islands, wrote the article she would dispatch by air to Durban.

One night at dinner, after glancing at Max Wilson sitting thoughtfully in his lonely corner, I turned to Aida and asked her how she had first become intrigued by the activities of this man.

'In South Africa', she said, 'we had mutual friends who told me that his new ideas were beginning to embarrass the travel trade. I had already heard rumours about this and suggested that the next time he came to Durban he should look me up.

'He walked into my office one day. I had not even seen a picture of him, but before he had time to open his mouth I exclaimed: "You're Max Wilson!" At the same time I knew that we were going to be friends. When later he chartered a Union Castle ship to take South Africans to England at cut prices, he gave me the story, and indeed from then onwards whenever he had a big story he gave it to me first. I found it exciting to watch his success, and in South Africa today there is a magic about his name. He phones me often from London at 3 a.m. That is typical of him. When he has something on his mind, he considers neither time nor distance.'

'From what I gather you're pretty good yourself at annihilating distance. Was it your idea to fly here to cover the story of this cruise?'

'I think that was an obvious one. I have already told you that in South Africa there is something magical about his name.'

'In principle, can you travel anywhere in the world to find material for your column?'

'Provided that I can convince my editor that I am going to bring him back something of value. For instance, I went to Russia because so few South Africans had gone there.'

'Do you feel that you must necessarily give a South African slant to whatever you write?'

'No, not at all, though it's possible that I may look at things differently because I am a South African, but I believe that universally people are longing to know what other people think and feel.'

'How long did you stay in Russia?'

'A month.'

'How did somebody as young as you, and what is still more wonderful, a young woman, get such a splendid opportunity?'

'I think it's a matter of knowing when you're up against your big chance, and then taking it with all your might. Most of us get one big chance. I was seventeen when I started journalism in Durban. My widowed mother was concerned about me. She said: "You really must try to make something of your life." She knew an editor. In 1953 I was sent to interview Dr Malan, then Prime Minister. He had a reputation for eating reporters alive, and so I fancy nobody else would go. Of course, I didn't realize at the time why I had been given this signal honour.

'Dr Malan was in his personal coach in Durban station. They called it the White Train. Mrs Malan received me. I was in such a state of nerves that she asked me what was wrong. "My dear," she said. "Don't worry. I'll go and talk to Oupa." That is South African for "grandfather". When she came back she took me by the hand and led me to him, and she said: "Oupa, you must be kind to this girl. She's nervous." He just laughed and said: "You had better have a cup of coffee!" and he held the train up for half an hour while he gave me a story—the story of the case that South

Africa was going to put up to the United Nations. That set me
a pattern.'

'Didn't you tell me that you had just come back from the Far
East?'

'I did.'

'What did you write about—politics?'

'I write about anything that interests me, sometimes quite
trivial things, the sort of things that a writer could turn into a
short story. In Hong Kong, for instance, I wanted to buy a piece
of jade. "Whatever you do," said my friends, "you must not buy
it in Cat Street." Cat Street is a whole hill of small streets tightly
packed. They said I would be robbed if I went there without an
expert. The trouble is that women are apt to do just the contrary
to what men advise. I went to Cat Street without an expert and
saw a lovely piece of jade. "But is it real?" I asked the merchant.
"People warned me not to come here." He smiled enigmatically
and answered: "The Chinese have handled jade longer than the
white man has existed." I bought it for £45 and showed it to the
experts.'

'What did they say?'

'They said it was bottle glass.'

'Were you angry?'

'No. Why should I have been? One buys one's experience.'

'What else did you do in Hong Kong?'

'I went to a fortune-teller. The life of a Chinese is governed by
the stars, and he would not dream of taking any important
decision without first consulting a fortune-teller. I went to an old
Chinese at the back of a barber's shop. Nobody saw me go in.
Nobody knew who I was. He asked me the day and the hour of
my birth and then there was complete silence while he made out a
horoscope. After forty-five minutes he began to speak rapidly.
He said that I came from a far away and very troubled country,
and added: "I feel that you are in communication with people
and that your business is to influence them. However, you are not
a teacher." He went on in this way, telling me many other things.
Finally he said: "In a short time, perhaps in a matter of hours,
you are going to have rather a fright. You are going to lose something very valuable—but do not worry, because it will be returned
to you." I left him, called a cab and asked to be driven back to my
hotel. There I had a bath and changed for dinner. It was then that

I missed the notebook I carried with me during the whole of my trip. Some of these notes, especially those on Red China, were irreplaceable. I went down to call the police, but at that very moment a page came up to tell me that I had left something in the cab and that the driver had brought it back. It was my notebook.'

I kept on coming back to a question that seemed vital to me. I said to this young woman:

'Do you believe it to be the main function of a newspaper writer to instruct?'

'As long as it is done gently. I think it is more important for journalists to travel than to sit at their desks and accept the ideas of others. Appreciating other peoples' problems is the root of the matter. Anything is worth while that helps to break down this terrifying wall of hatred that is continually being built up between one half of the world and the other.'

Two days later we ran into a small gale and the captain began to feel that we might not be able to anchor outside Monte Carlo. He hoped for rain as he thought it might calm the sea. Perhaps he even prayed for it. At all events when finally we reached Monte Carlo the gale had abated slightly but rain fell in torrents. Towards eleven in the morning we changed our anchorage, going from Monte Carlo to Villefranche, and the weather looked as if it might clear.

Reaching Villefranche for me was almost like coming home. I felt elated to be in the land of Milou, my father, and though it was a pity about the threatening skies I determined to have a good time. The village, built in tiers against the flank of the rock, is enchanting, and we had an excellent lunch in the company of two Dutch women painters in an unpretentious restaurant overlooking the sea.

We took it into our heads to go by train to Monte Carlo. The railway track, clinging to the sea coast, is far more picturesque than the road, and whereas a car would have cost us a great deal of money, the return fare by rail was only a few shillings.

The tiny station at Villefranche is in itself a thing of beauty. Deep red geraniums sprawled all over it and the paths that led to it were thick with little olives that the gale had blown off the trees. Rain had made the country smell delicious.

The trains that pass this way are of a superior kind. Most of them are international expresses that, having reached Marseilles at great speed, complete the journey to the Italian border by stopping at every delightful station. There are sleeping-cars that have the names of romantic cities written on them. It is very satisfying to step into a third-class coach attached to such a train.

At Monte Carlo we looked into the casino, where the great gambling-rooms were beginning to have a very old-fashioned air. Those wall paintings of Edwardian beauties with lilies and boats and swans, those great chandeliers, those grave attendants in knee breeches who wear their chains of office round their necks strike a pathetically old-world note against the batteries of fruit machines in adjoining rooms that bring to this august palace of chance the tinny vulgarity of Las Vegas.

The little railway station behind the casino was beginning to be overgrown with exotic verdure, and for that very reason had a charm as if it had been asleep since the days of its glory. Between the gnarled branches of fir and juniper one could look down over clusters of wild geraniums to the restless sea. The glass of the station roof had crumbled. Only the elegant trains passing through brought the present to the past.

'But the station is going to be pulled down,' said a woman on the platform to whom I turned for information. 'They will make the trains go in a tunnel under the casino so that they can build on this. They build everywhere. They are turning the whole place into what you see in American films, and we who were born here-abouts can no longer afford to live here. Misery, dear lady! Today is All Saints' Day and I've just been to place some flowers on the grave of my old man, and believe me, it'll be a wonder if soon they won't grudge us six feet of space to be buried.'

I was almost relieved to jump into the next Paris express and go back to Villefranche, but when the long train drew up at the little station the heavens opened and the rain fell as I have never seen it fall before. One had the alternative of going to Paris or getting drenched to the skin. On the whole it was better to get drenched, and there was not even much point in hurrying because we could never get wetter than we were the moment we set foot on the platform.

Down in the bay our ship seemed to be anchored half a mile away. She was even farther out than the great American warship that was flying the nuclear flag. The olives in the narrow lanes squelched under our feet, and I was terrified of tobogganing down the hill. The streets in the village were like lakes, and what inhabitants we saw were rushing from house to house as if the world had come to an end. A motor boat had just come in from the liner, but it was unloading a coffin. About a week out from Liverpool an elderly passenger had died at sea one evening while he was dancing a 'twist' with his wife in the first class lounge. The noise he made when falling, the anguish of the widow, still haunted me. Now this unexpected confrontation in the bay of Villefranche was doubly disconcerting. The body was, we supposed, being flown back to England.

To make matters more eerie a Frenchwoman with long white hair was standing by the water's edge bemoaning the weather.

'Dear, oh dear, oh me!' she cried. 'There's never an All Saints' Day but it pours with rain.'

One morning, as the ship was heading for Valencia, Max Wilson asked me to come and see him, and because of what Aida had told me about his youth I said:

'Aida claims that as a little boy you helped your father with his fruit and vegetable business in Johannesburg, and that when you are in a pensive mood you rather like to talk about it. If you are agreeable I should like to hear your story.'

He answered:

'My father had a wholesale fruit business, and when I had to go to school I got up at four in the morning to help him. When I didn't go to school I worked from 4 a.m. till 7 p.m.'

'Did you have a difficult childhood?'

'Father had strong ideas. He came from a village sixty miles from Moscow and he had no use for the cinema or any kind of sport. I had two brothers and two sisters. I was the youngest. At fourteen I ran away from school and joined the South African Navy. A year later my father pulled me out of it because I had given a false name. After that I ran away a second time and joined the army. I stayed there four months, then my father found out and pulled me out of that, so I joined the Merchant Navy in Cape Town and sailed for the Belgian Congo. That was during the last year of the war.'

'Presumably that didn't satisfy your wanderlust?'

'I got a lift in an aircraft carrier and went to England, where I stayed nine months. Then back to South Africa, where I started to sell property. I was then seventeen.'

'This is all very confusing. Aida said something about a trip to Australia. Could that be right?'

'Yes. I sold property for two years and then went to Auckland, where I started a woman's magazine called *Femina*. At the beginning I didn't think specifically in terms of a magazine for women. I just bought all those I could lay my hands on and tried to decide what was wrong with them.'

'Had you any capital?'

'I had £800 and some bank support. That was enough.'

'You might have become a press lord?'

'Perhaps.'

'But you got tired of it?'

'I suppose I did, in a way. I wanted to do some more travelling. I went to Canada and then went back to South Africa.'

'I know! One morning in Johannesburg you saw a pretty girl at a bus stop. You offered her a lift and eloped with her?'

'An over-simplification, but substantially correct. I was twenty-four at the time and living in the suburb of Emmerentia. It's common practice in the suburb where you live to offer lifts. But in fact I not only gave *her* a lift but I gave her father one also. He was a senior Afrikaner magistrate.'

'Was she pretty?'

'She was more than pretty. She was tall and lovely. She had in her everything that was good. She was feminine and serene. Her name was Monica Rossouw.'

'But there was parental opposition?'

'There was opposition from both sides. My father was living on the south coast of Natal—by the way, he was a complete agnostic. With him there was no question of colour or religion or anything. I took Monica to meet him. "Max, what are your intentions with this girl?" he asked. "If you harm a hair of her head you will never enter my house again."

'The fact is that when I first met her she was engaged to a doctor. My father considered that she was the nicest girl I had ever taken out. We stayed the week-end with him and before we left I told him that I would probably marry her. When later I phoned from Johannesburg, he said: "Don't worry to phone me again until you're married.'"

'Did it prove a runaway marriage in the end?'

'Yes, in the sense that her parents forbade me to see her. I was planning to go to Canada, so we met and decided to get married the following Saturday. This happened on the Tuesday. Later in the day she phoned me to say that we should get married immediately—but not in Johannesburg where her father was a magistrate. So we went to Brakpan, forty miles away, and were married. The date was the 8th April 1953.'

'How old were you both?'

'I was twenty-four and she was twenty-one.'

'That was when you both decided to come to London with practically no money?'

'We went to England, but not together. I sailed in the *Kenya Castle* and she flew. We were not exactly penniless. We had about £800, and another £1,000 from a farm. We took a flat in Notting Hill Gate, or, to be more precise, we started off with a flat. We spent the £800 on theatres, concerts and taxis. They were the happiest days of my life. London is a wonderful city when you are young and in love. We could never see enough. We walked for miles through the streets at night. Then when the money had gone we took an attic at £3 5s. a week. I sold space for a publisher, and Monica became secretary to a photographic firm.'

'Had you already decided to make a million?'

'I was sure I wanted to achieve something. I react best when the odds are against me. I thought of various things I could do, and finally hit on the idea of an overseas visitors' club. We started off in Templeton Place, Earls Court, with the £1,000 from the farm.'

'It was because your tiny flat was always full of lonely South Africans? They even slept on the floor. So you said: "We should have a place where people from overseas can meet?"'

'That is so.'

'Then you started the idea of cheap aeroplane fares for South Africans who wanted to come to Europe—from Lorenzo Marques, in Portuguese East Africa, wasn't it—and then there was that terrible accident in March 1962. Aida said it was one of the great crises in your life. You rang her up from London in the middle of the night?'

'It was a Sunday night. I had been ill. My wife woke me up to tell me the news. Of course it was a crisis, but when things like that happen you must either react or go to pieces. I decided to fly to Johannesburg but when I got to Zürich I had a haemorrhage and had to come back. An accident is a tragedy, but it doesn't change anything. We are now doing it through Rhodesia. You must always go forward.'

'You are reputed to be a millionaire. You bought a house in Johannesburg for £28,000 and one near London for £50,000 which is full of art treasures?'

'Not full of art treasures. Naturally I enjoy success. Life is short. One must make the best of it.'

Aida Parker, to whom I reported this conversation over dinner, said:

'He's flamboyant and hot tempered, but incredibly generous. One day at the Overseas Visitors' Club a young couple arrived so broke that they didn't know where their next meal would come from. News reached them that the girl's father had died suddenly in Johannesburg. Max, who was under thirty at the time, called them into his office. The girl was upset at the thought of her mother being alone and without money. How would she meet the funeral expenses?

'"What shall I do?" she asked Max.

'"You must both fly straight back to South Africa."

'"It's impossible!"

'"Nothing is impossible. Just wait a moment."

'He left the room and came back saying: "I've booked you both at my expense on the 6 p.m. flight to Johannesburg."'

Aida touched my arm lightly:

'That's the sort of thing he is capable of,' she said.

10

VALENCIA on a Sunday morning with all the church bells ringing. . . .

Our first sight of it was not perhaps inspiring—a corner of dockland with a café and gaudy swimming-pool for the seafaring men. They are of many nations and come to carry away in their vessels its rich produce of wine, raisins, olive oil, rice, onions and oranges. A tramcar, clanging its bell, set off up a wide avenue in the direction of the city which, being the third largest in Spain, was ringed with straggling industrialized suburbs.

A poet described Valencia as 'a piece of heaven fallen upon earth'. After several days at sea I longed to set foot on land again. I wanted to feel the pulse of cities, fill my mind with fresh thoughts, go out into the hills and breathe deeply the smell of rosemary, thyme, olives and pine needles lying on moss. I wanted to go to early Mass in the fifteenth-century cathedral with its pictures by Goya and Palomino. All this might not have been at all easy had not Aida invited us to accompany her in the car which she had taken the precaution of ordering in advance.

The centre of the city was a great deal farther from the harbour than I imagined, and if through ignorance we had tried to make the journey from El Grao on foot we should bitterly have regretted our folly. All along the wide avenue we drove, from time to time passing noisy clanging tramcars. Then, just as I was getting impatient, the city with its splendid fountains appeared. I should have realized, I suppose, that to enter even the smallest piece of heaven requires ten minutes of patience on a Sunday morning.

The cathedral was more splendid than I had even hoped to find it, and the magnificence and pomp of the service we were privileged quite by accident to attend will remain for long in my memory. I had not seen its equal outside St Peter's in Rome. The body of the cathedral was not crowded when we were there, but there were old women—and old men—in black, kneeling on the stone floor in attitudes that were worthy of the great Spanish painters. Had it not been for Aida, whose patience I was afraid to tire, I would gladly have remained all day in silent meditation.

Wisely, I think, we decided not to explore the city. The sun was coming up and we wanted to drive out into the orange groves. Our driver took us north to Sagunto. He thought we should see the ruins of the fortress the storming of which by Hannibal two centuries before Christ started the Second Punic War. Aida, who had a secret ambition to become an archaeologist, surprised us by climbing to the highest tiers of the nearby Roman theatre and picking up small pieces of stone which she put in her handbag to take back to Durban. Later we persuaded our driver to turn inland and head for the mountains.

The journey up to now had been mildly disappointing. There had been orange groves, quite a number of them, on either side of the highway, but the highway itself had been busy with traffic and I had been surprised by the number of lorries.

Now, turning inland, we suddenly found ourselves leaving the traffic behind and running into orange groves of a wealth and beauty I could scarcely believe. They grew without protection on either side of the powdery and deserted road, and when we stopped we could walk into them and pick the fruit, growing gold but tightly fastened to the stout stems and protected by savage spikes amongst the thick foliage. Nobody had ever told me that oranges could grow in such profusion, for miles and miles on every side. Some were green and some were gold, the green ones of the same deep green as the leaves, others like solid sunshine, blindingly yellow or sometimes as red as balls of fire. We picked them like children. We picked them off the trees, though not without difficulty—whole branches with the golden fruit tantalizingly hidden amongst the leaves. We picked them from the ground where the fallen fruit made rivers of gold between the trees. We ate them greedily and they were sweeter and juicier than I could ever have guessed—and we had scarcely time to travel another hundred yards in the car than we stopped to explore new wonders. This time there were tangerines in the place of the oranges and in our delight we started all over again.

Almost imperceptibly the orange and tangerine groves disappeared before our wondering eyes and, as we climbed higher and higher into the mountains, the smell of rosemary and thyme became so heady that it was as if we had entered by mistake into an enchanted land. The undergrowth became a carpet of sweetness; little fir trees grew among yellow prickly flowers, and above these were olive trees and those other trees that produce the manna which the Bible speaks of, hard but sweet when bitten.

We climbed and climbed with never a soul in sight. The rivers became dry, their wide beds full of dazzling white pebbles, but the vegetation all about us remained luxuriant and green because of the pools and artificial lakes which were visible everywhere, the precious water gleaming in the clear warm air.

The peasants (because it was Sunday) were doubtless in their homes. During the forty or fifty miles we travelled across the mountains, along roads that became steeper all the time, we never saw a peasant working in the fields or one leading a donkey or a mule—or a woman trudging home with faggots on her back.

The scenery was always changing. At times it reminded me of Greece. I could imagine myself in the Greece of the ancients. At other times the scenes were biblical. Aida was always saying: 'This is a South Africa in miniature.'

Most of us have had a dream that if we could but go on farther and farther along a certain road it would lead us to a paradise. Heaven is always just round the corner. But this is fulfilled only once or twice in a long time. I had the feeling this Sunday in Spain that the farther I travelled along this road the nearer we were getting to paradise.

I forgot to say that before we turned inland we lunched in a *posada*. We were each served with an omelette squeezed between two long strips of crisp white bread, and in front of us was a great bowl of sliced tomatoes in fresh olive oil and another bowl full of freshly picked olives. With all this we drank a wine of rare magnificence. We also bought for less than ten shillings a basket of tangerines so heavy that the men had to put it into the back of the car. We did not know, of course, that in another ten minutes we could have picked all the tangerines we wanted from the groves along the road. I took them back to my cabin where they shone like a piece of the sun fallen upon earth.

As we were not sailing till very late at night, we left the ship again in the early evening and took a stroll along the docks.

Docks and warehouses could not rob the quays of this beautiful harbour of its romantic air. The harbour of El Grao has been one of Spain's chief seaports since the Middle Ages. There were ships from many parts of Europe, amongst them two from London, and into these were being loaded thousands of cases of tangerines for Covent Garden. One of the ships put out to sea. We watched it go, and a fine sight it made in the setting sun. I promised myself the pleasure of catching up with the tangerines when next I walked along the Strand, perhaps in a fortnight's time. It would amuse me to see them displayed on barrows.

Before returning on board we found a little wine-shop where we drank wine from the cask in tiny glasses, wine that tasted like the nectar of the gods.

So like the Greeks in ancient times we set off again across the sea.

The fact that we had arrived at Valencia on a Sunday disappointed some passengers who were unable to buy presents to take home. They pointed out that we had arrived at Corunna also on a Sunday, and that in Villefranche and Monte Carlo the shops were closed because of All Saints' Day.

It was therefore decided that we should put in for a morning at Gibraltar and make up for this extra call by increasing speed through the Bay of Biscay on our way home.

Gibraltar's Main Street is ideal for shopping. Narrow, noisy and picturesque, its bazaars are packed with European, Indian, Chinese and Japanese merchandise, and as all the merchants speak English (as well as a dozen other languages) and gladly accept any currency, tourists feel at home.

'Consider', said an old woman in the fish and vegetable market, 'that we get an average of three great liners a day pouring out hundreds of people intent on spending money. Their only problem is how to spend it fast enough!' To those of us who saw the Rock during the grim years of the war, its transformation into a European Hong Kong was almost unbelievable.

On this particular morning the sun was hotter than anything we had yet enjoyed, and I would have liked to spend a week here making excursions into Spain, revisiting Ronda and Malaga.

A P. & O. liner homeward bound from India and a great

Russian ship flying the Red Flag were anchored beside us and due like ourselves to sail at midday.

Looking back across the Bay of Algeciras we set out on the last lap of our journey. Aida Parker would spend only one day in London before flying back to Durban. Already I think she was homesick. One evening while we were making heavy weather in the Bay of Biscay she told me about an assignment in London which she had finished a few days early.

'I found myself standing in Piccadilly Circus,' she said. 'I had never travelled on a London tube. I went down the steps, bought a ticket and stood at the top of the escalator. It was a terribly wet November day and I was depressed by the thousands of people pushing past me, not one of whom I knew, and my mind was so filled with a longing for sunshine that I ran up into the street again and booked a seat on the 3 p.m. plane for Johannesburg.'

Dear Aida! How happy I was to have met her! But curiously enough her story made me homesick too. I longed for the ship to hurry so that I could find myself in Piccadilly Circus and feel all round me the excitement of a cold rainy day in November.

II

MY GREAT adventure began on the morning of 19th November little more than a week after my return to London from the Mediterranean. The formalities had suddenly been speeded up, the visa granted, the reservation by Aeroflot confirmed. I was to leave London aerodrome just before midday and arrive at Moscow some three and three-quarter hours later which, because of the difference in time, would be about half-past six in the evening.

There were so few passengers in the bus that took us from Cromwell Road to the airport that when we arrived I had a sudden fear that I would misunderstand the loudspeaker instructions and miss the flight. In Rome once, and on another occasion in Geneva, my stupidity nearly caused me to be left behind—and I fancy that I am not the only persistent traveller to whom such misadventures occur.

Three men were talking Russian. One of them (who limped) wore an oversize tweed cap that gave him a squat appearance; the second would have passed unnoticed in any mid European country; the third was young, gaunt, very tall, strange in his expression and attire, with an overcoat that reached down to his ankles, and a black homburg. His eyes were dark and sad and his lips wide and prominent. They had a camera and were taking pictures of one another. I approached softly and tried discreetly to attach myself to them on the theory that four people together were unlikely to be left behind, but when I said something to this effect they made me understand by gestures that not one of them spoke English, and that far from taking me under their protection they were counting on me to direct them.

In this way I became the leader, and when finally the loud speaker invited us to follow the green lights my companion accompanied me with a confidence that was almost touching.

Now in the little bus that took us across the tarmac to th

aeroplane I experienced the extreme politeness that I was to find during the whole of my stay in Russia, for every traveller on entry greeted those already there with the soft spoken 'stratvouite', which before long I was to learn to say so often myself.

The aeroplane was a considerable distance away, like a liner anchored a quarter of a mile from shore. Then as we approached I had the satisfaction of being able to decipher the Russian characters which spelt out the word AEROFLOT. The air hostess was small and her fair hair was done up in a bun. She conformed more to the Slav conception of feminine beauty than to the Anglo-Saxon, being plumpish and wearing no make-up. She had a rather sweet smile and soft, comforting white hands, wore a somewhat vague uniform which did not detract from her personality, and had high (but not too high) heels. Was it Negley Farson who described his first view of Russian women thus: 'What a joy to see those lovely bosoms!'? It was a joy for me too to find that my figure resembled theirs, whereas in England I am often unhappy because I am different.

The air hostess took my coat, arranged it on a hanger and went off with it. This also is very Russian. On returning she gave me a newspaper, *The Moscow News*, printed in English, saying: 'This is for you!' as if she had the feeling that it would be good for me to improve my mind. This was the moment when we climbed into the sky and said goodbye to London as it lay stretched out below us with the Thames running like quicksilver through it. It is always a sad moment for those who love the great capital, but my sadness soon vanished, for from the very start these Russians, my first Russians on what was technically Russian territory, were endearingly gay and talkative. If there is a barrier between us it is one of language, never of unwillingness on the Russian part to communicate. Their clothes may occasionally appear drab to those who set out to criticize, but they have a gaiety that I had almost forgotten existed.

Soon we were flying at a great height. The sun was more powerfully hot than on the hottest summer day. Beneath us a sea of cotton wool stretched to infinity. The passengers appeared to be behaving quite differently from those I had observed in the past. They treated the aeroplane like the sun veranda on a ship. They got up, introduced themselves to one another, and moved about without any of the restraint which generally glues people

F

to their seats in aeroplanes as if they were afraid that otherwise they would upset the equilibrium.

A young woman showed her smart red umbrella with the transparent handle to a friend. She wore her hair pulled tightly back from her forehead and made into a bun, and by an altogether strange coincidence this had been the hair style I had adopted for some years. The air hostess brought a board and some chess men. The young woman was asked by her friend to play, and accepted with alacrity. Others also decided to play chess and their companions gathered to watch.

I was curious to know what we would be served for lunch. I might have guessed. There was Russian caviare! I had not tasted Russian caviare since before the war, since those unforgettable nights at the Embassy Club when we ate it greedily and youthfully on thick rounds of hot toast and butter to the accompaniment of champagne. I thought that perhaps it would never taste the same again. I now rediscovered its exquisite goodness. The wine was Russian, and excellent. The main dish was roast chicken with the sort of peas that come out yellow instead of green, being cooked in butter and lightly flavoured with sugar, a speciality in former times on French express trains, especially on the Golden Arrow in its glamorous days. To complete this Russian meal we had fruit, Russian apples, cakes, more wine (but of a different kind), sweets and coffee.

Less accustomed than my fellow passengers to walking about in the plane, I set off with some trepidation to repair my make-up and to wash my hands. Subconsciously I was always trying to decipher Russian words, first to read the writing, then to puzzle out the meaning. I felt like a child of five for whom the world is unfolding, for whom everything is a matter of splendid delight and surprise. It was with some satisfaction therefore that I discovered the sense of what was written on the taps over the basin, repeating each word aloud, savouring the sound. I put a finger on the tap and hot water gushed out. If my reaction was to be childishly pleased it at least showed that I was starting my journey in the right mood, with no prejudices, anxious to learn and to enjoy, not to criticize. Adjoining the toilet was a room large enough for passengers to change their clothes in.

I had, I suppose, thought so much about this journey that it was bound to take on an atmosphere of its own. I had wanted to travel to Moscow by Aeroflot for this reason. The unknown is what excites the imagination. Perhaps I shall never again experience that wonderful sensation of being new in a new world, deliciously receptive like a photographic plate to quite ordinary things which would be below the notice of those whose hearts have grown dry. For a multitude of reasons this may come more easily to a woman than to a man.

I had the impression while making my way slowly back to my seat of being carried on some magic carpet towards an unknown country. The sun to my right was still high and looked like a great red ball, but to my left the sky seemed to be growing darker. For some mysterious reason the sight of this fiery sun fascinated me. I saw it start to sink and then to my great surprise I caught a glimpse of the moon coming up like the crescent on a Turkish flag. Soon the sun fell spectacularly. It was as if a child had thrown an orange over a wall. The orange just disappeared out of sight. This was so unexpected that I remained wide-eyed. Then the pale crescent of the moon took possession of a sky that had turned midnight blue.

An hour or so later we began to lose height. Scattered lights appeared through breaks in the cloud, then more and bigger lights, and people exclaimed that we were over Moscow. The blonde young woman who had been playing chess looked out of her window, took up her smart red umbrella, removed the sheath and started slowly to unfurl it.

Now we had arrived. Steps were wheeled into place and the door swung open. The air hostess in bidding us goodbye explained that she was keeping our passports for the moment. We would get them back later. This information gave me a sudden chill, which increased when I became aware that it was raining in sheets as it had rained that day at Villefranche when my husband and I were soaked to the skin as we tried to run over paths made greasy with fallen olives. I had never thought to see such rain again, and this if anything was heavier, more relentless; and there stretched before me a great distance to the airport building, across which I read the word in giant letters of crimson light: MOSKVA—letters that in reflection danced weirdly on the tarmac that had become a lake.

I could imagine no more miserable welcome to the land of my dreams. With this journey in mind—and at the last moment so as not to tempt providence—I had made two major purchases in London. The first was a pair of fur-lined bootees and the second a magnificent leather coat as supple as doeskin and lined with natural fur. It had a voluminous black fur collar to frame my face and give me warmth. By coincidence it was Hungarian and had thus come from a satellite country. The heat in the aeroplane was such that I had exchanged my bootees for ordinary high-heeled shoes. In these I slipped and slithered over the wet tarmac while this torrential opening of the heavens soaked my fur collar so that long before I reached the airport building I had the impression of having a wet animal round my neck.

In this sad condition and feeling thoroughly disillusioned I stood dripping in front of a customs officer trying to answer a long questionnaire. Had I brought any U.S. dollars? Any jewellery? Any gold? Platinum? Shavings of gold or platinum? Any firearms? Answer only yes or no.

So I stood there, feeling once again like a schoolgirl, trying hard to put the right answer in the right places. I must not make a mistake, I thought. This is very important—like an examination paper in which one must not fail. My fountain pen, after its journey through rarefied air, spilled ink. Now I must append my signature. Was the document neat enough? Did my signature betray signs of nervousness? The customs officer bent down, examined the paper and said: 'You have not answered here . . . and here. You must answer all the questions.'

The passport which I had abandoned on the plane was now very courteously and with great dignity returned to me. From now on it was continually to be taken away and returned, but though I was to appreciate the scrupulous way in which these things were invariably done I never could rid myself of a pang of fear when I was temporarily left without it.

An official from Intourist took my bags and led me to a waiting car. The rain had not abated and I felt like a fly in a bowl of water. The Intourist man seated himself beside the driver and a moment later a woman, an employee of Intourist doubtless taking advantage of a lift into town, came to sit beside me, and we set off.

The journey took much longer than I had expected. The rain continued mercilessly. The car was fortunately heated, which made me feel as if I were in a Turkish bath, my fur collar emitting steam round my neck. The car windows were also steamed up so that it was only occasionally that one could see in the lights of an approaching lorry the birch woods on either side. The two Intourist employees talked incessantly, ignoring my presence as if we were part of a fairy story and a sorceress had made me invisible. I felt sorry for myself, even pretending to be miserable, though I would not have given up my place for all the gold in the Urals. 'Didn't you want to come to Russia?' I said to myself. 'Well, you're here.'

After an hour's drive we crossed over a wide bridge. The Intourist girl, who was neither pretty nor ugly, but whose features had lit up with the sheer joy of her animated conversation, turned to me and exclaimed: 'La Moskova!' and I thought of Napoleon and his army, who had come all this way on horseback. The car drew up at the kerb and the young woman, thanking us all profusely, got out. Anxious to show off the only English word she knew she smiled at me and said: 'Good-by-ee.' A moment later the car stopped a second time to allow the man to get out. Now I was alone with the driver.

Rubbing the vapour from the window pane I peered out. Gorki Street, I read. Then: Karl Marx Avenue. Finally we drew up in front of the Metropole.

There was a revolving door. This was like almost any hotel in the world. At the top of a flight of marble steps I read in Russian letters the word: Administrator. Here several guests were already patiently waiting for the woman administrator to instruct them how to fill up yet another questionnaire. When we had all done this—and the proceedings as usual were carried out with the most dignified cordiality—we were each informed of the number of our room and directed to the lift.

The lift woman had a fine bosom and her hair was done up in a large wholesome bun. She reminded me of Mme Bayard in my village in Normandy, and I almost waited for her to cry out: 'Ben, ma'am Henrey, and how are you?' I made signs that I wanted the fourth floor, and upon leaving the lift I found myself face to face with the floor governess, who inquired my name and handed me the key of my room. This floor governess, known as the *Dijournaia*, sits at a bureau beside the lift. Her function is to guard all the rooms along the corridor.

It is she who keeps the keys, hands them to the rightful guests and takes them back when they leave the floor. In fact no one need lock their room, for nobody could escape her vigilance; and there is a floor governess on duty both by night and by day. Her function is slightly reminiscent of the French *huissier*, that important individual in evening dress with chain of office, picturesque reminder of another age, who can still be seen in French ministries seated at a bureau to guard the privacy of senior civil servants.

My hotel room was charmingly but most unusually planned. Picture a perfect square of which one quarter is prettily curtained off to make the bedroom, the remainder serving as a sitting-room, a dining-room or a writing-room according to one's needs—a most ingenious solution to every problem.

According to Moscow time it was past the hour for dinner. I put on dry clothes, tidied myself, and examined the room, which was old-fashioned but comfortable, warm and spotlessly clean. Outside it was still raining, but I was longing to explore the hotel, listen to people talking, have something to eat in the restaurant. I gave my key to the floor governess. 'Spasiba,' I said shyly—my first attempt at conversation. 'Pajalousta,' she answered, smiling.

The lift attendant's coat and skirt intrigued me; the jacket was too small for her, which made her appear stouter than she was, but she had beautiful expressive eyes, tiny well-shaped ears, the lobes of which were pierced to receive childish-looking ear-rings. She was subjecting me to the same sort of scrutiny and finally asked:

'American?'

'No, French, but my *muje* is English.'

'Ah!' she said, 'the husband only is English.'

Though my attempts to speak Russian were so far very slight, I felt hopeful and made up my mind to persevere.

RESTORAN. Here then was the hotel restaurant, but the loud strains of an orchestra playing dance music almost made me turn back. On the point of doing so I caught sight of an empty table, changed my mind and sat down. 'No, not here, but over there where there are more people.' I rose obediently, chose a smaller table and found myself for want of imagination once again asking for caviare. What else does one order in Moscow? Ah, perhaps, *poulet à la Pojarsky*, to which as a penniless manicurist at the Savoy in London I was introduced when I was twenty by General Tchermoeff, whose strange story I told in *The Little Madeleine*.

May he rest in peace! Whoever would have believed at that time that the day would come when I would be ordering *poulet à la Pojarsky* in the land of his birth?

'Squeeze lemon on your caviare!'

The voice was that of a man in the act of seating himself at my table.

'You don't mind me coming here?' he asked without waiting for an answer but spreading out a fine linen napkin. 'From your English which I overheard just now I take it that you are French? As for me, I am Belgian. Brussels is the city of my birth. Have you just flown in from Paris?'

'No, from London, where I live with my English husband. This is apt to confuse people. I am French, but I am English. Suppose you tell me about yourself?'

'I am here on business,' he said. 'My Russian colleagues have just entertained me to an excellent dinner, but I thought I would drop in here for a last glass of *tchai* before turning in for the night. Amazing, the amount of tea I drink in Moscow. Their tea is delicious. You will soon find that out for yourself. And life is agreeable here for those of us who are driven half crazy by the traffic in Brussels, Paris or London. You will also find here more politeness, a slower *tempo*, a chance to stroll, just like it must have been along the *boulevards* in the days of Napoleon III or in London when there were broughams and hansom cabs. I'll wager that however short your stay is you'll go home rested, I might even say with your nerves calmed. Time is a valued commodity here. People are taught to enjoy it.'

People were dancing in the middle of the room, and to my surprise they were predominantly Russian. I had thought of the hotel as a sort of oasis for foreigners. I had said to myself: 'I won't see any real Muscovites till tomorrow when the rain stops and I can go out.' But I was wrong. One has to change all one's preconceived ideas. There were foreigners like myself and my Belgian acquaintance, but the people dancing were Russians and most of them were not staying at the hotel.

At first one is tempted to subscribe to the general misconception that Russians taken *en masse* are drab, but this is a *cliché* which is wildly misleading, for though a person's clothes may be sombre, even poor, it is his character and his capacity for open enjoyment that matter.

So at first I noticed with a touch of pity that the sheer nylon stockings which we all take for granted at home were the exception rather than the rule amongst the women dancing. Their shoes were rather coarser than ours and the men often had jackets that did not match their trousers. A number of them wore open-necked shirts, some had sweat-shirts like sailors wear, under a pullover. In the days of my childhood when a man like my father went out without a tie it was usually because he was exhausted by sheer physical hard work and could not pluck up the energy to shave and make himself look presentable. But here in Moscow I think that what struck me most was the relaxed expression on the faces of the dancers. If they occasionally wore open-necked shirts, for instance, one surmised that it was because it was thus they had wanted to come, and one ceased after the first few moments to notice anything except the gentleness in their eyes and the loving way in which they held their partners, not unlike the way Parisians used to dance in the Bal Musette. I think that before long I was thoroughly acclimatized. One would see a girl wearing a *lamé* shift in the arms of a young man in a woollen pullover, and it needed no gift of second sight to realize that each had dressed to please the other and that there could be nothing incongruous in an alliance that so clearly spelt love. Other things combined to delight me, such as the Russian tongue, which is so soft and tender that it fills the room with a nobility that far outstrips any question of dress.

The orchestra started to play 'Mack the Knife' by Kurt Weil, that genial composer who was to die so tragically young, and my thoughts suddenly went back to a winter evening spent with friends in 1936 in the grill-room of the London Savoy. There were Kurt Weil, Elsa Schiaparelli, Brecht, Henry Horne, my husband and myself. We had gathered to assess the chances of Kurt Weil's satirical operetta *My Kingdom for a Cow*, on which the curtain had just fallen at the Savoy Theatre. We spoke of Jean Cocteau and of Laure de Noailles. Our thoughts ranged from London to Paris, from Vienna to Berlin—where the shadow of Hitler's Third Reich made the future heavy with doubt. 'Schiap' believed in Kurt Weil and had put money in the operetta, but London audiences were not yet ready to admit that there was danger from across the Rhine, and the venture failed. Now I was listening to 'Mack the Knife', Kurt Weil's most famous air, in this lofty restaurant in the heart of Moscow, and because it is irresistible the dance floor quickly filled up. My Belgian friend leaned across and said to me:

'This will be the last tune. In Moscow everything closes down at 11 p.m. There are no night clubs, no strip-tease. There is something fundamentally clean about this country; because it is scientifically so far advanced, it can afford to appear old-fashioned in other ways. For me that is the charm of Moscow. You can't imagine what a pleasant contrast it makes to the cynicism and brashness of West Berlin, which has become more depraved than before Hitler's time.'

Now the dancers were returning to their tables. It was very gay but not noisy. The lofty restaurant with its pillars and playing fountains in the centre had an air of 1900. My companion claimed it had been put up by his compatriot Marquet at the beginning of the century—Marquet, whom I once met in a restaurant car while travelling between Monte Carlo and Paris and who besides owning a great string of hotels across Europe had financial interests in Brussels.

I asked my Belgian friend if he travelled a great deal. He said that he did, but that his travelling was confined to Central Europe —Moscow, Kiev, Riga, Warsaw, Budapest and Bucharest. He had become something of an expert on these cities.

A young woman brought me a bill and when I explained that I had no money, not even the coupons that Intourist would presumably have given me if I had not arrived at such a late hour, she said: 'Don't worry. I'll make myself responsible for you and you can pay in the morning.'

While the orchestra was packing up and the lights were being dimmed, we drank a last glass of tea. I then invited my Belgian friend, who lodged on the same floor as I did, to come and fetch a copy of the Paris newspaper *Le Figaro* which I had bought in London. This he did before wishing me good night.

I now drew aside the dividing curtain and, passing into the alcove, took stock of my bed. A square of highly starched guipure lace with flounces covered the pillow which, as in France, was a perfect square. A rectangular piece of similar lacework was arranged prettily over the rest of the bed, which thus gave the impression of being in two parts. The bed was not made up as English beds are—if anything it more closely resembled a German or Austrian one. A thick woollen blanket entirely encased in a giant envelope of magnificent Russian linen reposed on the bottom sheet. This linen envelope, incidentally, had a diamond shaped opening cut in the centre of it and beautifully hemmed. Through this the blanket is introduced. The blanket fits the linen envelope perfectly and as part of its woollen surface is visible through the aperture the whole thing looks like an ace of diamonds playing card. The advantage, of course, is that the blanket in its linen covering always remains clean. I thought this contraption might tend to slip off during the night, but it never did, and I found it warm and snug.

I had placed an order with the *Dijournaia* for breakfast at eight, and at eight exactly there was a knock at my door. I leapt out of bed, but there were two locks, and as soon as I opened one the other closed. A babble of musical sounds came from the other side of the door, and when at last by pure chance it opened I found myself confronting a little maid in a black dress and apron and a tiny cap on her blond braided hair. She was quite convulsed with laughter, so it was in a state of considerable merriment that I began my second day in Moscow.

The bread was white and excellent, the coffee weaker than in Paris but much nearer the French taste than what we had been given on the *Empress of Britain* and which, though I could never get used to it, apparently found favour with Canadians.

Tui . . . tui . . . tui, and there on the zinc covered ledge of the open window were two Moscow sparrows asking to be fed. Their tiny feet made a tinkling noise as they hopped about on the zinc. They were as graceful as ballet dancers, and as I fed them so they were joined by more until I had over a dozen of them outlined against the grey uncertain sky.

My window opened out on a courtyard where two women were engaged in moving long wooden planks; a third bore on one of her sturdy shoulders a crate of wine bottles. All three wore iron-grey kerchiefs tied in a knot under the chin.

I dressed hurriedly and left my key with the *Dijournaia*, who was seated at her imposing desk surrounded by several laughing chambermaids. I saw her open a drawer and place my key against the number that corresponded with it. She had in this drawer a horizontal replica of the sort of key-board one sees hanging up behind hotel inquiry desks at home. The Russian system has the advantage that no unauthorized person can obtain a key to a guest's room.

The Intourist Bureau was situated in a gallery next to the administrator's office. One is obliged before going to Russia to settle all the details of one's projected journey, and the Soviet Embassy will not even think about granting a visa until everything has been paid for in full. When all this has been done and the visa granted, the London office of Intourist issues one with a contract. I had now to present mine to a young woman in this gallery. She in return would give me vouchers for my hotel room and *pension*, a car for three hours a day, the services of a young woman interpreter, and the rail and sleeper tickets I would eventually need to go to Leningrad.

'Oh!' cried this young woman, when I showed her my contract. 'What a pleasant surprise! We all expected you to be a *man*!'

If this employee was surprised, I was even more so. All sorts of communications about me had already passed between London and Moscow, and I took it for granted that they knew all about me and about the books I had written. I was even under the impression that I was to meet a number of distinguished Russian women writers. This employee's naïve surprise made my unimportance clear, but though I remained puzzled I was curiously relieved. I wanted to see and not to be seen, and it does one a great deal of good from time to time to be faced with the realization that a very limited success in one country can pass entirely unnoticed in another.

'Your name was forwarded to me as Mrs Robert Henrey,' said the young woman. 'Married women in Russia do not use the prefix Mrs—and so . . . well, you can see for yourself why we got a wrong impression.'

She broke out into the same sort of laughter as the chambermaid who, on the other side of my bedroom door, could not make me understand how to unlock it. This love of laughter was quickly helping me to take to the Russian way of life. Their brand of gaiety seemed very like my own. I was relieved that the mistake about my sex had been satisfactorily corrected. It was not until later that I found out to what extent the discovery of my true identity was to facilitate my stay.

The Intourist girl wrote at a speed that filled me with admiration. Her pen, tracing the difficult Russian characters, raced over the paper. She gave me a book of vouchers to pay for meals. They were for set amounts. The ones for breakfast were for one rouble and ten kopecks; those for lunch for three roubles and thirty kopecks, and for dinner for two roubles and thirty kopecks. Incidentally a glass of tea cost thirty kopecks. They were all interchangeable, and if one ate for less than the voucher was worth one was given the difference in cash.

I was now to be introduced to the young woman who was to make my stay in Moscow a pure delight.

'Come and meet your guide,' said the Intourist girl.

Unknown to me, my guide had been seated at the far end of the gallery. I saw her get up and come lightly towards us. She was wearing a tweed coat. Our eyes met.

'I'm Nina,' she said.

'I'm Madeleine.'

'Where do you want to go?' she asked.

'Everywhere!' I answered, and we both laughed.

We became at that instant firm friends. I slipped an arm under hers and we went off joyously in the direction of Red Square. We both wore head scarves and were about the same height.

The Metropole is on Sverdlov Square, and between it and the famous Bolshoi Theatre are flower gardens and fountains. The first frosts had already come and the fruit trees were bereft of leaves. Nina led me past the magnificent statue of Karl Marx carved out of a giant block of granite. The avenue bears his name. The morning was not cold and my fur-lined coat was almost too warm.

'Winter's late in coming,' said Nina; 'which is a pity because there's nothing like an early winter and plenty of snow to prepare the ground for a good harvest.' She looked at me anxiously to see if I was listening, and added: 'The harvest was a great disappointment to us this year.' Her little face had taken on a serious expression. She looked like a good little girl in a Victorian story book. I thought: 'She's right. In London we would probably have been talking about something futile like make-up or nylons.'

'Nina,' I asked, 'how old are you?'

The sudden change of subject disconcerted her. Then a look of fun lit up her dark eyes and she exclaimed:

'I'm terribly old. You'd never guess.'

We had agreed from the start to speak English, but we could not fail to notice that we each spoke it with a different accent and this formed a link between us, preventing either from having a feeling of superiority.

The avenues through which we passed were crowded; most of the women wore head scarves in dark colours; the men had fur toques or cloth caps. There were a great many soldiers whose long overcoats reached almost down to their ankles. The front of their fur hats bore the red star and a minute hammer and sickle.

Now suddenly all my dreams had come true.

Here we were in Red Square with the crenellated walls of the Kremlin in front of us. Its ramparts and towers, built under Ivan III, glowed a warm russet colour. I was not prepared for the beauty of the scene that met my eyes. I had heard too much about Red Square being a place of grim, rather frightening, military reviews. I had imagined a huge parade ground, a sea of asphalt. Nobody had told me that it was a scene of infinite beauty, that it was paved as romantically as the streets of old Paris and that it was first called Red Square hundreds of years ago—not, as you might well think, because of its politics but because the Russian word for 'red' and 'beautiful' have the same root, and because the square, which is really oblong, is just about the most lovely thing that anybody could imagine.

Trees of majestic stature add splendour to the wall of the Kremlin, whose dark red bricks have the same endearing warmth as those of St James's Palace and Hampton Court. Not till later did I catch that much wider vista of the Kremlin which you get from the far bank of the majestic Moskva river. From Red Square one sees only one side of it, but how evocative of all that is greatest in Russia's past and present! Maxim Gorky wrote that Moscow was the heart and brain of the country. The highest legislative and executive bodies, the Supreme Soviet of the U.S.S.R. and the Council of Ministers, are situated here in the Kremlin as well as the fifteenth- and sixteenth-century palaces and churches of the czars whose golden spires and domes dazzle one.

But Red Square, which was once a great market-place, has other marvels. The most unbelievable is the cathedral of St Basil the Blessed or, more correctly, the cathedral of the Intercession on the

Moat whose bulbous domes glow with a myriad colours. This fantastic church (of which the cathedral at Nice is supposed to be a copy) was built in 1554 by Ivan the Terrible to commemorate the conquest of Kazan. The story is told, no doubt too often, that Ivan had the architect's eyes put out so that he should never build anything so beautiful again. Whether this is truth or legend, the czar's sadistic cruelty gave rise to appalling scenes of torture in this very square where, on this November morning, people were arriving from the most distant republics to visit the mausoleum of Lenin, a dark porphyry building beside the Kremlin wall.

Nina now took me under the tower and through the great gate into the Kremlin. We found ourselves in a courtyard as one might upon entering Windsor Castle. Now even on this dull, grey day the domes of the cathedrals and churches shone fantastically in gold and silver, making one think of a huge wedding cake made for giants.

We went into a white church with a golden dome. It was the Assumption cathedral, the most wonderful of all the churches in the Kremlin.

'This', said Nina, whose English occasionally took on strange corruptions of her own, 'is where the czars were coronated!'

'Here also', I might have added, 'Napoleon stabled his horses.'

These churches have now all become museums, and I was continually surprised by the numbers of Russians visiting them— soldiers of the Red Army, old women with peasant faces, old men, young men and young women too, and a host of children.

All these people were absorbed in their anxiety to understand —touchingly so at times—so that one oscillated between feelings of admiration and surprise. They moved slowly about the museums which were so packed with treasures of a regime that could only be a fable to them that one could but look in wonder. The incredible gold and silver of Ivan the Terrible, his ivory throne, the amazing baubles of Peter the Great, the crowns of innumerable czars great and small, countless diamonds of incredible size—truly countless, for they run into tens of thousands—imperial sledges and jewelled whips and bridles, all the jewelled masterpieces of Fabergé (whose work occasionally comes up at a sale at Christie's or Sotheby's) the treasures of Catherine the Great, and many more such wonders displayed so closely one next to the other, but in perfect taste, that in the end one's brain can no longer take them in, and one had the impression of walking through a richly laden store in Oxford Street on a Saturday morning.

The churches are golden inside; the icons are of unbelievable beauty and yet savage in aspect. One can well imagine how these haunting figures painted on wood with long, drawn figures, fierce beards and often cruel eyes must have shone frighteningly by the flicker of candlelight as the faithful knelt in front of them. This experience is like no other. Those who in their youth were impregnated with Russian literature developed a passionate longing to see the country they read about in Turgenev and Tolstoy. The curious thing is that the past and the present manage to dwell together in new-found understanding, like the biblical promise of wolf and lamb, of leopard and kid. Some will consider that to travel so far to see churches turned into museums is a poor palliative, and yet, watching the Russian people in these places, whether church or ornate czarist palace turned into some breath-takingly beautiful museum, watching peasants perhaps from the Ukraine, or from the Caucasus or from the Urals, watching the slow steps of old men and women, the serious expressions of young eager Muscovites, one knows that the experience is more than rewarding. They walk slowly, but there is wonderment in their eyes. The new regime has given them such an intensity, such an awareness of the present and the future, that they can safely ponder over the curiosities of the czars, and project themselves into these dreams of the fantastic past.

One is surprised also by the contrast between uncouthness on the one hand and natural politeness on the other. In no other country have I seen men make way for one with such dignity. The smiles also that illumine the faces of Russian women betray a mixture of gaiety and tenderness. When one speaks to them they listen with exemplary patience—even when one maltreats their beautiful language.

I have already written how immediately on entering the Aero-flot plane at the start of my journey I was relieved by the air hostess of my fur coat which she arranged on a hanger and put in a special place. Here in the Kremlin I was to receive a further lesson in the importance that Russians attach to the removal of their outdoor clothes before they go indoors. Fundamentally this is due to the severity of their winters. They wear thicker outdoor garments, and their homes and public places are better heated, but there is also in this custom an element of good manners that it takes us some thinking about fully to appreciate. To remain even for a moment with one's coat on indoors would be as impolite in their eyes as for a guest to grind out a cigarette on a carpet, or even in the gilt interior of an eighteenth century silver bowl—which has happened to me at home.

Thus women as well as men take off their outer garments on entering the Kremlin museum, and these are left with one's other impedimenta in a vast cloakroom in the crypt. Jute sacks and miserable looking bags may be standing dejectedly at the foot of their owners' drab coats. Here we were called upon to do even more. In another part of the basement were wooden packing cases filled with carpet slippers of every size, and under the careful but twinkling eyes of museum attendants, who were prodigal in encouraging talk, we dipped into the nearest case to find slippers to fit us.

Thus shod, we shuffled away to visit the wonders prepared for us, and as we were all wearing the same monstrosities we no longer thought anything about it.

Firearms, bejewelled swords, crowns bordered with sable, royal gifts to princes and foreign ambassadors, snuffboxes in a dozen different coloured golds with beautiful designs upon them, clocks of complicated and surprising design, and the gorgeous dresses of the czarinas—of Elizabeth, wife of Peter the Great, of Catherine the Great herself. But what is most evocative of all are the superb sixteenth–seventeenth-century coaches such as the one with its leather doors that was sent as a gift to the czar by Queen Elizabeth I of England. There are French coaches with the body-work painted by François Boucher—who never had a rival for painting the drawing-rooms of elegant eighteenth-century ladies, though some of his pictures were as suggestive as they were gracious; German coaches, strong and yet elegant, and sleigh-coaches, one of which was designed to be drawn by twenty-four horses, and carried Catherine the Great from what was then St Petersburg to Moscow for her coronation. This journey is said to have been accomplished in only three days.

Poor Nina had started her first cold of the winter. I was happily just finishing mine. The more I made her talk, the thicker her normally soprano voice became. I kept on meaning to observe what for her would have been a beneficial silence, but my curiosity got the better of me and off I would start again.

Having come to the end of our sight-seeing we removed our carpet slippers and put them back in one of the wooden cases. A crowd of schoolgirls, shepherded by a mistress, stood in front of another and their laughter echoed happily against the grim walls.

There was a restaurant where people were drinking tea in glasses; others ate ices, which in Moscow, both winter and summer, has become a national pastime. There are scores of different flavours, and they taste better than any I remember since those delicious maple syrup ices that I used to buy for five cents in Montreal and during our excursions into the Laurentian mountains.

I asked Nina to take me to see the Moskva river, from the opposite bank of which there is such a superb view of the Kremlin. She said that we would have to walk. Unfortunately we had no sooner left the museum than it began to rain.

So, arm in arm, well pleased with each other, we set off in the rain and soon came upon a long crocodile of little children, the oldest of whom could not have been more than five years old.

They all had little coats either in fur or in material tightly belted to keep in the warmth of their bodies, balaclavas (well named in this country) and fur-lined bootees in gay colours. They looked like a collection of those Russian wooden toys representing men or women that come apart in the middle and reveal other painted people and yet others till the last one is quite tiny. They were all holding on to one another by the ends of their scarves, and made the prettiest, gayest crocodile it has ever been my good fortune to see. I bent down and made friendly overtures to the littlest of all, whose eyes became large and interested. The mistress said that it was a pity about the rain because she was taking her charges to play in the gardens of the Kremlin. The rain, which was not yet very heavy, did not seem to have any effect on the children, who made the same sort of happy chirpings as the sparrows who had come to share my breakfast at the hotel that morning. The Kremlin with its trees and birds and little laughing children seemed a very different place when one was in it from the grim picture one draws of it on the other side of the Iron Curtain

Nina wanted to show off her knowledge of history and informed me that we were about to pass through the gate by which Napoleon left Moscow at the time of his disastrous retreat, adding that it was about the same time of year and that the first snows were falling. Then, by one of those disconcerting *non sequiturs* by which women of all races distinguish themselves, myself included, she added naïvely: 'I'm so glad you're French. You don't frighten me so much.'

'Because you beat Napoleon?'

'No,' she said gravely. 'I mean you laugh and cry, and you're rather intense like we are.'

'I've heard you laugh a lot. Do you also cry?'

'Well,' she said. 'I've cried quite a bit. Who hasn't? But I've been alone for a long time.'

She paused.

'Oh, not because I haven't friends. I have a great number of friends who are intelligent, charming and gay. When I said I've been alone I referred to the heart. Do you understand?'

'I think I understand.'

'My father was a doctor. He caught typhus while working in the hospitals during an epidemic and died. I was scarcely a year old at the time. My mother was a nurse. She sent me to my grandmother in order that she should be free to go on with her nursing, but she too contracted typhus and died. I'm afraid I came into the world at a difficult moment.'

'Was this during the revolution?'

'Yes, it was during the revolution. My father was Armenian. I don't know much about my paternal grandparents. I was brought up by one of my mother's sisters and when I grew up I was fortunate enough to be sent to the university. Then I married, but the marriage didn't work out. So I was left alone—in the heart, do you see?'

'I see.'

'And you?' she asked anxiously. 'Are you happy? Does your husband love you? Do you love him?

'Yes,' I said. 'We are happy and we love each other.'

'Oh, I'm so glad for you, Madeleine.'

Declining the verb to love can bring sadness as well as joy. Poor Nina looked sad, but she also had a shocking cold which

was getting no better in the rain. So I said to her: 'Nina, something tells me that you are on the verge of experiencing a great
love.'

'Oh!' she cried. 'Do you really think so?'

It was getting late. Nina had an important meeting at her office.
She left me within sight of my hotel, saying:

'I must run. *Svidania!*'

'*Svidania*, Nina!'

The *Dijournaia* looked at my fur collar as she handed me the
key, and exclaimed: 'Idet Dojd!' ('It rains!')

My door and I were not made for each other. The locks were
far too high and still failed to synchronize. I had to battle with
them but when I finally succeeded I took a linen hand towel and
rubbed the rain off my fur collar. By the time I finished lunch it
would be dry.

The restaurant was crowded. The nervousness I had felt on the
previous evening had now quite disappeared. I was beginning to
feel at home in the hotel and was no longer surprised by the slight
differences in custom and etiquette. I chose a table for four at
which two men were already seated. Of what nationality would
they prove to be? This doubt added spice to the adventure. Still
rather shy of using the childish Russian I knew, I said hopefully:
'Good morning!' and then: 'Bonjour!' My companions turned
out to be Russians and answered: 'Stratvouite!'

A waiter arrived to serve them and then took my order—
caviare, a steak and a glass of tea. The beautiful Edwardian room,
with its pillars and tall ceiling, its fountains playing in the centre
and its palm trees, was very gay. The incongruous thought
suddenly struck me that this room must date from about the same
time as the very ornate interior of the gaming-rooms in the
casino at Monte Carlo to which the pre-1914 Grand Dukes were
so addicted. Both locales had suffered a great change, but this one
had certainly more vigour and more gaiety. There were, as in so
many restaurants in London at lunch time, more men than
women. People lunch very late in Russia, just as they do in Spain.
Three o'clock is a perfectly normal hour to arrive.

There is something else. I heard it said that the Russian service
was appallingly slow—well, so it is in a way, but this, if anything,

is an advantage. There is not that sense of rush that one gets in London, mostly because the West End restaurants are predominantly in the hands of Italians who have always put speed above anything else, claiming that business men don't know what they are eating and never have the patience to wait. So often the food is cooked the day before and merely heated up in an oven or in a frying-pan when the order is given. The Russian system takes one back to the quieter days of our grandmothers, when people had time to do certain things like eating quietly. One has the feeling moreover that life is really able to run smoothly along, that things don't have to begin and end at arbitrarily fixed hours —a system that too often makes seven-eighths of the population do little else but watch the clock for closing time.

I settled the bill with my first Intourist voucher and, as I had apparently not eaten to its full value, I found with the receipted bill a number of kopecks, coins of such minute size that they reminded me of some Victorian silver pennies which my mother-in-law once gave me, and which were struck, I think, during the Great Exhibition of 1851.

While waiting for Nina I looked into the cloakroom where, beside a long row of outer garments, the *schlapkas*, or fur hats, were ranged, looking for all the world like great sleeping cats. There was the usual souvenir shop with amber necklaces and bracelets, black boxes illuminated with vividly painted Russian scenes and, of course, the wooden dolls that contain other wooden dolls of diminishing size—those toys which the children at the Kremlin had put me in mind of, and which in France we call *des poupées gigognes*, after the Mère Gigogne, the French equivalent of the old lady who lived in a shoe and had all those children.

There were also *schlapkas* for sale, which made me reflect that a fur hat transforms the most ordinary-looking man into a potentially romantic hero. No wonder they had come into fashion in England. Here in Russia they were mostly made of shorn lamb, black or grey astrakhan or some fur that imitated sable—but which, of course, was not. I found it amusing during the few moments I spent here to watch men trying on *schlapkas* with an almost childish delight. There is nothing quite so endearing as to see the important male giving way to vanity.

The big hotels in Moscow resemble modern caravanserais— one finds everything in them: post offices, banks, shops of every description. At a furriers I even saw a pair of magnificent sables that I would have liked to be rich enough to buy. Of all furs none is more beautiful, more flattering, uplifting. The skins were of course in their raw state, which made them all the more romantic and desirable, for if by some magic they could have become mine I should have had felt I was acquiring some of the romance which as a child I injected, thanks to *Les Malheurs de Sophie* and the *Général Dourakine*, into the limitless forests of Siberian Russia.

Raw and unmounted as they were, I put them round my neck (the shop girl did not mind a bit—I think it amused her) and murmured: 'What fun to be a queen!' and then burst out laughing at the enormity of such a thought here in Moscow! But why do they put such temptation in one's way? I was perhaps not alone in these reactionary thoughts, because the salesgirl, in order to impress upon me the beauty of some silver mink, put some round her own neck and I caught a quick flash of excitement in her eyes as she felt its loveliness and warmth.

I must turn my back on dreams of sable and mink and buy some picture postcards. Perhaps one day I will boast of having put on a pair of Siberian sables in a Moscow hotel. Perhaps when I am very old. Somebody in my village in Normandy had told me the story of a peasant woman who at the age of eighty went to confession. 'I behaved very giddily at harvest time,' she said to the priest. 'I did things with the boys I should not have done.' 'What!' he exclaimed. 'At *your* age?' 'Not at my age *now*,' she said. 'When I was twenty—but it does me good to talk about it.'

Having addressed my cards I took them to the girl at the post office. A girl beside her was drinking milk straight from the bottle. I had no need to count my change; the smallest transactions are effected with scrupulous honesty.

Nina arrived as I was posting the cards. I had told her that I wanted to look at the shops and she had ordered a car.

We drove down Gorky Street and away into some new suburb with beautiful squares and trees and wide avenues in which the traffic moved smoothly along. There were splendid new apartment houses going up everywhere, and large stores to serve the housewife. Quite clearly the authorities were building for the future when there would be more apartment houses, more customers and more merchandise, and most important of all, more trees, more gardens, more air. 'In a few years', said Nina, we shall all have an apartment of our own, with our own kitchen, bathroom and central heating.

'For the moment I have a room with a divan, easy chairs and a fine German wardrobe large enough to hold all my clothes. I have to share the kitchen, but as I get on well with the others that is no hardship. I am fortunate to be in the heart of Moscow, only a few yards from the Bolshoi, the Maly Theatre and within easy walking distance of Red Square. When I have my own apartment it will almost certainly be farther out, so that what I gain in comfort I may lose in convenience. Moscow, like all great capitals, is expanding fast.'

Some of the stores in these new parts of the city reminded me of those in Oxford Street. One especially was magnificently lit up and I asked Nina to stop the car and let me visit it. We might have been in D. H. Evans except that some of the colour was missing, but it was beautifully warm and there were moving staircases, perfumes, knitting wool, dresses—and crowds of shoppers.

'Our lingerie is improving,' said Nina. 'Some of it is very pretty. These mauve slips, for instance, come from East Germany. Oh! I want to show you the gloves. These fur-lined ones from Czechoslovakia are beautifully warm.'

As I followed her from department to department, I was intrigued by the noise of wooden disks being manipulated by agile fingers—a sort of symphony against which one heard all the normal noises of a busy store, the voices of women, the cries of children, the tread of feet. Then suddenly I understood. Every girl cashier used an abacus to tot up the value of a customer's purchases, and all this sliding of wooden disks heard together produced this curious noise. I had, of course, seen in nurseries and primary schools those frames with parallel bars along which children slide coloured beads when they are learning to count. I remembered that this device was called an abacus, and that it was a derivative of that simple but highly effective calculating machine that the Greeks and Romans used and which even now is still to be seen in shops and offices in China and Persia.

I watched a young cashier swiftly sliding a number of disks from one side to the other. The first three rows represented kopecks; the rows above them roubles. The customer, watching the cashier manipulate these disks, could herself quickly check that the total of her expenditure was correct. After every operation

the cashier would lift up the abacus and with a graceful movement shake the disks back into place, so that the machine was
ready for the next addition.

One was flabbergasted to see this primitive method still so
widely used in a country that leads the world in space travel, and
whose scientists had invented computers every bit as complicated
as those of America's I.B.M.

But there was no question about it. The abacus was highly
efficient, and what could be prettier than to see these nimble
fingers dancing across the parallel bars as if one were in a kinder-
garten watching little girls learning to count! In truth, how old
was the abacus? Some people claim that it was used in China some
twenty thousand years before Christ. Others point out that one of
the earliest was a board strewn with sand (*abaq* in Old Semitic) on
which rows of pebbles were laid.

'The porcelain', Nina was saying, 'comes from Dresden . . .'
and suddenly I remembered a shop in Bond Street where antique
porcelain shepherdesses fetched thousands of pounds. 'Dresden
china!' the owner once murmured reverently, putting into my
trembling hands one of these marvels that I was terrified of
dropping. Dresden, I thought. How far removed from our lives
has this great city behind the Iron Curtain become!

I bought a pack of playing cards.

I love patience and telling fortunes and I try to buy playing
cards wherever I go. The German and Austrian packs are
particularly fine. Now I wanted a Russian pack.

This was how you made a purchase. You told the salesgirl what
you wanted and then you went to a cashier, who ran the total up
on her abacus and handed out a receipt which you took back to
her and against which she handed over the goods.

My playing cards were delightful.

The king has a K marked upon the card. The Russian for
'king' is *Karol*.

The queen has a D for *Dama*, the Russian for 'lady', but queen
in the cards.

The knave has a B, which is the Russian V for the French *valet*.

Looking at all these royal personages, I said laughingly to
Nina: 'It's all very V.I.P.!'

'What does that mean?' she asked suspiciously.

'It was a wartime invention in England', I said, 'to designate

politicians and generals or high-up civil servants without reveal-
ing their names. It stands for "Very Important Person".'

'You can't imagine', cried Nina, 'how glad I am to know this.
I feel that I have added to my knowledge of English, But, heavens,
how gay you are! You're not a bit like an ordinary tourist—and
when you laugh you're very pretty.'

'Amusing, perhaps, but not pretty. Let us not exaggerate.'

'I assure you', said Nina, 'that all the girls at the office tell me
how lucky I am to be looking after you. Now I shall be able to
inform them what V.I.P. means.'

'What I would like next', I said, 'is to buy a Russian calendar
for the coming year.'

I was surprised by the number of book shops in Moscow. Did
people read so much? They at least gave the impression that their
reading was channelled into books rather than into newspapers
and magazines. Apart from *Isvestia* and *Pravda* there were few
newspapers for sale in the kiosks or news-stands and, of course,
none of the scandal-sheets that form such an integral part of mass
reading in London, New York and Paris. The Muscovites in their
taste in books, in their preoccupation with opera, ballet and
serious plays—even in their love for what they have always
excelled in, the puppet show (the Moscow Marionette Theatre is
unique)—remind one in some curious way of what Paris must
have been during the Second Empire. The country's desire to
fashion upwards the artistic appreciation of its young people
rather than bring down the level of taste for financial benefit, was
not unlike what Mondadori, the eminent Italian publisher, proclaimed as his policy when I talked to him in Milan.

Night fell quickly during these last days of November.

The Hotel Metropole was very animated. I was now finding my
way about it as easily as I had learned to do on the *Empress of
Britain* after two or three days. There was everything—shops,
entertainment, restaurants, dancing. It was pleasant to recognize
faces and to receive welcoming smiles on one's return. I felt
almost too happy and murmured: *Merci, mon Dieu!*, though this
sounded curious in a city whose loveliest churches were turned
into museums.

Groups of men and women whom in my ignorance I mistook

for Chinese turned out to be Russians from Mongolia and Vladivostok. On the other hand there were quite a number of Indian women wearing saris and a Japanese family dressed in European style.

I went up to my bedroom to rest for an hour.

Fastened to the clasp of my handbag was an inch-tall golden charm that Julia Chapman, the Russian-born wife of an Englishman living in São Paulo, Brazil, had sent me after reading *The Little Madeleine*. The charm was in the form of a tightly closed hand and was called Figa. The gold was Brazilian. Figa, I fancy, kept her golden hand in this continual state of tension so as not to allow the slightest suspicion of good fortune to escape either from her or from me. Dear Julia, did you guess that your Brazilian charm delivered to me in my London flat by your husband in person would one day accompany me to the land of your birth? I brought no other jewel with me.

'Don't try to learn Russian,' Julia had written at the time of the gift. 'You'll never succeed.' But I did go on learning Russian, though my success with it was so far terribly limited.

Figa and I rested on my Russian hotel bed, the golden hand against my right cheek. I did not try to sleep, but a pleasant torpor stole over me.

At 9 p.m. I got up and did my hair and, with the agreeable feeling that if I were lucky I might be asked to dance by some good-looking Russian, I put on some light shoes and, feeling happy and refreshed we set off, Figa and I, for the restaurant.

I sat at a table alone. A Russian came to sit beside me. When after a few moments he noticed that his cigarette smoke was stinging my eyes he made elaborate efforts to turn his head each time he emitted smoke. His contortions became after a while so pantomimic that he ended by laughing. Unfortunately our acquaintance was short-lived for, seeing friends for whom he had doubtless been waiting, he made me a bow and went off.

I was not alone very long. A young man every bit as good-looking as the one I had imagined while doing my hair came to ask me in Russian if I would dance with him. Now that my hero had materialized I had a moment's hesitation. Wouldn't he have done better to find somebody younger, prettier? But fortunately he insisted and we danced round and round the illuminated fountains. He danced well, and I was too absorbed to bother about polite conversation. The little Russian I knew deserted me. When I asked him anything he smiled and said *Niet*, but when finally he saw me back to my table he bent over me and pressed his lips into the palm of my hand in a way that I had imagined could only happen in a film. I watched him go back to his own table. Then all his fellow guests—both women and men—turned to me and smiled politely.

A moment later another young man came to ask if he might sit beside me.

'Of course,' I said.

We fenced for a common language, for of French or English he knew *niet*. But German, yes. Did I speak it? Well, perhaps, enough to get on with. In this way he informed me that he was twenty-seven years old and from Riga in Esthonia. Both his parents had been killed in the war, with the result that he was alone in the world. But he had his music. He played the violoncello and the clarinet and occasionally percussion instruments, and had come to Moscow to perform chamber music. The concerts had been very successful and he was making a lot of money. There was plenty of money for food and drink.

Our dance orchestra was at that moment striking up 'Smoke gets in your eyes'. We danced. I was enjoying myself, and even the orchestra seemed excellent, but my tall partner turned up his good-looking nose and said: *Nein! Nein!* the orchestra was not good at all. It was *schlechte*!

'No,' I objected. 'Aren't we enjoying ourselves? Then the orchestra *must* be good. Besides, can't you imagine it playing military marches in the park? Or waltzes at a village wedding? I think it's a fine orchestra.' I think I amused him, but he looked at me with an air of slight pity.

We ordered supper.

He asked for a *Pojarsky* cutlet, and while waiting for it gulped down in the traditional way little glasses of vodka. My Belgian friend, who spoke perfect German, suddenly appeared and asked if he could join us. A few minutes later a second Belgian (a friend of the first) arrived. There were introductions all round—and so we were four.

Bottles of wine were ordered and made their appearance—

excellent red and white Georgian wines. The men spoke German and, with my wit sharpened by the food and the wine, I quickly fell into this language that in Moscow is far more useful than French or English.

We danced quite a lot and then the Esthonian noticed a very pretty girl at a nearby table. She was accompanied by three young men. The girl's hair was platinum and she wore it in a sort of beehive, European fashion, and her neck was long and elegant. She was dressed modestly in a beige sweater and a dark skirt. The young group was drinking, smoking, laughing.

The Esthonian's eyes were fascinated by the girl's shapely back and white nape. As it is considered perfectly good manners in Moscow for a man to invite a girl to dance with him if he feels like it whether she happens to be with other men or with only one, be it her *fiancé* or her husband, our Esthonian got up and went over to her. We stopped talking to watch him as in his beige sweater and dark trousers he stood in front of her making a little bow. To his obvious surprise he was met with a curt, almost scornful, refusal. On his return to our table he had difficulty in hiding his vexation, and one of the Belgians said to him in German: 'If instead of being only in a sweater you had been wearing a jacket she would certainly have agreed to dance with you.'

He made up for his disappointment by going over to the extreme end of the room to ask another girl to dance. Meanwhile the two Belgians continued to speculate on the reasons for the girl's refusal. The second one said: 'Perhaps the men at her table are conducting some sort of business, and the girl is the bait.' As he spoke an elderly man, turning bald but extremely well dressed, rose from a nearby table and like the Esthonian stood before the girl and asked her to dance. She accepted with alacrity and we watched them take the floor.

A crowd of young Canadians now came in. They were in Moscow to play ice hockey against the Muscovites and were guests of the city. Wherever they went they were fêted, wined, dined and thoroughly spoiled. Several came to join us and though some were from Toronto, speaking only English, others were from Quebec and Montreal and spoke French-Canadian.

They were amateurs, they said, and therefore had no illusions about the result of the match. Also they were playing according to Russian rules, which were slightly different from their own, and this would require a period of adjustment; but they were having a superb holiday and were quite overcome by the warmth of their welcome.

The pretty girl who had now finished dancing with the well-dressed middle-aged man was surrounded by young Canadians for whom she had nothing but smiles. Our Esthonian forgot his earlier disomfiture by attacking an enormous helping of roast turkey, so rich that when he stuck his fork into the meat we had to take quick action to avoid being sprinkled with gravy and stuffing. He explained that the more he ate the hungrier he became, and as we were anxious to encourage him we told him to take up the bone in his fingers. The Belgians added that this was considered quite the thing to do in Bucharest and in Budapest, even in Warsaw. 'When one is in Eastern Europe', they said, 'there is already a faint echo of the Orient.'

A new pretender now arrived to ask the pretty girl to dance. She gave him a curt refusal but when, some moments later, he saw her get up and prepare to be whirled away in the arms of a Canadian, he became angry and tried to come to blows. The men at the girl's table rose in her defence, but just as we expected a battle to ensue the intruder was invited by his adversaries to sit down and soon he was drinking generous glasses of vodka in their company.

They spoke calming words to him and were doubtless forgiving him for his pugnacious attitude because perhaps he had been drinking too much. Then to my amazement one of them got up, took him in his arms and gave him a fraternal but resounding kiss on the lips. Peace was thus restored, but soon afterwards two of them took him to the door and with much waving and good wishes put him on his way.

The orchestra now played a 'twist' and for the first time I saw the Muscovites let themselves go. The scene had become very warm, very gay, very young, and by any standard the evening could not be counted anything but a tremendous success. The girls from Lancashire who had 'twisted' so enthusiastically night after night on the *Empress of Britain* would have found themselves no less at home on this Edwardian dance floor in the heart of Moscow.

The pretty girl was now surrounded by quite a collection of

young men, amongst whom were several more Canadians. She was the centre of attraction, the queen, but from time to time I surprised the quick smiles she gave to the well-dressed man with whom she had danced earlier in the evening. He was obviously an important business executive, and by the way he smiled back at her one sensed an incipient romance.

The Esthonian continued to devour large portions of food and the rest of us went on drinking the excellent Georgian wine which kept on being renewed. I had the feeling of momentarily living in a film. Everything was new except for the delirious frenzy of the 'twist'. The men at my table discussed machinery for washing raw lambswool, and how in payment for it the Russians were giving them the choice of anthracite from the Donetz Basin or marble from the Urals. They talked about a Russian discovery for making stronger steel and said how proficient they had become in making synthetic diamonds for industry.

They treated me as a woman amongst business men, but they paid me the compliment of not talking down to me but expecting me to understand. I found it restful to be far away from newspapers, from the radio, from household problems, from the eternal gossip about bank hold-ups, political scandals and take-over bids. Gorky, whose magnificent statue is one of the sights of Moscow, was right to say that the best university was the street and the people one met and talked to. Though this might not prove sufficient for a man in these highly competitive days, it suited a woman like myself.

The playing of 'Mack the Knife' was again the prelude to the end of the ball. A young man who had drunk too much was being taken away by two companions, but as he was not in a fit state to look after himself he would be taken in an ambulance to a hospital, where a doctor would apply a stomach pump and then put him to bed. The bill would be sent to his employers, who would deduct it from his pay. Drunkenness was frowned on in Moscow. The Russians have a different conception of liberty from ours. They do not like to see it abused.

Our Esthonian friend was paying his bill from a great wad of roubles. Chamber music, in his own words, fed its man, and he proclaimed himself hugely delighted with his supper.

The clock struck eleven, the music stopped and the chandeliers dimmed.

12

THE next morning Nina and I went to GUM, the state department store which is on the side of the Red Square where there are houses and shops. I had imagined GUM to be an immense store like Selfridges. It is nothing of the kind. Imagine a labyrinth of lanes and alleyways, crowded and full of life and colour, like a cross between a stage setting for Bartholomew Fair and an oriental bazaar. It is entirely covered over and beautifully heated. There are fruit stalls and sweet shops. You can buy pans, kettles and samovars, porcelain and textiles, hats and lingerie, and here and there in this market place, village, *sok*, or whatever you like to call it, you come across squares and fountains. When the sun shines as it did on this particular morning it is visible together with patches of blue sky through the glass roof. I had much admired the Galleria Victor Emmanuel at Milan, but this surprised me more. There were children, pretty and warmly dressed, wide-eyed as they held a grandmother's wizened hand.

I fell in love with a child's small wooden chair lacquered in red and illuminated with beautiful designs in silver, gold and green, like an icon. I thought it one of the loveliest toys I had ever seen, ideal for a little girl to use, and as the price was within my means I asked the salesgirl, whose natural blond beauty would have been quickly noticed in New York or London, to put it aside for me, which she smilingly did. Neither Nina nor I had enough roubles with us. There was a smell of newly picked apples and nearly all the women had apples in their string bags, but there were also many vendors of lemons, because sliced lemon is an integral part of the Russian's glass of tea.

The children ate ice-cream, as they do all the world over, and chattered continually, but their voices are musical rather than raucous as they are in America. I found to my surprise that I was increasingly able to understand snatches of conversation. Nina, to whom I communicated my joy, took this opportunity to ask me if in London intellectual workers spoke a different language from that of others. She said that many of the guides who had learned at Moscow University to speak English perfectly had been surprised on going to London to discover that newspaper sellers and barrow boys in the streets spoke in a way that they found impossible to understand.

If you follow this side of Red Square you come to a fine new bridge across the Moskva river. This we did.

Part of modern Moscow's noble look comes from its wide avenues and bridges, its newly planted trees and gardens, its almost stately silence (for there is no ill-mannered hooting of motor horns—in Moscow as in Paris this is strictly forbidden), and its cleanliness. No Muscovite would dream of throwing a cigarette stub, still less a piece of paper, in the street. He would quickly be reprimanded; and everywhere one sees old women with birch brooms sweeping the pavements.

The British Embassy is one of the larger buildings on the far side of the Moskva river, and from its balconies one has the most magnificent view of the Kremlin with its trees and churches. Russian soldiers in long coats and big fur hats stand guard outside the embassy. I had been advised to sign the visitors' book, though I was doubtful what good this would do. Probably the more one kept away from embassies the better, but all the same I rang the bell and signed the book. The porter said: 'Don't forget to take a look at the view, madam. It's a piece of fairyland, like something out of the opera *Ivan the Terrible*'—and yes, it was superb, perhaps the most wonderful view I had ever seen. The sun had come out and the domes of gold and silver behind the crenellated walls on the other side of the river were unforgettable.

I lunched at the National. This hotel, which faces Manezhny Place (named after a Russian victory over Napoleon) was nearer to Nina's office. It was another relic of pre-revolution days, magnificent, shabby, incredibly Edwardian, but comfortable, friendly and scrupulously clean. Like the Metropole, it was filled with the most surprising links with the old regime—massive furniture, stained-glass windows and old pictures. In the cloak-room where I went to leave my coat a servant was trying a new lipstick in front of a mirror and saying to a colleague who was watching her: 'It only cost a rouble.'

The restaurant was full of sunshine, and in contrast to the Metropole there were waitresses, not waiters. Almost as soon as I had ordered lunch a man came to sit beside me, putting a large case containing a camera on a chair between us. As he looked friendly I asked him if he was a tourist on his first visit to Moscow.

'Oh, no, not tourist,' he said, shaking his head vigorously. Then, in laborious English, he explained that he had just arrived from Mongolia where he had spent several months in his embassy. Had it been very cold? Yes, very cold, but the country was unbelievably beautiful and incredibly interesting. 'The world is full of wonders,' he said, with the air of a man whose eyes had been opened by a long journey to undreamed-of lands. He had also been to China, and that was still more interesting.

I asked him what the food was like, for the sturgeon that the waitress had served me was cold and tough and the sauce ill-mixed.

'In China', he said, 'the food was fair, but as in Mongolia they ate too much meat—meat and caviare. That gets monotonous, and one craves for fresh vegetables. So when I am in Moscow and Prague I catch up on green things.'

He talked at length about his impressions of China, and it was not till the end of the meal that I had an opportunity to ask him about himself. He said he was born in Prague, and that was where he lived.

He had a young wife and a small child, a boy, and as he spoke of him the voice of this man (who was incredibly ugly) changed and became very tender. He had married late in life, and that was why he had this very little child, who was such a joy to him.

I think it was because of the boy and the sudden tenderness in his voice that I asked him to tell me about the churches in Prague. Were they full or empty?

This question clearly embarrassed him. 'We are supposed to be a Catholic country,' he said, 'but people go to church less and less.'

Pursuing my thought, I asked if his little boy went to church. Had he been baptized?

At this point he turned his head and called for the bill, and as soon as he had settled it he left almost hurriedly, as if we had not spent this last half hour in conversation together. A moment later he came hurrying back. In the speed of his departure he had forgotten his camera, which was still sitting on the chair.

Nina was waiting for me at the Intourist Bureau, which was similar to the one at the Metropole. A tall, bearded African whose ebony face shone under his *schlapka*, making him look like one of the Wise Men from the East, was looking for a match to light his cigar. I must have seemed very small, very blonde, beside him. He spoke English so, asking him to be patient, I searched in the bottom of my voluminous handbag where I found some book matches that I had been given at the opening of the London Hilton. He accepted them with a big smile, saying that he would keep them as a souvenir.

Nina and I took the underground which, like its Paris counterpart, is called the Métropolitain, or Métro, though of course written in Russian characters, which makes it more romantic. As in Paris the fare is uniform whatever the distance travelled. I had heard much about its luxuriousness, the cleanliness of the trains and the stations built of marble. All this is true. But when one has seen the Franklin Roosevelt Métro station in Paris and Piccadilly Circus in London there is little left to surprise one. On the other hand, while Nina was buying the tickets I went ahead of her in a direction I should not have taken. With a speed faster than the eye could see a metal arm sprang out from the side to bar my way. I must have looked surprised, for Nina laughed and said: 'I had no time to warn you!' Apart from its beauty, which takes one's breath away, Moscow surprises chiefly by the unexpected—the abacus, oldest of all known adding machines, and a moment later an electronic device that pulls one up with a feeling of terror.

The Moscow Métro carries several million people every day. I noticed specially a good many soldiers and also great numbers of women with dark woollen scarves over their heads and carrying heavy parcels. The Paris Métro does not smell good, the London Underground has that peculiarly acrid smell of English cigarettes, the Russian Métro, for some curious reason, has virtually no smell at all.

Making our way on foot to the Pushkin Museum we came upon the largest open-air swimming pool I had ever seen—at a guess as large as the whole of Trafalgar Square. The water was heated, with the result that on this particular afternoon when the temperature was just under zero a white vapour hung lightly over the pool, which was a tropical blue. There were portions reserved for children and elderly people, there were long channels marked off with white cordons as one sees in newsreels of swimming championships at Olympic Games. In spite of the biting cold, or perhaps because of it, I longed to go swimming in this warm lake. There were many bathers, though it was too large for it ever to be crowded. 'One is obliged to take a shower before going into the water,' said Nina. 'We in Russia are very jealous of our privileges. Nobody is allowed to abuse them on the grounds that he has the right to do what he likes.'

This immense pool is in a hollow, and from the surrounding gardens one looks down upon it. Everywhere are plants and beautiful perspectives. There is an ice rink, and in the distance one sees the amusement park with a great wheel like the one at the Prater in Vienna. 'In summer', said Nina, 'all this is very gay because we divide up our work into shifts. A waitress or a shop girl, for instance, will work two very long days and will then have two days' holiday. This is what gives Moscow its look of animation. The shops don't all close at the same time as yours do. At whatever hour you knock off work you can be sure of finding shops open. Thus you can buy what you need in comfort and without having to hurry. That is real liberty. And on the days you don't work you are free to stay at home, or go swimming or skating, or to visit the museums. The same thing applies to school children. That is why you see so many of them in our museums and parks. They go to school either in the morning or in the afternoon. This is much less monotonous than the old-fashioned systems, both for the children and for the teachers.'

While we were watching the people swimming, children were playing in the park that stretched all round it. New parks, new trees, new flower-beds. I remembered a week earlier seeing one of the loveliest plane trees in Green Park near the Ritz Hotel being cut down to make way for the giant works connected with the new Victoria underground line. It had not been long since a great slice of Hyde Park had been cut off to make the new motor way between Hyde Park and Marble Arch. How long would Londoners allow the theft of their green lawns and the cutting down of their trees?

I had brought with me some crumbs from breakfast which I threw to the sparrows. They were as friendly and as greedy as their London cousins and followed me along the paths. This intrigued Nina. I told her about my London flat and my Pekinese, about my son and my husband. She was prodigiously interested in my private life and from time to time would exclaim like a little girl: 'Oh, I'm so happy that you are content in your home life!'

The Pushkin Museum is a large building in a garden. The gardeners were getting the rose trees ready for the long winter. 'These roses', said Nina, 'are superb and smell delicious. They are being wrapped up in straw and sacking so that when the snow comes they will sleep snugly under their eiderdowns. In spring the dead leaves will be cut off, the trees will be pruned and summer will see the roses in bloom again.'

We had come to look at the French impressionists: those which we at home have known only in reproduction—the Gauguins, for instance, which were done in Tahiti. Moscow women in their thick clothing and dark woollen head scarves stared at the canvases which were aflame with tropical flowers and sunshine. There were Renoirs and a quantity of fine Boudins in which I could smell the salty tang of those golden Norman sands where I had spent the summer. How curious to find myself confronted with these evocations of my homeland!

But what struck me most of all was an early Picasso—a bedroom scene. A man and a woman were standing in front of a wooden bed in a poor lodging (one of those beds in which bedbugs used to lodge before they were replaced by iron bedsteads) and the man, hefty and broad-shouldered, was clasping tightly against his body a woman whom he was greedily kissing. His large, ungainly hands were crossed over her tiny waist so as to make a huge belt of love. This was Picasso in all his youthful vigour—the most superb example of his work. There were rooms upon rooms of these marvels—a priceless heritage for this old and wealthy country that has so much in common with France. But most surprising of all was to see these peasants from all over Russia in contemplation before these paintings. I thought of my own village in Normandy and what Ma'am Déliquaire or Ma'am Bayard would have said if I had suggested to them that they should go and spend an hour looking at the 'Mona Lisa' in the Louvre! But Nina said: 'There comes a time in the lives of all

Russians when they feel that they must visit Moscow. So they come from everywhere and meet in the Kremlin or in the museums.' But suddenly Nina broke off, and explained that she also had unfulfilled desires. 'I would like to see Venice,' she said, 'because of the Canalettos. I would like to go to London—but most of all I would like to go to Paris!'

'Be patient,' I advised. 'It will come.'

Nina, having seen me back to my hotel, returned to her office. I took the lift to my room, thought it might be pleasant to have a glass of tea, decided against it, and felt a sudden desire to show my independence by going out for a stroll by myself.

Night had fallen and the flower-beds in the Sverdlova Place were in shadow. The street lighting in Moscow is as it was in London and Paris before the war, soft, mysterious, romantic. Street lighting that eliminates shadows removes poetry from our midst. I felt adventurous but not brave. There were a great many barbers' shops. I peered into one of them and it amused me to see all these men so trustingly offering their bared necks to the barber's murderous knife. I shivered and then laughed at my folly. I thought for some extraordinary reason of Casanova, who came to the Moscow of Catherine the Great and had all those terrible adventures. Why should I imagine *him* in a barber's shop? There were some cafés whose windows were so clouded with smoke and vapour that the men inside looked like charcoal figures without shape or expression. From the top of a building in the Kremlin an illuminated red star shone against the dark sky.

On my return to the hotel I met my Belgian friend, in whom I confided that having arranged to spend a couple of days in Leningrad I was leaving by the midnight sleeper. On the other hand I was sad to leave Moscow even for a few hours.

He had himself been to Leningrad earlier in the year and said: 'At midsummer Leningrad has eighteen hours of daylight. I could never prevail upon myself to waste time in sleep. One can walk through its gardens all night, the air heavy with the scent of roses. It is a city of poetic splendour and unsurpassed courage. Remember when you first set foot upon its streets that six hundred thousand of its inhabitants died during the nine hundred days that the Germans besieged it.'

'I wonder', I said, 'if I could ask you to keep one of my heavy travelling bags. I need so little for the journey.'

'I was on the point of suggesting it,' he said. 'In that way you won't need to trouble the administrator. Incidentally, insist on being put up at the Metropole when you get back to Moscow. Intourist has the right to lodge you where it likes.'

We spent an hour together, drinking tea and talking about his family at home. He had new plans for improving his house in Brussels. He would put in oil-fired central heating and fix double glazing in all the rooms. 'My wife will make objections at first. Women—forgive me for saying this—are invariably opposed to change. They hate the idea of having workmen about. What appals them is the mess the workmen make, the tread of heavy shoes, plaster on the carpets, dust on the furniture. One can't make them look beyond that to the ultimate good. But my arguments will prevail. Then next winter we shall be warm.'

He left me to go to some friends with whom he was dining. While I was casting round for a table in the restaurant I came upon an American woman to whom I had been introduced earlier in the day by Nina.

She was a free-lance photographer, making a series of pictures to illustrate a book, and was leaving for Vienna at about the same time as I was leaving for Leningrad. I asked if she was pleased with her day's work. 'I would have preferred a little more sun to take the *kodas*,' she said, 'but on the whole I am well satisfied.'

She talked about her profession in a pleasant Southern drawl, and I was glad to have such an intelligent companion for the evening meal. She said that her greatest worry on such assignments were the camera and the tripod, which needed constant watching for fear that by some brusque movement or sudden clumsiness one or the other might be damaged.

'They give me more trouble than a child,' she said.

Because of the amount of travelling she did, her other problem was how to cut down her baggage to a minimum. Photographers attached to agencies or newspapers might well travel as much as she did but their firms paid their bills. They never need worry. As a free-lance it was up to her to avoid unnecessary expense. So she tried to store as much as she could in her handbag and virtually dispense with luggage. Would I like to feel the weight of her handbag? How would I like to carry that around all day?

She consulted the menu and asked me what I intended to order. She felt like caviare, but would only order it if I were having some too. And fish? She would like fish, but what kind? She invariably had butterflies in her stomach before a long train journey. It was curious to reflect that here we were having dinner together, and that at midnight, or about midnight, we would get into trains that would take us in completely different directions.

There were not so many people dancing this evening. Perhaps there was something important going on at the Bolshoi. The pretty blonde of last night was at a table at the far end of the room, and she still wore her beige pullover and tight dark skirt. She chain-smoked.

My American friend said that she must remember to take a couple of rolls from the table to eat on her long journey to Vienna. There was no *Speisewagen*, and a journey that took all night and half a day without food was exhausting. One could generally manage to buy a glass of tea or a bottle of that excellent Russian mineral water, but food was out of the question. Besides, there were the customs. If by chance you did see a station buffet you could be sure that something would happen to prevent you reaching it—passports, or money inspection, or customs.

She took her roll of bread, and mine too, and then began to search in her huge handbag to find a piece of paper in which to wrap them.

'Take one of the serviettes,' I suggested.

'Oh no!' she exclaimed. 'I couldn't do that. It wouldn't be honest.'

She went on searching, and after a little while discovered one of those long envelopes which American firms use and for which the notepaper has to be folded over into three.

'This is just what I need!' she exclaimed, laughing. 'I can put the rolls in this.'

But on opening the envelope she gave a cry of surprise.

'Oh, my goodness!' she said. 'What a catastrophe!'

She pulled out a twenty-dollar bill.

I was puzzled. If ever I were to find a twenty-dollar bill in an old envelope I would certainly not call it a catastrophe. But my companion said:

'Before leaving Vienna I changed a cheque for a hundred dollars. My fare cost me sixty dollars. I therefore had forty dollars left of which I took twenty dollars for petty cash. Ever since then I have been trying to puzzle out what happened to the other twenty dollars. I was so worried I scarcely slept. I did my accounts over and over again but I never could account for that twenty-dollar bill. And it had to be this evening, on the very night I am due to leave Moscow, that I find it in this old envelope. Whatever shall I do?'

'But aren't you glad?' I asked, puzzled. 'It's a sort of present.'

'You don't understand,' she said. 'It's a catastrophe.'

'Explain!'

'To leave Russia with money that one did not declare on entry is a serious infringement of the law. When I crossed the frontier on my way in, I could only find twenty dollars—so that was all I declared. As soon as I reached Moscow I changed it officially into roubles at Intourist. So they know all about those twenty dollars. But this twenty-dollar bill? How am I to explain *that*?'

'I remember,' I said. 'It was the questionnaire that included such items as firearms and shavings of gold and silver. I had to sign that too.'

'I wish I had never found this twenty-dollar bill,' she said. 'The Russians don't joke about false declarations. But I won't tell a lie. I shall leave the money in the envelope just as it is and if they ask me about it I shall tell them the whole truth. It's very worrying, but what else can I do? And now all this leaves me without any paper in which to wrap up my rolls.'

'You're getting me worried too,' I said. 'I think I'll run up to my room and see if the luggage is ready and check up on the time of my train. By the time the fish arrives I shall be back.'

Everything was in order, but as I was closing my bag I discovered a wad of paper serviettes which the steward had given me on the *Empress of Britain*. They were very smart and had 'C.P.R.' written all over them in big blue letters. I brought them triumphantly to my friend.

'This is just what you need!' I exclaimed.

She was delighted, but smoked cigarette after cigarette.

'Aren't you excited too?' she asked. 'I mean, the journey to Leningrad . . .?'

'Yes, I'm excited.'

'And you don't feel the need to smoke? How fortunate you

are! I hope they put you up at a comfortable hotel in Leningrad. One never knows in advance which one Intourist will choose. I took some wonderful pictures of the Neva. Leningrad is one of the most beautiful cities in the world—my dream is to go back there. The people are so friendly, so simple and yet so wonderfully intelligent.'

'From an American woman that is a compliment.'

'We are spoilt at home,' she said. 'Too much liberty, too much merchandise in the shops, too much of everything. What pleases me about Russia is that one has the impression of being taught all over again how to appreciate certain things which cost nothing, like peace, the absence of noise, politeness, slow living, trees and gardens, things which in our countries are apt to be smothered in the fury of living. I don't suppose you can understand what I mean?'

'I feel much the same,' I said.

While waiting to be driven to the station I sat rather sadly in a chair in the foyer, like Cinderella before going to the ball. Not that the hotel was sad—far from it. A crowd of Japanese had just arrived and were standing in front of the administrator's office. My American friend had told me that I might have to tip the porter at the station, and so I had put some twenty-kopeck pieces in my coat pocket. The problem of tipping had never presented itself. Mostly if one offered a gratuity it was politely refused.

The administrator now gave my American friend and myself small pieces of paper that we were to hand to our respective car drivers. She was going to one station, I to another. We bade each other farewell and I went first.

The night was dark and the red star shone high in the sky. We drove quickly, passing motor buses filled with workers whose fur hats nodded quietly as they half slept. Were they going to work? Or coming away from work? Or returning from the theatre or ballet? One saw the naked trees in the gardens, the white statues, the flower beds. The street lamps cast shadows against the walls of buildings. Moscow looked enchanting and mysterious.

Here was the dome of the railway station—'LENINGRAD-VOKSALL'. A porter wearing a *schlapka* took my bag, but for no apparent reason started an argument with the driver of my car. He was a big, hot-tempered fellow but he finally calmed down and asked to see the number of my sleeper. The train was waiting, all lit up and with crimson velvet curtains. Written right across it were the words 'LENINGRAD EXPRESS'.

We had no trouble in finding my compartment, and when I gave the porter his twenty kopecks he thanked me nicely. My compartment was fit for a princess. It was all done up in crimson velvet. Two beds were made up just like the bed at my hotel, with the blanket inside the white linen envelope, leaving a diamond opening in the centre. There was a big square pillow case. The linen, like everything else, was scrupulously clean.

The corridors also were decorated with crimson velvet and there were bevelled mirrors on the walls. All this cherry red glowed like rubies, and it was warm. One felt like a pearl in a red velvet case.

The train was filling up and I went back to the compartment. There was a radio, a table lamp whose light cast a warm glow on the table's shining surface, a luxurious *cabinet de toilette*. The radio gave out the late news and then began to play some Russian songs, including 'La Belle au Bois Dormant', from Tchaikovsky's *Sleeping Beauty*. Suddenly it stopped and I heard: '*Govarit Moskva* . . .' ('Moscow speaking . . .') and midnight sounded on the bells of the Kremlin, bells that sounded as if they were of silver.

Without any warning, without any guard whistling, but merely because the train was due to leave at midnight, and midnight had sounded at the Kremlin, the train slipped quietly out of the station.

I was to be alone.

The radio now played a selection of songs—'La Mer' in French, 'O Sole Mio' in Italian, 'Paloma' in Spanish, a song which brought back to my mind that evening with Gemma in Verona in her big music-room when she played for me the song

> Nina, quand tu verras une colombe se poser
> sur ta fenêtre, ce sera moi.

Then some Russian songs.

The music lasted half an hour. I undressed, slipped into bed and allowed myself to be borne over the smooth rails towards the city of the czars.

13

'WOULD madame like tea?'

The radio had been playing for the last half-hour. I dressed, and pulling the crimson curtains aside saw flakes of snow gently hitting the window while night changed slowly into grey dawn. It was eight o'clock. We were running through the suburbs of Leningrad, which looked no different from those of any other great city—a factory here and there, grey streets, lighted windows, an occasional motor-car speeding along a road.

I drank the tea the attendant had brought me and went out into the corridor, where I leaned against the window bar. A Red Army officer who was doing the same bade me good morning.

'Leningrad,' I said as a statement rather than as a question.

'Da.'

Then, more bravely:

'Idet sniek!' ('It snows!')

'Da, da!' he answered. 'The first of the winter.'

Now slowly the train pulled into the station.

'Mme Henrey? I'm from Intourist. Good morning. You see it is snowing . . . the feurst snows of thee year!'

A young man took me gallantly by the arm so that I should not slip on the icy surface of the platform. He asked me if I had enjoyed the journey. My accent intrigued him.

'You are not English . . . not American . . .?'

'I was born in Paris, but my husband is English.'

The matter always puzzled my Intourist guides. As our tickets had been collected before the train left Moscow we were free to leave the station without any formalities. The change in temperature from that of Moscow was considerable. Here it was several degrees below zero and the snow whirled about us, but I enjoyed it and took a great breath of this invigorating air which I liked to think had swept across the Neva.

My companion sat beside me in the car, but when we reached a certain part of the city he asked the driver to put him off. Then bidding me goodbye he gave instructions that I should be taken on to the Astoria.

The city was grey, snow continued to fall and the pavements were crowded with people hurrying to work. Motor buses also were full. As we drew up in front of a red traffic light I saw a charming thing. A young mother on the edge of the pavement kissed her little girl of seven or eight, and then lovingly watched her cross the road in front of the halted traffic. When the little girl had safely reached the other side, she looked back at her mother and then put up a little gloved hand to wave goodbye. She was wearing a toque of Mongolian lamb and her eyes were full of love. Then suddenly she turned and ran off in the direction of a building which I took to be a school. Her mother waited a moment longer to be certain that her little girl was safe and then went off and was swallowed up in the dark, hurrying crowd.

How often on grey mornings like this when I was a little girl of eight in Paris had mother and I set off through streets that smelt of hot bread, *croissants* and black coffee! Sometimes, when mother was rich, she would stop at a little café bar and order a cup of coffee and then she would dip a piece of long French sugar in the coffee, and give it to me to suck. How delicious it tasted! And the *croissants*! How warm and full of butter!

Matilda would have been so happy to know that I was in Russia—that country which after England she and I had longed most to visit.

A few moments later we were driving along the Perspective Nevski, and now I remembered as a girl of twenty standing beside General Tchermoeff in his suite at the London Savoy and hearing him say: 'The Perspective Nevski, mademoiselle, is the most beautiful street in Europe.' It was in the days when I was a manicurist, and he used to ask for me because he spoke French but no English. His drawing-room had a corner window-seat, access to which was by two or three little steps. On grey November mornings he liked to look across the embankment gardens at the Thames which, he said, reminded him of the Neva.

At the Astoria I was shown by a porter (whose name I think was Ivanovitch Mikhailovitch) to Room 111—*adin, adin, adin*. To the chambermaid in her black dress and white apron and cap I turned for coffee and buttered toast. The room was old-fashioned but light, and as at the Metropole at Moscow the bed was in an alcove.

Though the windows had paper stuck against the rims, blasts of cold air came in.

St Isaac's Cathedral, which the hotel overlooked, had a dome like that of St Paul's. There was a thin film of snow over everything, but now the sun had made an appearance in a blue sky. There was a little garden with trees near the cathedral and here and there bits of green lawn shone through the snow. Women pulled infants along in toboggans, a big boy was trying out his skis, a younger companion tried to copy him.

Breakfast was excellent, the coffee hot. Pigeons paraded on the outer sill of my window, but as the double windows were firmly closed for the winter with tape across the chinks I had no opportunity to feed them. There were little trap windows called *fortoshka* which could be regulated to let in the air. Only one of them worked, and there was too much cold air already.

I finished breakfast, tidied my hair and went down into the hall.

At the Intourist office a young woman took down my particulars. Would I like a guide who spoke English or French? English, I said. Then please would I wait a moment?

Two workers were sticking long strips of paper over the edges of a tall window in the hall, sealing it for the winter. One of them was a woman. She was dressed in a workman's blue overall and a man's jacket. Her hair was covered by a kerchief and she was mixing paste in a bucket. When she had done this to her satisfaction she laid the long strips of paper on two planks supported on trestles and ran the paste brush over them, after which she handed them up to her mate on the top of the ladder. She had bright dark eyes, well-shaped lips without any make-up and she wore pretty ruby-coloured ear-rings surrounded by tiny diamonds. In spite of her man's jacket and trousers and the nature of her work she was very much a woman.

The young woman from Intourist now came towards me, followed by a colleague.

'This is Ella,' she said. 'She is to be your guide in Leningrad.'

Ella was so beautiful that I was slightly taken aback. She was a brunette with blue eyes and a camellia complexion, and her lips were made up like those of a film star. Her big fur hat poised over her forehead gave her a feline expression. She wore a black coat, but in contrast to Nina she had no handbag. Nina's handbag was almost a valise.

Beauty intimidates. It would never have entered my head to slip an arm through Ella's and to hurry her joyfully into the street. I felt that in her mind I was just another assignment—and probably rather a dull one.

'We will take the car and drive round the city,' she announced. 'I will point out the streets and the places of interest. After lunch we will visit the Hermitage.'

The weather was beautiful but very cold.

'This fall of snow won't stay,' said Ella. 'The first never does. It's generally the third or fourth that stays.'

'As in Canada,' I said.

Her eyes betrayed a glimmer of interest. She spoke with an American accent and had by now certainly detected that I also had an accent. In any case she was probably in possession of my dossier.

The traffic was heavy, but as the streets were wide we were seldom held up. The snow ploughs were out, driving the snow into the gutters where it was loaded into trucks and discharged into the Neva.

Ella was an intellectual and her discourses resembled lectures by a university don. She did not realize how limited were my powers of reception. We had a woman driver, and from time to time she also would join in my education—but in the nicest way. She had a habit of opening the driving door a little to see what was coming up from behind. She wore a turban and ear-rings and drove with prudence. She was obviously a strong character.

We all got out to admire the Neva and afterwards we went to look at the statue by Falconet of Peter the Great, who founded the city. The statue stands on an immense piece of granite which Ella said had come from Lake Ladoga, probably on rafts, and she conjured up a picture for us of how the block must have been dragged or pushed into place by thousands of men. 'Everything in Russia is on a vast scale!' she said.

The statue shows Peter the Great about to spring forward on his charger whose forelegs are raised into the air. But the horse's hind legs stand on the coils of a snake, doubtless to illustrate the perfidiousness, the treachery and the dangers of his reign. This statue pleased me, for I have always liked monarchs who have had to fight against difficulties. Those who reigned without trouble are uninspiring and one quickly forgets about them.

The sun was superb against the buildings of the city. Ella was looking forward to spending week-ends ski-ing in the country. She said that her husband was a scientist.

'He is very intelligent and we have friends, a young married couple of our own age, who own a car, so we all go off together.'

I asked if she had any children.

'No,' she answered. 'We are in no hurry. My brother is only twelve and my parents are still young, so I have the advantages of a family without having to start one. Besides, I love my work. I have our apartment to look after. I knit, I sew, I read, we entertain and we visit our friends. I never waste a moment.'

It was a joy to watch Ella talking. She had the sort of mouth that lends fragility to a beautiful face—small, delicate, the lips perfectly shaped like those that a doll-maker paints on a doll, and yet strong. Russian, the most gentle of languages, seemed even more caressing when, to the driver for instance, she spoke it. Sometimes she turned to me to see if I was following what she said, and I smiled at her encouragingly, but it was almost a begging smile, urging her to go on. The truth is that I wanted to pierce her armour and make her more human. I would have liked to see her break out into real, uncontrolled laughter, though that was unthinkable. Yet had she not talked to me about her husband, that intelligent scientist? I ought to count that as progress. She even admitted that he had a tiny fault, that he smoked too much, whereas of course she did not smoke at all.

Feeling courageous, I said to her:

'Ella, you are wearing a delightful scent but, try as I may, I cannot place it. Is it a Russian perfume?'

'No,' she answered. 'It's Revlon.'

'If it ever comes my way again', I answered, 'I shall instinctively think of you.'

'Look at this small but beautiful palace,' said Ella becoming professional again. 'Nicholas II gave it to his favourite dancer.'

'Poor Nicky', as the members of his family called him! How long ago it all seemed!

'Tell me, Ella,' I said. 'The place where the czar and all the members of his family were assassinated—is it far from here?'

'Yes,' she answered in a flat voice, knowing all about it but showing no interest whatsoever. 'It was in the Urals.'

The façades of the Leningrad houses reminded me of *His Hour*, that novel by Elinor Glyn, which she gave me and which my mother and I read in Normandy. Futile, romantic thoughts passed through my mind, but Ella was beside me.

'During the war', she said, 'I was too little to understand everything that was taking place, but what surprised me was to see and to hear so many aeroplanes going backwards and forwards but never stopping—like birds that would never come down to rest. I said to my grandmother, for it was she who looked after me: "Why do these aeroplanes never stop flying?"

'That was not the only thing I was too young to understand. There were others—that children who were born in the morning were dead before nightfall, for instance.

'But I was a little girl who felt herself to be protected by her parents. What is wonderful about being a child is that one is quickly afraid but, when one has parents, just as quickly consoled.'

We were all three on the banks of the Neva looking at the Winter Palace. The Russians who did away with their czar now scrupulously respect his former homes. The façade of the Winter Palace has that warm green tint that was the favourite colour of the Italian architect Bartolomeo Rastrelli, who built it.

'Whenever you see a palace of this colour,' said Ella, 'you can be sure that it was designed by him. Another colour which will constantly strike you in Leningrad and which also helps to give the city its peculiar character is Carlo Ivanovitch Rossi's golden yellow. Later I will show you the Senate, the beautiful Pushkin Theatre and the Ballet School, all of which he built. Rossi was the son of an Italian *ballerina* who lived in St Petersburg.'

Rossi's yellow is the colour of Van Gogh's sunshine—the sunshine of Arles. The street in Leningrad that bears the architect's name, though short, is of great beauty, and Ella said that a certain V.I.P. whose name I did not catch was never happy if he had not walked along it at least once every day.

From now on I shall think of Leningrad in terms of Rastrelli's green and Rossi's yellow, just as I think of Florence's rose palaces and Valencia's red earth, the earth in which the orange trees grow.

From my hotel window I looked again at the gardens in front of St Isaac's Cathedral. There were young women wearing coats of bright colours which I had not seen in Moscow, and some of them were pushing smart prams shaped like gondolas and painted pale blue or cream. Children threw snowballs, happy that winter was on its way. There were as many pigeons as in London.

I could also see that equestrian statue of Nicholas I about which there is a story. It faces the palace which he built for his wife Maria, but Maria would not live in it because she complained that her rooms faced the back of the statue, and it shocked her to look out of the window and see her husband's back and the hind portions of a horse.

The hotel restaurant had ceilings so high that I found myself shivering. I therefore ordered borsch and some *bœuf Stroganoff*. Alas, both were served to me tepid. There is no possibility in Russia of complaining if a dish or a meal disappoints. The waiter or waitress assumes that one is fortunate to have a meal at all, which perhaps one is. Also it is a country of all that is most illogical—the worst meal can be followed by one that is a poem.

The shops at the Astoria were much the same as those at the Metropole in Moscow and there was the same animation, except that there seemed to be more foreigners. A group of Italian men, presumably there on business, succumbed to the *schlapka*, which they wore with Roman haughtiness. I asked one of the girls selling these hats how much they cost. She answered in French that there were two prices: the cheaper ones were of sheepskin, the more expensive of astrakhan. When she found that I was French she expressed delight, explaining that her colleague, to whom she introduced me, was the English-speaking salesgirl, whereas she dealt with those who spoke French. It was her dream to go to Paris, just as mine had been to go to Moscow. Her golden hair, though *bouffant*, framed her face like a narrow gilt picture-frame, and her eyes were blue. I told her she was pretty and she said that men did indeed pay her many compliments, but she never knew whether to believe them. She had a daughter of fifteen who would soon be going to the university.

She left me to serve a customer and then I saw Ella who said that she had not wanted to disturb me while I was talking to the girl about *schlapkas*.

'She was telling me about her daughter who is going to the

university,' I said. 'Do you find me very inquisitive? I like people.'

Ella made no comment, so I went on:

'I make myself sound as if I were a vampire. Are you afraid of me?'

'Oh no!' she cried, throwing her head back and laughing.

'At last!' I cried. 'I've made you laugh, and you are even prettier when you laugh than when your face is in repose. I hope your husband keeps you happy and gay.'

We then drove to the Hermitage, but our car was not the same, and instead of being driven by our *citoyenne-chauffeur* we had a *tovaritch*:

The Hermitage, built by Catherine the Great, is connected to the Winter Palace by an aerial bridge. This gives the narrow street between them a slight resemblance to a Venetian canal. One thinks of the Bridge of Sighs that connects the Palace of the Doges with the prison from which Casanova made his daring escape. Casanova incidentally went to see Catherine at the Hermitage, so I was again reminded of him.

The Hermitage and the Winter Palace together form a Russian equivalent to the Louvre, in which are housed some of the greatest paintings in the world, and such priceless treasures as jewels from the Egyptian tombs, Greek carvings in solid gold and the fabulous personal belongings of the czars. In one gallery I saw gigantic vases carved out of single blocks of lapis lazuli; others were made of amber and gold, yet others were carved out of a green stone which Ella said was in her opinion the most wonderful of all, like some rare marble which on being quarried would have taken on the tint of fresh grass.

We saw the great rooms in which the czars gave their glittering balls. Théophile Gautier has described how as an uninvited guest he watched the Czar Alexander II arrive for such a ball, how it started with a polonaise and how it went on with quadrilles, waltzes and *rédowas*. If there had still been a czar of Russia what chance would Ella or I have had to look upon these wonders? As it was we were free to go where we liked. We saw the dining-room where Nicholas II used to take his meals surrounded by his family, and it needed little imagination to people it with ghosts, the czar so like our own George V, the czarina, the czarevitch. . . .

Ella's dream was to find a shop where she could buy a fragment of the green stone she liked so much, so that she could have it mounted on a ring. She told me the name of the stone, but because there was so much to remember I forgot it. On the third floor, for instance, we came upon the most incredible thing of all —a garden, yes, a garden on the third floor with shrubs and flowers and lawns, like the hanging gardens of Queen Semiramis in Babylon which the ancients numbered amongst the seven wonders of the world.

Ella was surprised because I told her that I could look at pictures for only a limited time, even those by Titian or Rubens. She said that Catherine the Great liked to wander alone at night through her picture galleries knowing that she and the mice were the only ones to enjoy this privilege.

Thinking again about Nicholas II and his family round the dinner table, I said: 'I have a great pity for him. He was the czar of my girlhood.'

At that moment I twisted my ankle, not seriously but enough to make me wince, and I exclaimed: 'There you are! Lenin did that to me for saying that I pitied Nicholas II!'

Ella smiled an icy smile. She said: 'I think I have shown you enough for one day. Shall we go and fetch our coats?'

We went down a magnificent white marble staircase on which new carpets had just been laid. 'Every time I bring somebody here', said Ella, thawing, 'I find new improvements. All our former palaces are being restored to their original state, but the cellars and attics are still full of masterpieces for which there is not yet space.'

As in the museum of the Kremlin we had been obliged not only to give up our coats but also to put on felt slippers. Three old women dressed in grey and seated in a row were in charge of the baskets. They were gossiping and laughing.

Leaving the Hermitage, we waited for our car on the embankment that overlooks the Neva. I was glad of this diversion, for I could imagine nothing prettier than to watch the street-sweepers sweeping away the snow with their brooms. On this grey afternoon the picture was as beautiful as anything we had seen on the walls of the palace. A man and a woman passed us, arms linked, cheeks gently touching. The man, whose eyes were Mongolian, was speaking soft and loving things to the woman, and his breath turned to vapour in the cold air. 'They are terribly good looking,'

I said to Ella, 'and it's nice to see lovers on the banks of the Neva.'

'They are good looking,' said Ella. 'They must come from one of our distant republics.'

'Good heavens!' I exclaimed. 'You *do* sound rich with your "republics" in the plural. We in France have only one! You make me feel like a poor cousin, a little down at heel!'

Two boys arrived with haircuts exactly like those of the Beatles. They had come out of the Hermitage wearing the statutory slippers, with which they tried to skate over the snowy surface of the pavement, and their laughs echoed against the historic background. They were the first youths I had seen in Russia who looked like those who have created so much controversy in Paris and London. They hurried into the palace again, for they had left their overcoats inside; also they probably felt the censure in Ella's beautiful eyes.

The women sweeping the snow continued their rhythmic movements and the Neva flowed deep and dark—and now our car arrived. We drove to the opposite bank to look from that side upon the Hermitage, the Winter Palace and the Palace of the Admiralty, and the tall golden spire which is visible from every part of Leningrad.

'Hitler tried his best to destroy it,' said Ella. 'He had sworn to lay Leningrad in ruins. The city's name was doubtless sufficient to make him froth at the mouth, and he had already printed the menu of the victory banquet which he had planned to hold at the Astoria, the hotel at which you are staying. The menus were in a German army packing-case left behind in the great retreat.'

Now night had fallen. Those beautiful lamp-posts which we have been tearing up in Paris and London, the ones that shed such soft mysterious light from big round globes, made the Neva look infinitely wonderful. This sight was one of the things I had waited a whole lifetime to know.

Having ordered a glass of tea in the restaurant of the Astoria, I was surprised to find it poured out in front of me into a cup of fine china, but the teapot was not left on the table. The dining-room struck me once again as decidedly depressing and I thought about Hitler whose spies must have been singularly badly informed to advise him to hold his victory banquet here.

At the post office where I went to buy some stamps a large Russian, his elbows spread out, was composing a telegram while the girls behind the counter were preening themselves as girls do the world over in the presence of a male. From time to time he looked up and talked to them, and from time to time he would again apply himself to the task of writing the telegram, his tongue peeping out from between his lips like a good student doing his lessons. When at last his telegram was written he handed it to the girls, who counted the words and figured out the cost. When he had gone (he was carrying under one arm a child's pictorial map of Russia which looked delightful) the girls broke out into fresh laughter. What had the telegram said? Why were the girls laughing? I would dearly have liked to know.

There was a shop that I had not seen before which sold small silver things, and those silver holders in which you put a glass of tea. On a piece of black velvet were some very light thin bracelets or bangles, some of gold and some of silver. The salesgirl, not knowing any other language, patiently explained to me in Russian that I could have four for two roubles and forty kopecks, and five for three roubles. As this was all the money I had on me I took the five and immediately put them on.

Feeling rather pleased with myself I showed them to another salesgirl with whom I had become friendly. She was not impressed at first but I said to her: 'When I tell people in Paris and in London that I bought these in Leningrad, they will be interested.'

'Will they?' she asked.

It was then that I noticed for the first time that this pretty blonde limped. Indeed, one of her legs seemed quite stiff.

'I was wounded during the siege,' she said. 'I was at the front helping to bring in the wounded, and I got a shell splinter. As I was scarcely twenty then, I have never known what it is to dance.'

The way she put it went straight to my heart. One needs to have been a girl of twenty to know what she meant. She went on:

'Nine hundred days and nights—do you realize what that means? And nothing to eat. Nine hundred nights and days—and famine! And not knowing what had happened to our loved ones or even if we should have a country left to call our own. Those at the front worried about those in the cellars. Those in the cellars worried about those at the front. Do you realize why we all so desperately want PEACE? I have a daughter. I want peace for her.'

'Have you a flat of your own?'

'We live with our grandparents, and if it were not for the fact that I have just lost my mother I would be more than happy. I loved my mother so much.'

Suddenly her eyes filled with tears. She did not try to check them. They flooded her cheeks. She gulped:

'I thought it would get better, but it doesn't. I miss her more and more every day. My daughter is grown up now and she doesn't need me so much, so I would like a baby. A baby always needs one. Only in that case I would have to leave my job, and I love working here.'

'But you could come back?'

'Yes, but I would have to stay away for two years. It's the rule. If one wants one's baby to be strong one mustn't tire oneself out at work. If my mother were still alive she could look after the baby for me. Everything would be easier, but then if my mother were still with me perhaps I would not want the baby so much. The years pass quickly. Suddenly one day I shall grow old.'

She said all this slowly. I did not want to see her pretty blue eyes so full of tears, and mine were far from being dry. I asked her gently what she liked doing. Did she sew? Oh yes, she said, she made all her dresses. So I said: 'I'll run up to my room and bring you down a French fashion magazine in which there are some excellent patterns.'

When I brought it to her she looked calmer. She was balancing her till, as I used to do when I was holding the till for the cashier at the Savoy. That was always my last job of the day, but when I was a girl we worked till seven or eight at night. Another girl was doing the same thing. Both used an abacus. One heard the click of wood against wood as they ran their fingers lightly over the disks —now the kopecks, now the roubles.

All the salesgirls in all the little shops started to count the day's takings. Occasionally a customer would appear and then the girl into whose shop he had walked would immediately break off her calculations and smilingly await his good pleasure. This is what struck me particularly—the immense politeness, the eagerness to serve, the smiling faces of the younger generation.

I had decided that five silver bracelets were not enough to make the desired effect so I went to the bank to cash a traveller's cheque. Before the teller could count out the roubles I was required to produce the declaration I had signed at the airport and on which I had listed the money, both in cash and cheques, that I had brought into the country. Every subsequent transaction was entered on this document. I now understood why my American friend had been so worried about her undeclared twenty-dollar bill. I hoped most sincerely that by now she had arrived safely in Vienna and that her pictures had proved a success.

The theatres in Leningrad are as famous as those in Moscow, and so is their ballet. Next to the hotel lift was a list of attractions. I tried to decipher the Russian characters and felt immensely happy when I had succeeded in reading, for instance: *Othello* by 'Chekspeer'. They were also playing *Eugen Onegin* by Pushkin and the *Lac des Cygnes*. The lift door opened and a high Russian Army officer walked out. He looked terribly imposing in his tall fur hat with the red star, his coat reaching to his ankles and his breast covered with decorations. He must have been a general, and I thought he was one of the most martial beings I had ever seen. A young man in the foyer of the hotel hurried towards him. The officer opened his arms wide, gathered the young man into them and kissed him resoundingly on the lips. I was more and more glad to have come to Russia.

I was getting tired of dining alone. I walked resolutely into the restaurant and looked round for somebody interesting to sit next to. This at least was one Russian custom that offered possibilities to a woman alone. She could choose her man.

A young Japanese was alone at a table. I thought it likely he would speak American and I decided that it would be fun to discover what he was doing in Leningrad. Brazenly I smiled and sat down beside him. Small, good-looking, bright-eyed, he bowed the Japanese way. Did he speak English? Yes, a little, but please would I not talk too fast. His English might not be distinguished, he said, but at least it was better than his Russian—but then he had only been in Russia for six months. What was he doing? He was professor of Japanese history at Leningrad University. As his appointment was for two years he had enough time to improve his Russian, though he delivered his lectures in Japanese. That was the way the Russians wanted it. It allowed them to learn history and Japanese at the same time. Everything they did was done the hard way.

'At least your contemporary history must be easy to teach,' I said. 'The men of your generation are moulding the new Japan.'

'That's true,' he said solemnly.

We were still waiting to be served.

'Does one have to wait as long as this in Tokyo?' I asked.

'Oh no,' he said. 'We are many people in a small country—here there are a very few in a vast one. Even the corridors in this hotel are as long as a road in Tokyo—and look at the height of. these ceilings! We in Japan measure every centimetre.'

After dinner I thought I might as well have a hot bath and go to bed early. The borsch had been cold again and my Japanese friend had gone off to an appointment.

There was no attendant in the lift. I sat down patiently on the red velvet seat to wait. The lift was very large and in one corner there was a vase of white chrysanthemums. This was the only flower I saw at this time of year. One occasionally met people hurrying along the street with two or three white chrysanthemums done up carefully in paper. Sad flowers, I thought, mindful of cemeteries in France. I don't like them.

The lift attendant arrived slowly. He was eating an apple. Slowly he took me up to my floor. Now for the hot bath, I thought.

The bath was large enough to accommodate a giant, but when I turned the hot-water tap only a trickle came out of it. Perhaps I was not sufficiently conversant with the mechanism. I put on a housecoat and went to fetch the *Dijournaia*, who came back with me into the bathroom. She turned the tap and after a while the same trickle arrived of cold, black water. We hoped that patience might remedy the situation but when, after five or six minutes the water became neither clearer nor warmer, the *Dijournaia* broke into a laugh that must have echoed all down the corridor. I have seldom seen anybody laugh so loudly or so happily. Before long I was laughing too, and anybody would have thought that we were part of a music-hall act. All this, of course, was accompanied on her part by cries and gesticulations, grimaces and shakings of the head.

'Good night!' she said suddenly. 'Tomorrow I'll make a report.'

I was so cold that I jumped into bed with my housecoat on. I covered my head with a scarf, bound another round my feet and opened *Tom Brown's Schooldays*, a copy of which I had slipped into my bag before leaving London.

14

I WOKE to sunshine, and probably because I had slept well all my ill-humour had disappeared. Ella and I were going to Tsarkoye-Selo, the Czar's Village, sixteen miles from Leningrad which, during the siege, had been the scene of the fiercest fighting.

I breakfasted hurriedly and found her waiting for me in the hall. We had no sooner passed through the swing doors than the intense cold whipped our cheeks and gave our complexions a glow which no beauty treatment could have produced. Ella was prettier than ever, but I also felt snug and happy in my fur coat, and the sun that had greeted me on waking was shining out of a blue sky. Ella's perfume added to her general air of sophistication. She told me she had spent the previous evening with friends.

We drove past the mosque, which is a faithful replica of the one at Samarkand, and once again I thought of General Tchermoeff, who was a Muslim and who probably came here when he was a young officer. We also passed the Smolny Institute, which was originally a school for the daughters of the nobility. Lenin used it in 1917. The convent was designed by Rastrelli.

Now we left Leningrad behind us. 'This', said Ella, 'is where we enter the battlefield. You have in front of you the scene of the bloodiest battle of the entire war. We are driving across sacred ground.'

The country as far as the eye could reach was absolutely flat. I thought of Waterloo, that dismal plain, as Victor Hugo called it, but what stretched before me would have dwarfed that historic field. 'The vast German armies camped here,' Ella was saying, 'and it was from here that their aircraft took off to pound us night and day.'

Now this battlefield, that will live as long as Russian is spoken, has become acres and acres of apple orchards so that though poignant it is smiling rather than dismal. The apple trees are young and straight. There are also greenhouses that produce tomatoes and cucumbers for the people of Leningrad. The earth was covered by snow, but the road was wide and we drove at speed.

We passed a few trucks and an occasional cart drawn sometimes by one horse, sometimes by two, with those half hoops over the harness that one associates with *troikas* and which are typically Russian, but the drivers were no longer bearded but clean-shaven and so muffled up in furs that I was never quite sure whether they were men or women. This was the road to Moscow. The milestones were unusually large, and at first I took them to be pillars put there to commemorate various phases of the battle. The girl I spoke to at the hotel, who had gone to the front as a nurse, was presumably wounded here.

The entrance to the Czar's Village is through the Egyptian Gate. We found ourselves in a birch wood that added a curiously unreal quality to the scene. We drove through this to a small square in the centre of the village, where we got out. In front of us was the prettiest white and gold palace, and with the sun shining and snow all round it looked like that sugar-icing house in the fairy tale. The village had of course been entirely rebuilt, so that one could truthfully say that the Russians had brought all this to life again out of the ruins of a battlefield. When we entered the palace (which was beautifully heated) we were asked to wear slippers, but this time they were made of cotton, not of felt. There were splendid reception halls, then a pink room, a yellow room, a green room. The rose traceries of the ceilings were reproduced in different woods on the marquetry floors. A few fragments of the original palace were found in Nazi trucks during their flight. These had been reintegrated, and it said much for contemporary workmanship that the new was every bit as beautiful as the old.

The admirable silk curtains, for instance, were exact copies of those that had hung there in the time of the last czar; a fine marble chimney piece had an almost imperceptible break in the centre. Ella who pointed it out to me said that one half had been taken from a German truck, the other discovered buried deep in the ground.

We went to the music room where the boy Pushkin, when attending the Czar's Village school, came with his fellow schoolboys to sing. The gallery where they stood and the palace church are all that remain of the original building. The church itself surprises by its light blue colour, which was doubtless chosen as a compelling background for the icons and sacred paintings.

As we were leaving the palace we came upon a small group of Italian and French visitors, all men, and one of them who had already seen Ella in Leningrad told her in Russian that she was beautiful. Ella blushed and afterwards she said to me:

'That young man was cute!'

'Cute?' I queried, wondering exactly what she meant by this word.

'Yes, cute,' she answered, 'but you may have noticed that he employed the Russian "thou".'

This unwarranted familiarity had grievously shocked her and when we were back in the car Ella, after remaining silent for a while, came back to what was on her intellectual mind and said:

'A foreigner should not risk employing the "thee" and "thou" until he is much more proficient in the language. On the other hand, love stories in English must have lost a great deal by the disappearance of the more tender mode of address. "You" is a very cold substitute for "thou" and "thee".'

'The English still employ the "thou" and the "thee" in their prayers,' I said. 'That is the highest form of love. They are also brought up to appreciate its full beauty in the New Testament, which for most of them is the basis of their thought and education.'

Ella turned her head to look at the birch trees and the snow. The subject I had dared to raise was, alas, a curtain between us, but I had too much respect for her right to think as she wished to want to seem rude, so I added:

'If I were to answer you in my capacity as a Frenchwoman, I could tell you that I also have the "tu" and the "toi". This would put us all square, would it not?'

Ella turned to me and her eyes were full of laughter.

'One can never get the best of you,' she said.

This, of course, was a politeness on her part, for I was convinced that secretly she had no doubt about her superiority. Later when discussing what we had seen she referred to the Czar's Village as 'Pushkin's Village', and I began to realize that the great admiration that the Russians felt for Pushkin had something almost religious about it and was not likely to decrease. Thus Tsarskoye-Selo would doubtless figure on future maps as Pushkin Selo, and it was indeed charming to imagine Pushkin as a little boy playing in the snow amongst the birch trees or seated on a school bench—this Russian Byron who was to achieve fame with *The Prisoner of the Caucasus* and *Boris Godounov* and to lose his life at only thirty-eight in a duel.

The road along which we travelled back had become glorified in my mind and I could not help comparing it with the Sacred Way to Verdun, which from the first day I saw it with tears in my eyes had remained for ever implanted in my memory.

I was to leave for Moscow on the afternoon train. I had thought it would be a good idea to make a long day journey across Russia. I had not realized that most of the journey would be in darkness, and that I would merely be subjecting myself to an exhausting adventure. But it was just this sort of adventure which more than any other was likely to give me an insight into the people of whom up to now I had seen so little.

As I had gone without lunch I went to the restaurant and ordered an omelet and some toast. Remembering my cold borsch and execrable service I had by now no great opinion of the Astoria's dining-room, but within ten minutes I was brought one of the hottest and most succulent omelets it had ever been my good fortune to eat. I ranked it with one I had eaten many years earlier in the town of Saverne in Lower Alsace.

Enchanted by this sudden change I gave the waiter twenty kopecks and tried to explain to him that I had been warned that there was no restaurant car on the day train to Moscow and that I would be glad if he could bring me a few pieces of toast to take with me.

At first he understood nothing, then some minutes later my meaning dawned on him and he arrived not only with the toast but also with a paper serviette to wrap it in. I asked how much I owed him.

'Niet! Niet!' he said. 'Pajalousta. Bon voyage!'

Now suddenly the restaurant struck me as more sympathetic.

I bought some more silver bracelets, so that I then had nineteen in all. The girl who had been wounded on the Leningrad front came up to bid me goodbye. I told her that I had been to 'Pushkin Village' and had thought about her on the battlefield. 'I also thought about you,' she said. 'You are charming.'

This compliment I would not repeat were it not that I took it as a sort of prophecy of the affectionate relations which one day would surely exist between our two peoples.

The train had very long coaches and the seats were arranged as in a motor coach, in twos all facing the front with an aisle in the middle. The windows and doors had freshly ironed white curtains, the lights were excellent and on the back of the seats in front of one, as in an aeroplane, a table could be fixed. A radio played some music, but not aggressively.

The activity on the platform became increasingly great and soon attained such proportions that in my imagination I saw myself transported to Nijni-Novgorod on market-days in Jules Verne's *Michel Strogoff*. Part of the reason lay in the fact that another train had just come in alongside us and was emptying itself of a great concourse of men, women and children all carrying heavy packs and parcels done up in reconditioned paper and salvaged string or rope. Some women carried sacks of potatoes on their backs. A few wore flowered cotton dresses, because these were obviously all they possessed, and to help keep the cold out they wore over their poor little dresses coats or jackets lined with kapok or filled with feathers and sewn criss-cross like an eiderdown. Two boys dragged a heavy case, much too heavy, for every few yards they were obliged to stop and rest. It left a white trail behind it which made one suppose it might contain flour.

Our train was filling up fast. Doubtless it would be crowded to capacity, because when I had asked the Intourist man if I could change my seat to one with a better view he told me that every seat was numbered and booked long in advance, and that I would have to content myself with what I had. Soon I had a companion, whose imitation leather case, having lost its handle, was tied up with rope.

Our guard or conductor proved to be a martial woman who wore a dark blue costume and a magnificent otter skin bonnet which had seen much valiant service. Her eyes were clear and blue, her tongue sharp and active as she sped from one end of the coach to the other like a gadfly.

I looked out of the window again. A mother was arriving with her young soldier son. She wore spectacles and seemed confused by the crowd pressing round her. The young soldier took her in his arms and embraced her. They remained thus for a long moment and then the soldier hurried into our coach. His mother stayed on the platform but each came closer to the window until only the plate glass separated their faces. I watched the woman's eyes become misted behind her spectacles. The muscles of her face twitched with the efforts she was making to keep her emotion in check. The soldier spoke words through the window that she could not hear, words that men invariably use in such circumstances. 'Go home quickly and try not to cry!'

She must have understood for, overcoming her desire to remain till the last moment where she stood, she began to move away. Then turning round she raised a gloved fist to give him the Russian greeting that up to this moment I had supposed was the sign only of hatred and revolution. I never knew that in Russia it could be used, this tightly closed fist, by a mother to show all the overflowing love that was in her heart at so poignant a moment for her darling son. What tenderness there was in this gesture! The fist had been raised very slowly to the level of the elbow, not higher, where it remained quivering—like the gesture of a baby about to run a chubby pink fist against tired eyes. Now suddenly those eyes became drowned in tears, but before they had time to roll down her cheeks the woman bravely turned and with tiny steps hurried away down the platform back to what I could only suppose was her little Leningrad room.

Then came a younger mother with her baby who from a distance looked like a small bundle. An eiderdown enveloped its soft body, obliging it to keep upright like a stick. Two men now arrived in the coach looking for their numbers. They sat down in front of me and one turned to ask me something I could not understand. 'Ne ponimoyo,' I answered. 'Perhaps you are French?' he asked, but as he spoke the train started to move.

The guard arrived with bottles of beer and mineral water with which she did excellent business. My neighbour, who appeared restless, got up and walked along the corridor, and I took advantage of his absence to put twenty kopecks into the hand of the guard with the request that she would allow me to sit in a vacant seat behind, which looked much more comfortable and from which the view of the countryside was not obscured by any impedimenta in front of the window. With smiles and amicable gestures, and *pajalousta* repeated a dozen times, she personally

supervised my change of place so that when my former companion returned in search of his seat he might not have found it
had it not been for the valise he had left on the floor.

The guard now returned with newspapers and games of
draughts, which she distributed. At the far end of the coach a
group of young soldiers, drunk with their sudden liberty, laughed
and sang. They had removed their overcoats and tunics, and were
now in their shirt-sleeves. They did not look like soldiers any
more, but were simply carefree young men in their gay shirts
which were rather light and pretty. The guard or *tovaritch* chief had
also quite changed her appearance. She had removed her fur
bonnet and now exhibited light blue stockings that were rolled up
to below her knees, and she had brought a brush and pan and was
keeping the coach clean with the same pride as if it had been her
own home. No stray piece of paper was allowed to remain where
it should not be.

Now that night had fallen I could not help being impressed by
the way the lamps were ideally placed for reading and writing. I
arranged the table in front of me and played patience with the
cards I bought in Moscow.

The soldiers at the far end of the coach had been drinking. One
of them, scarcely more than a boy, was being held up by another
who had slipped his friend's arm round his neck as in those
pictures of the First World War showing a wounded soldier being
helped out of a shell-hole by a comrade. The one who was drunk
soon allowed his head to fall limply against the shoulder of his
companion, who murmured tender words to him and was
rocking him as a mother rocks her child. They behaved as if they
were still children, and the mother who tried to prevent herself
from crying while saying goodbye to her son would doubtless if
she were here now cry a great deal more. What does youth not do
to waste its best years! From time to time the movement of the
train threw the two soldiers against the seated passengers, and on
such occasions the *tovaritch* chief would arrive with her brush and
pan and vehemently abuse them, for she was obviously no
respecter of soldiers, and after telling them what she thought of
them would look round to us for moral support.

The drunken soldier was at last seated and one saw the almost
childish contour of his smooth neck. Poor baby, I thought, and
remembered a certain grey morning at the Gare St Lazare when I

saw, seated on his luggage, a French sailor so young and so drunk that unless somebody took pity on him he would probably catch pneumonia.

As in the aeroplane from London to Moscow passengers went from group to group arranging parties of draughts, chess or dominoes. The hours passed slowly and I read another chapter of *Tom Brown's Schooldays*. His journey by stage coach to Rugby was not unlike mine.

The train stopped at a station, but I was not able to read its name. Some passengers got out, a dozen soldiers came in. They sat together in twos along one side of the coach and, having taken off their overcoats and fastened the belts across their tunics, they proceeded in a very orderly way to peruse the illustrated papers that the *tovaritch* chief gave them. When they spoke it was in low tones.

From time to time the noisy soldiers, on the way to quench their thirst at a drinking water tap, passed the well-behaved soldiers who looked up from their magazines with a slight air of censure. The noisy ones drank the clear water out of paper cups as in America, and one of them, discovering the electric light switches, decided as a practical joke to plunge the whole coach into darkness; then repeatedly and quickly he put the lights on and off to give us the illusion of lightning in a storm. The *tovaritch* chief spoke angry words to the young soldier, who answered her with such happy laughter that she stood still, confounded. The chess champions could be seen when at last the lights went on again with their fingers poised above their chess men, the well-behaved soldiers tried not to look amused and the *tovaritch* chief and I were the only two women in the coach.

The elderly man who, just as the train was leaving the station at Leningrad, had asked me if I was French now came to kneel in the chair that I had vacated in order to resume our interrupted conversation. This was the only way that he could face me, and he looked like a carved figure on a medieval choir stall.

He said he was a research scientist in iron smelting, and that the iron works in Moscow where he was employed often sent him to their foundry at Leningrad. He had learnt French at school, and when he was in the navy he had even spent a few days at Marseilles—though that had been a long time ago.

I thought him extremely good looking in a paternal way, his

hair clipped short, his dark eyes bright and intelligent, the sort of man one meets in hotels all over the world. He asked me how I was enjoying the trip in a day coach and said: 'Six and a half hours in a train is nothing for me, for I am often sent to Irkutsk, which takes four or five days and as many nights. I love it. One gets into the train at Moscow, one eats and drinks and sleeps, one looks out of the window, and the countryside, the most beautiful in the world, just rolls by. I so much prefer it to travel by air.'

My companion's French was not much better than my Russian, but he was a patient man and we never had any real trouble in expressing ourselves. He was married, his wife worked in an industrial concern, and they had a comfortable apartment in Moscow which they shared with his aged parents. I asked if he had any children. Yes, he said, a married son who had children of his own, so that he was a grandfather.

His passion for research in steel was such that he spoke of his work with burning enthusiasm. They were on the eve of great discoveries and their steel works were unrivalled.

Our train was approaching what looked like a large city.

'This is Kalinin,' said my friend, looking out of the window. 'As far as steel is concerned Kalinin is a satellite to Moscow and the two cities, which are seventy miles apart, are joined by a magnificent motor road.'

The *tovaritch* chief took our arrival at Kalinin as a sign that the long journey from Leningrad was nearly over. Ten minutes after we had passed it she appeared with dark stockings instead of light blue ones and she was wearing her dark blue uniform and the fur hat which was at a slightly rakish angle, a curl escaping from the side. She looked like a *cantinière*, one of those stalwart women who followed the French armies with food kitchens during the Franco-Prussian war of 1870. The fact that she had put on her fur hat did not prevent her from appearing again from time to time with her brush and pan in case somebody had dropped a piece of paper or other rubbish on the floor. Her sharp eyes were everywhere. She turned the radio on low, and as the passengers seldom smoked, perhaps because cigarettes were expensive, the air remained comparatively sweet and clear.

The noisy soldiers dressed. The well-behaved ones folded their illustrated papers and put them carefully into their bags. Newspapers and magazines were too precious to be lightly thrown

H

away. One of them began to rub the metal clasp of his belt, rubbing it and blowing on it alternately, and all with such vigour that my companion laughingly told him that unless he took care he would rub the metal away; to which the soldier answered that he would get into trouble with his superiors if his belt did not shine, from which it would seem that the rule of 'spit and polish' is the same all the world over.

Now at last we ran into the terminal at Moscow, where the passengers hurrying off our train joined the crowds already on the platform, so that for a moment I felt a wind of panic not knowing where to turn. A moment later a voice murmured 'Intourist' in my ear and a man relieved me of my bag and led me to a waiting car.

My joy at seeing Moscow again was indescribable. It was almost as if I were coming home.

'The *Dijournaia* still sat at her desk on the fourth floor. She welcomed me as an old friend. 'The administrator has changed your room,' she said. 'You have a much better one facing the Place Sverdlov and the gardens of the Bolshoi.'

This was one of the most agreeable results of Intourist's discovery that I was not, as they had first supposed, a man. I think they were trying to make up for that curious mistake that had set them all laughing the first day. My room was enormous, with what in France we call a 'ministerial bureau' or huge writing-table with leather top and gold nails. These date from the days of Napoleon III and are a status symbol for French cabinet ministers. The inkstand was of green marble, the blotter bound in leather and stamped with gold, the pens large and heavy. Drawing the blinds aside, for it was night, I saw a huge red star shining in the sky. The apartment was beautifully heated and, when I turned the hot water taps on, boiling water gushed out. The bed in the alcove with its brown velvet curtains looked most inviting, and the whole apartment was so Second Empire that I quite fell in love with it. I peeled some clothes off—a cardigan, a sweater, a pullover —and suddenly I felt young and slim again, and ready for the Saturday night rejoicings at the restaurant.

The female restaurant director hurried forward to meet me and, putting a hand on my arm, said in a confidential whisper: 'You are expected. The gentlemen are waiting for you!'

'The gentlemen? What gentlemen?'

But the noise of the orchestra which warmed my heart drowned her answer. At the table to which she led me I found my Belgian friend with another man unknown to me.

'Ah!' exclaimed my Belgian friend. 'I was afraid you might have missed your train. I've put a bottle of Russian champagne on ice in your honour—but first let me introduce you to this gentleman, who is from the British Embassy.'

The gentleman in question made a slight bow. He wore a tweed jacket of good material but rather worn at the sleeves.

'I went to the embassy the day following my arrival to sign my name in the register,' I said. 'I must say you are well housed.'

The Englishman laughed.

'We are,' he said, 'but, alas, not for much longer. We are obliged to vacate it and it won't be easy to find anything with half as fine a view.'

'Just now', said the Belgian, 'we had a Russian gentleman at our table, but when he heard that my companion was from the British Embassy he fled.'

'I am accustomed to that,' said the Englishman. 'I make it a point of honour to tell people who I am. When a stranger sits at my table I say to him: "I am connected with the British Embassy!" then if he wants to leave he can. Some Russians don't like to be seen with members of a foreign embassy or legation.'

'Well,' said the Belgian, 'forgive me if I say that I am not in the least frightened of you. You could be from fifty embassies for all I care.'

'And I shall certainly not get up and go,' I said, laughing. 'On the contrary I am delighted to have this opportunity to speak English, but as for that visitors' book at the embassy, my opinion is that nobody but that nice porter ever looks at it.'

'I wouldn't say that,' said the Englishman prudently. 'No! No! I am sure it is carefully perused.'

I asked him if he liked Moscow. He said he liked it very much. I said I supposed he had a motor-car. Yes, and it was a pleasure to drive a car in Moscow, and at least there was never any problem as to where to park it.

'And now', he said, turning to my Belgian friend, 'I must ask your permission and that of the lady to leave, for whenever I am at all late my wife gets very anxious.'

He hurried away as if I in turn might have endangered his peace of mind. My Belgian friend and I were left to open the champagne by ourselves. It was excellent, and we drank it in tall narrow glasses of a kind I had not seen before but which are known as 'flutes', from which comes the expression much used in my girlhood in France, 'une flute de champagne', and which until now had never quite made sense to me.

The caviare was magnificent and from time to time the female restaurant director came to talk to us. The ball was now at its zenith. 'Mack the Knife' was played and replayed and every table in the big, high-ceilinged room was filled with gay laughing guests. The dance floor was packed. This was Saturday night at its happiest and most democratic.

The pretty blonde who had intrigued us before my departure for Leningrad was at a large table surrounded by men, and it struck me that not since Edwardian nights, at the Café Royal or Romano's for instance, could any girl have been the centre of so many male glances. Two young men got up and left the restaurant. They were no longer wearing the ties I had seen them wearing a moment earlier when they arrived.

'Am I imagining things?' I asked my friend.

'No,' he laughed. 'They have either sold them or exchanged them for something else. There's an element of strip poker in Moscow. This evening, for instance, as I was leaving the hotel a man came up to ask me when I was going back to Belgium. He wanted me to sell him my clothes before I left. I'm afraid there's a black market for these things.'

'Did he expect you to go back naked?'

'As near naked as I dared. But I'm far too old a hand to fall for these tricks. I'll have nothing to do with them. If somebody has been specially nice to me I will occasionally give them a tiny present, something of no value like a packet of razor blades or a lipstick, which are easier to obtain at home than in Russia. But as for accepting money—never! Besides, what would I do with it?'

My Belgian friend went on:

'In a year or two, perhaps much sooner, the Russian people will have everything they want, and these anomalies will disappear as they disappeared in our own countries. We had them, if you remember, for quite a time after the war. It's not for us to criticize.'

The music became more hectic. From time to time a waiter would escort to the door some guest who had drunk too much. One guessed that for many it was pay day. The scene was noisy, colourful, friendly, and there was an atmosphere of live and let live that was perhaps the most striking part of it. Within reason a person could do what he liked without incurring critical glances from his neighbours. At a table next to ours a party of Russians were laughing, drinking, eating roast chicken with their fingers, dipping bread (as the French like to do) in the sauce. Innocent-looking vodka, clear as water, was poured frequently into their glasses and drunk in one long thirsty gulp. At some tables guests began to sing, then the orchestra took up the tune. I was deliriously happy because this was what I had always wanted to see. There was no longer any such thing as class. Nobody cared what his neighbour did or how he was dressed, and if a man wanted to take off his coat and give it to the stranger opposite that was his business—not ours. But the vodka flowed, the music played and those who wanted to sing did so. This was Saturday night in Moscow, and I was in the middle of it, drinking Russian champagne.

Later in the evening I saw my companion casting an anxious glance at a group of merry guests making their way out. He had been sitting opposite me. Now suddenly he rose and came to sit beside me. He was just in time. As the group passed us one of its number vomited on the back of a *maître d'hôtel* who was bending over a menu taking a guest's order. The drunk hurried out before the *maître d'hôtel* had time to discover what had happened. It was my friend who called him over to whisper in his ear: 'Go quickly and clean yourself up with a damp towel!'

'But,' I said to my Belgian friend, 'what made you so suddenly change places?'

'Merely the fact that I spend half my time travelling across Central Europe,' he said. 'Budapest, Bucharest, Moscow. . . . Men who can afford it eat and drink on Saturday night. Sometimes they drink more than they eat. I have learned to see what a man looks like when he can't hold his drink any more. The muscles of his cheeks twitch. Then it's only a matter of seconds; so when I can I get out of the way.'

The pretty girl lit another cigarette. The men at her table were getting rowdy, but she remained imperturbable, observing them clinically as she puffed at her cigarette. She looked like a spider watching its victims, her eyes cool, clear and cruel.

I had a steaming hot bath in the ornate bathroom and then, putting on a housecoat, knelt in front of the larger of the two windows—the one that had a radiator in front of it—and looked out into the night. The illuminated red star on top of the Kremlin burned like a ruby. Cars came and went in the square and turned into the Avenue Karl Marx.

Moscow night.

How could I perpetuate the memory of this night that seemed so different from every other night I had ever known? What strange thoughts passed through my head! I wondered what my feelings would have been if I had found myself during Napoleonic times overlooking the Place de la Concorde. Would I have felt the same sort of emotion as I now experienced—the blood bath that had happened, the blood bath that had passed—and now the exhilaration of looking forward to the future?

The room was immense and, in spite of its high ceiling, beautifully warm. The velvet curtains were russet brown, nearly crimson, like hot red wine, and the alcove with its Victoriana, its silver and bronze corners, looked like a large family picture album, massive, heavy, bound in leather, with silver clasp and bronze corners. I knew that I would always cherish the memory of this night and that Moscow had more than fulfilled my dreams of a lifetime.

When I was in bed propped up against the big square pillowcase of cool Russian linen, I heard in my imagination the noise of the Leningrad day train pounding, pounding on the rails. I thought of the young soldier who had drunk too much. I recalled a final glimpse of him on our arrival at Moscow. He walked unsteadily along the platform, leaning against his comrade. I hoped that the future would allow him to taste more satisfying joys than those of alcohol—the joys of love, of happiness, of beauty, of creation. I was tired and yet in no hurry to fall asleep, for there are occasions when sleep is a waste of time. I picked up that cheap edition of *Tom Brown's Schooldays* which had followed me from London to Normandy, from London to the Mediterranean, from London to Russia, and which was always providing me at stray moments with glimpses of an England of stagecoaches, unspoiled country and hearty breakfasts of beef and ale.

I seemed to be living in several countries and dimensions at the same time.

Sunday morning.

The bells of the Kremlin should have been ringing, and I should have been going to church, but instead my Belgian friend was taking me to a matinée at the Bolshoi. This was the first time in my experience at least that the word 'matinée' made theatrical sense, for this performance of Tchaikovsky's *Nutcracker Suite* was due to begin at eleven o'clock.

The Bolshoi. I first saw this famous theatre at the far end of a little park with the Sunday morning crowd converging upon it, masses of officers broad-shouldered in their long overcoats, women wearing cotton dresses and long jackets padded like eiderdowns, and numbers of children warmly and prettily dressed. Occasionally we were stopped by a girl or a youth asking us to sell our tickets.

The theatre was like any other of similar importance—the Monnaie at Brussels, the Scala at Milan, the Paris Opéra, Covent Garden—but there was a buffet and the coffee smelt delicious. We had two places in a box, a *Loga*, and my friend took my seat and gave me his from which the view was better.

The adjoining box was suddenly filled by fifteen or sixteen children, little girls and little boys, accompanied by a mistress in a simple black dress and a rope of pearls reaching down to her waist after the fashion of Mlle Chanel. I wore my Chanel suit and felt happy in it. The little girls had long fair plaits with a great number of bows placed at the top, the bottom and in the middle, and made of such light and transparent ribbon that they looked like butterflies ready to fly away. Most of the girls had little black skirts, blouses with starched white collars and charming frilled pinafores like those worn by children both in France and England in the nineties. Everything was crisp and beautifully laundered. The boys had round-shaped heads and hair cut very short. They must have looked well in *schlapkas*.

The theatre was warm and softly lit and the stalls, instead of being fixed to the floor, were like small armchairs that could be easily removed to turn the *parterre* into the setting for a ball. The orchestra took their places. I recalled how, during the Russian

lessons of the B.B.C., I had been slightly vexed by being made to
learn the names of so many different string and wind instruments.
They must have guessed that the time would come when those of
us who were following the course would visit Moscow and go to
the Bolshoi, and that we should accordingly be glad to know the
Russian for flute and trombone. By leaning over the red velvet rim
of the box I could see the musicians' scores with Tchaikovsky's
name in Russian characters. I again had that extraordinary
impression of being a little girl and discovering the joys of
reading for the first time, spelling a word out laboriously and
perceiving its sense. The children in the box next to ours were of
the age when the delights of reading are new and fresh. By
travelling back along my life I was building a bridge between
myself and them.

To thunderous applause the conductor, dark and rotund,
arrived, bowed several times to the audience, sat at his lighted
desk and raised his right hand. Now the curtain went up to show
guests arriving for the Christmas party at the home of President
Silberhaus. They were wrapped up in their furs, for snow was
falling and it was cold. Tchaikovsky finished the music for this
version by Dumas of Hoffmann's fairy tale in the spring of 1892,
only eighteen months before he died from cholera in St Petersburg
after drinking a glass of water. How crowded those last months
must have been for him! St Petersburg, Vichy, Brussels, his new
country house at Klin (where he composed a symphony, destroyed
it and started another), London, Cambridge to receive the degree
of Doctor of Music, back to St Petersburg and that fatal lunch.

Now the scene had changed and we were in the home of
President Silberhaus with the presents and the lighted candles on
the Christmas tree. This was the moment for Councillor Drossel-
meyer to arrive with his dolls which moved as if they were alive,
and for Marie, the president's daughter, to receive the German
nutcracker made in the shape of an old man who broke nuts in his
jaw and which, after her brother Fritz and the boys had broken it,
she caressed and fussed over as if it had been a real invalid,
rocking it to sleep.

The ballet was originally arranged by the celebrated Marius
Petipa. None more subtly evokes the spirit of the old German
Christmas, its snow, its fir trees, its toys, its fairies, its honey
cakes and sugar plums. The Russians guard such fairy tales as

carefully as they treasure the former palaces of their czars, their museum-churches, the jewelled Easter eggs of Fabergé, the relics of Peter the Great.

But the Christmas tree in President Silberhaus's drawing-room has become, as in many Western countries, merely a decorated fir tree, magical in this case because, if you remember, it grows when the toys come to life. To call it a Christmas tree is perhaps a misnomer, for in the eyes of an eager new generation it can have nothing whatsoever to do with Christ's Mass.

I was always being struck by points of similarity between the Paris of Renoir and Degas and the Moscow of today. Though in many ways Russia is the country that looks most vigorously to the future, that is most advanced in its scientific knowledge, it retains the beauty of light and shade and slow movement. The French Impressionists would feel at home in the Moscow of today. When the curtain fell on the first act of the *Nutcracker* the mistress in the box next to ours seated her children round her and lectured them on the composer, on the dancing, on the music, on what they were to expect in Act Two. Their intent little faces were a joy to see. For a long time I listened to the mistress talking, the children asking questions. These were the Russians of tomorrow. Of all the pictures of Moscow that will remain in my mind, this one of intelligent, eager childhood fascinated me most.

15

THIS was my last day in Moscow. I had asked the *Dijournaia* for an early breakfast so that I could take my time over it, feed the sparrows, and look at the people in the square. Evening would come soon enough. I had slept well and now felt relaxed in this warm, cosy, tall Edwardian apartment with its plush curtains and fringed table-covers. Kneeling on a chair by the window, my forehead pressed against the pane, I murmured childishly: 'I am in love with Moscow!' I remembered one Sunday morning some two years earlier meeting a woman in the Pincio, that beautiful part of the Villa Borghese where Roman children play as London children once played in Kensington Gardens; she said to me: 'I am in love with Rome!'

A maid brought breakfast, laying everything out carefully on the table with many gay compliments, followed by *spasiba* and *pajalousta*, but she had no sooner gone than I discovered that she had forgotten the hot milk for the coffee. I hurried out into the corridor. She was not in sight, but I recognized her crystal laughter against a background of tinkling china. A moment later she appeared with a milk jug and a look of infinite amusement on her young face. She came back with me and started to pour the milk into the cup. Alas, it was tepid. Patience, she exhorted me, she would hurry to the pantry and heat it up. Let me exercise only a little patience, she would be quick, quick, quick! I was so convinced that she would not come back, at least before the coffee in its turn became cold, that I decided to breakfast in the res-taurant. To my surprise within a few moments she arrived with a tray on her shoulder—fresh milk, freshly made coffee, all piping hot, and a thousand excuses, *spasiba*, *pajalousta*. We bowed to each other like wives of tribal chiefs. The coffee was excellent. As she was about to leave the room I took from my handbag a lipstick I had bought for myself in London before my departure and gave it her. It was a small thing, but because I was not allowed to give her a tip I hoped it would amuse her, and I was more than rewarded by the happiness it gave.

The phone rang. It was Nina. I hurried down into the hall, where I found her wearing a different coat—a black one with an astrakhan collar. 'I have a *schlapka* to go with it,' she said, 'but it's not quite cold enough yet, and they do disarrange one's hair. It's lovely in the street. You'll see. The sun is shining.'

We drove along avenues, past gardens, in the direction of the old city. As it was Monday, shops which had been open over the week-end were closed. Even in the old city the roads were wide and many of the houses were new. On the other hand one occasionally had glimpses of eighteenth-century houses that had inner courtyards, into which a coachman could have driven a carriage and pair, as one sees in the older parts of Paris. Nina asked me about my trip to Leningrad and talked about Chaliapin. I said that Ella had pointed out to me the house in which he had once lived. His memory was greatly honoured, and both Ella and Nina were surprised when I told them that we spent some of the most enchanting evenings between the wars in his company either in Paris or London, and that after dinner he would sing the 'Song of the Volga Boatmen', the strains of which still haunted me. He was proud of his peasant stock, claiming that he never went to school but at seventeen joined a touring company, making his operatic *début* at the Maryinsky in what was then St Petersburg. *Boris Godounov* was his great role, and he once told me that during the revolution he was paid in sacks of flour because money had ceased to have any value. He died a year before the war in Paris. Afterwards I went to seek out his last resting-place in the Batignolles Cemetery. In *Milou's Daughter* I pointed out that this was at Clichy, five minutes from where I was brought up as a girl. I wrote:

I do not need to close my eyes to see again the tall, fair-haired giant with the big hands whose palms were so soft to the touch. On a slab of rose-tinted marble stands the double cross of the orthodox faith, and I read these words:

Ici repose Feodor Chaliapine, fils génial de la Terre Russe.

And now here I am at last on this Russian earth from which he sprang.

The maternity hospital, which was in a growing and populous

part of the city, differed in few respects from similar hospitals elsewhere. Perhaps what struck me most was that instead of a large waiting-hall for patients there were many small rooms each with a couch and one or two nurses. The nurses wore starched white linen toques and blouses tied at the back. We were taken immediately to the doctor's private room.

The doctor, a woman and extremely pretty, welcomed us with great gaiety. To me she said: 'So you want to see a little Muscovite born?' She went on: 'This maternity hospital is not one of the largest in Moscow, but it is the one that happens to serve this part of the city. Every district has one of its own. We are constantly building new ones, but we are always short of beds.'

I asked her the reason for the small waiting-rooms, and she said it was to cut down the risk of infection from colds, influenza, sore throats and anything else that might jeopardize the health of future mothers. She pointed out that this particular hospital was an old building but that the methods employed in it were extremely modern.

Her eyes were dark and laughing, her face full, her mouth small and well proportioned and she wore her toque slightly back from an arched forehead. Her movements were lively, and it was fun to watch the eager expression on her face as she answered questions.

From a tall cupboard which she unlocked with her own key she took two blouses, two masks and two toques for Nina and myself. When we had put these on she locked the cupboard and the door of her room and we set forth. Seeing her walk briskly beside us I reflected that she had none of the drabness that some people impute to the inhabitants of Moscow. She wore olive green high-heeled shoes and her legs were well shaped and her ankles slim. Her eyes were just sufficiently slanted to give her an intriguing expression. Her son was also going to be a doctor and had already done three years in hospital.

We went to the first floor, a long corridor with wards of five or six beds and glass walls. Here and there on a table by a patient's bed were a few chrysanthemums in a vase. The newly born babies, some only a few hours old, some several days, were in little cots ranged one beside the other in a glassed ward of their own, into which we were only allowed to peep. They were protected from any contact with the outside world. The mothers themselves, said the doctor, were not allowed to receive visitors while they were in hospital. This might sound cruel, but she felt certain that it was a wise precaution.

There was a room in which a plastic baby lay on a cot with next to it all that was necessary to dress it in the Russian fashion. Thus expectant mothers from distant republics could take lessons in baby-dressing and welfare. We saw the operating theatre for Caesareans and afterwards were taken to witness an *accouchement*.

Back in the doctor's room we took off our masks, blouses and toques, and the doctor smoked one of those long Russian cigarettes which smell so good. I had wanted to send her flowers to thank her for giving me so much of her time, but I feared that she would be tired of those white chrysanthemums one saw everywhere, and so I asked her if she would accept a rather amusing new shade of nail varnish that I had bought in Paris and which perhaps she had not yet seen. She accepted it very gracefully and slipped it in her drawer. On the way out we passed many expectant mothers waiting for consultations. Most of them were very young. They looked tired and anxious and did not even glance in our direction.

The driver of our car was engrossed in a paper-back. I asked him what he was reading (this question was in a delightfully illustrated Russian phrase-book I had bought in Leningrad) and he said it was a thriller by Simenon, and that it was *ochem Karacho!* We set off and in the distance we could see the dome of the university building. I told Nina that I wanted to buy a tea-cloth because the Russian linen in the hotels seemed of excellent quality but slightly different from what we had at home. The driver said that the only place to go on a Monday was the ZUM.

The ZUM was a store in the Western sense, a sort of Selfridges and very animated. The tea-cloths were charming but expensive, and Nina, seeing me hesitate, offered to pay half 'in order that you should have something to remember me by', as if I could ever forget her, but refusing her kind offer I decided to buy a piece of plain linen which I would embroider with cross-stitch.

Nina said that she had some material and wanted to make herself a dress. Ever since I was back from Leningrad she had planned to ask me how to cut it, not that her own head was not full of ideas, but she thought it would be more fun to talk things over with me.

'We could design separates,' I said; 'a rather close-fitting black blouse with darts and a skirt. I'll show you.'

On leaving the shop we found the driver still engrossed in Simenon.

'My goodness,' he said. 'Already?'

Time had gone quickly for him, but he inquired whether I had found what I wanted. Some moments later, as he was driving along a fine avenue, he said reflectively:

'This Simenon mystery takes place in "Parije". I would be much interested to go there.'

Nina said:

'Madeleine was born there.'

Her use of my Christian name was not a familiarity, for in Russia there is no 'Mrs' or 'Miss'. One is either called by one's Christian name or referred to as *citoyenne* or 'comrade'. Nina's revelation concerning the city of my birth greatly intrigued the driver. I did not ask which Simenon he was reading or what the citizens of 'Parije' were up to in the tale, but I had a terrible feeling that he must now imagine me to be a murderess, an immoral woman, an heiress or the potential victim of a spy ring.

'Ask him if he's married,' I whispered to Nina.

'No,' he said, 'and I'm glad not to be, because what I want to do most is to travel, and a wife would embarrass me.'

We drew up at the Metropole and Nina dismissed our comrade-driver with many thanks, but as we still had time in front of us we walked a little in the sunshine while Nina asked me questions about the model I had in mind for her separates. I made her a drawing at the back of her pad. 'Yes,' she agreed, looking at it critically. 'That looks pretty, and if I make it without sleeves as you suggest I can go dancing in it.'

A woman and a little boy who had been following us heard us speak English. As they turned into one of those houses with the large courtyards I described the boy cried: 'Goodebaille!' and blew me a kiss. His mother also waved, saying 'Goodebaille!' Then their two *schlapkas* disappeared out of sight.

We laughed about this and the friendliness of the Muscovites, but I was sad to think that in a few hours the goodbyes would be real. Already it was time for Nina and me to part. We kissed each other.

'*Adieu*, Madeleine!'

'*Adieu*, Nina!'

As I was not hungry, and as I had been told that I could exchange my last food vouchers for caviare, I went in search of the lady restaurant director, who not only made me a splendid parcel but insisted that I should stay to have a borsch, which proved excellent and piping hot. I gave her my own lipstick and what remained of the make-up in my handbag, knowing that because it had come from Paris she would invest it with special qualities. I would have done the same in Rome or Madrid.

My Belgian friend came in to have a glass of *tchai*. His stay had proved longer by two days than he had expected, but it was a great success.

'I have worked well for my masters,' he said, and this expression amused me because one of his companions had told me some days earlier that they considered him socialistically inclined.

'That doesn't surprise me,' he said laughing. 'As soon as one confesses to one's love of Russia people interpret it in a political sense. In politics I am both to the left and to the right, as in life one makes use of both one's hands, the right and the left! I respect and admire my employer in Brussels but I like to see people share prosperity. Russia thrills me because it is in a state of flux, and as I deal in complicated machinery and new inventions I feed on progress. I wish you a happy journey home—and don't forget to ask for a carrier bag, so that you can buy some more caviare and a bottle of vodka at the airport before taking your plane. That's what *I* always do.'

I went up to my room and looked out of the window at the people in the square. What a wonderful day, this last day in Russia! The *Dijournaia* bade me *bon voyage*. Two chambermaids were discussing TV. At the administrator's office new guests were arriving, handing in their passports: *Stratvouite! Goodebaille!* Life in this grand hotel flowed forward like the waters of the Moskwa, even when the surface was iced over. The porter had brought my baggage down. The little chair I had bought at GUM was here with a smart tie-on label. I was given the number of my car. Now it was the long drive through the woods to the airport.

MOSKVA

The letters in red across the airport building burned against the night sky. It was bitterly cold, several degrees below zero. Passport officials were courteous, but our Roman writing must be puzzling. Often in Vienna after the war I heard people laughing at the Russians, saying their soldiers could not read because they had a habit of turning passports this way and that in their efforts to understand what was written on them. British soldiers might have been equally puzzled by Russian writing.

This was nearly the end. Had I any roubles? I was reminded that Russian money must not be taken out of Russia. The few roubles I had were exchanged against American dollars. Then through customs—a mere formality—to the shops, where for foreign currency one could buy vodka, caviare, amber necklaces and dolls. Two English business men were waiting for my flight. I asked them to take me under their wing, but when a few moments later our departure was announced first in Russian, then in French (but not in English) it was I who had to take them under mine. 'How on earth did you know?' they asked.

A bus took us across the tarmac to the Comet. I was flying back by B.E.A. As soon as I was seated an impeccably dressed air hostess asked me if I would like tea. She might have been a film star, so unaccustomed I had become to seeing young women made up in the Western way. 'Oh, please!' I answered, already unfaithful to *tchai* in a glass with lemon. Opposite me sat the young Russian woman, with hair pulled slightly away from her forehead and made into a bun, who had travelled with me in Aeroflot on the way out—the one whose smart red umbrella I had noticed.

We took off immediately and were soon travelling at so great a height that I was glad of the rug that the hostess brought me. I dozed a little. The plane was more than comfortable. Two hours later the flight bulletin was handed round. Captain Watson informed us that we had left Moscow at 6 p.m. Russian time and that it was now 5.30 p.m. English time and that we were flying over Hamburg. Dinner was brought—hors d'œuvre, Scotch steak, champagne, *marrons glacés*, coffee. We were served by the steward in spotless white and the air hostess, who was slim as a pencil and very pretty.

The lights of London came up at us at a quarter to seven. They looked like all the jewels in Aladdin's Cave, green, red and white, unbelievable after the comparative dusk of the great Russian capital. Then the drive to Kensington and my husband waiting for me with my Pekinese.

Thus it was that my dream came true.

16

I WAS delighted to be back in London, to be with my family and enjoy the warmth of the flat in Shepherd Market, but my thoughts during those first days of December were entirely on my journey to Russia. I had taken to working, as so many women do, at a corner of the kitchen table, having dropped into this habit in Normandy after my mother's death—the strict discipline of those long mornings of hard work in bed, a shawl round my shoulders, notes and papers strewn about me, having snapped when she who had been everything in the house had so suddenly gone from it.

Shall I not always regret those wonderful mornings when I got up first to let the hens out, to sniff the country air, to listen to the song of the birds? I would go back to bed to work. This was by tacit agreement. Matilda then got up, dressed with great difficulty because of her arthritis, and made breakfast, my share of which she would bring on a tray as far as the foot of the stairs, her slippered feet shuffling painfully over the black and white tiles. 'Coffee, Madeleine!' she would cry in her shrill piping voice. I would rush down to take the tray from her and return to work in bed, while below me and all about I would hear the noises of a waking house, the postman coming, the farmer's wife bringing the milk and discussing the events of the night, the hens scratching in the orchard, pots and pans being moved about on the stove, taps turned on and water running. All this finished when Matilda was no longer there to protect me from small interferences. There was nobody but myself to make breakfast or lunch or to take in the milk or the letters, so it was easier to work snatchily at a corner of the kitchen table.

On 11th December, my mother's birthday—she would have been seventy-seven that day—Patsy telephoned to say that my farm in Normandy had been broken into and burgled. It was she who had given me the news of my mother's last terrible illness. I had grown to fear these calls from Normandy, and was less resistant to sudden shock, which on this occasion almost paralysed me.

Police were in the farmhouse. They said that every room had been ransacked, drawers and cupboards broken open, all my possessions soiled and thrown into confusion. It was impossible for them to know how much was missing.

The joy of my Russian journey suddenly evaporated. My husband and I had taken to the farm in Normandy the greater part of our family treasures, not things of value, but manuscripts, portraits, pictures, photographs, letters as well as everything that had belonged to my mother and to his. The idea that a burglar had—as the police informed me—slept with his boots on in my bed, scooped out jam with his hands from jars in the cupboards and smeared it all over my pullovers, dresses, skirts; broken open champagne bottles, emptying the contents on the floor; thumbed through books, photographs, Bibles; spat out plum-stones into linen; soiled carpets—all this made me feel faint with disgust.

I had already known what it meant to lose a home. In 1940 when the Germans swept across France I left my farmhouse while the lunch was still cooking. I lost every single thing in the house—furs, dresses, hats, linen, books, pictures, glass, china. Not a single thing was ever recovered. To suffer this humiliation a second time was almost more than I could bear. I told my husband that I could not face it and asked him to go instead. I was afraid of taking a violent dislike to the house and never wanting to live there again. He took the night boat *via* Le Havre on the evening of the 12th December, promising to return the following night.

I was glad to be spared the sight that met him on arrival the following morning. Jacques Déliquaire, our farmer, and Georgette, his young wife, were in a state of excitement, remorse and fear. The house had been broken into in three different places and the burglar had been seen, but not identified, by the farmer one morning when roasting a stolen goose on an open fire in the middle of one of my orchards. In his flight he left behind a number of objects stolen from the house, amongst them a tin of English salt and a pepper mill to flavour the goose, five fountain pens, several packets of English cigarettes which I kept for friends (not smoking myself), a knife and fork, some woollen garments knitted by myself, and half a dozen boxes of matches.

He had, I think, spent at least three days in the house, sleeping in my bed and going through every room with meticulous care. Several sacks filled with my clothes were later found in a huge

empty vat in our cider presses. He had lit a log fire in the big room
of the farmhouse; in another room had upset a bottle of methy-
lated spirits and nearly set fire to the house. Would he return after
dark? The police believed that it was the work of some farm
labourer who knew the district well, for this was not his only
visitation. Other houses had been burgled in a similar way.
Georgette was now afraid to remain at the farm unless she knew
that her husband was around with his gun. Dared my husband
return by the night boat, or should he remain on watch?

This burglary had a most unpleasant effect upon me. I had lost
too much in the war not to be aware of the transitory nature of all
that goes to make a home, but what hurt me was that my little
treasures had been soiled. I had only recently in that same house
lost my mother. I must not allow myself to believe that the house
had turned against me. For if I were to believe that, what would
be left?

Depressed, I finished the chapters on Russia, and learned with the
rest of the world of the loss by fire of the Greek cruise ship *Lakonia*,
which cast a cloud on the memories of our recent cruise on the
Empress of Britain. It was then that I met a woman in Green Park.

A young woman wearing a three-quarter red coat was exer-
cising three tiny apricot French poodles in the park. One of them
made off in the direction of crowded Piccadilly. Appealing to me
to keep an eye on the other two, she ran after it. 'Thank you!' she
exclaimed breathlessly a moment later. 'I caught her just in time.
She might have been run over.'

'I like the colour of your hair,' I said.

'Oh,' she answered. 'It's a wig. In my profession they save a
lot of time.'

'In your profession?' I queried.

'Forgive me—I thought you knew. I've seen you so often in
Shepherd Market. We are virtually neighbours. I live in that
funny little white doll's house opposite the coster's barrow, the
one who sells fruit and vegetables. Yes, since before I was run
over by that bus in "Coronation Street" and killed. It was from
there I watched my funeral on TV.'

'Your *funeral*?' I said. 'When did you die?'

'About nine months after the start of "Coronation Street". Ida
Barlow was my name. Surely you remember me? That kindly
mum married to Frank Barlow, who was then a post office sorter

with two sons, Kenneth and David. Don't tell me you've never watched "Coronation Street" on TV.?'

'Why did you have to die?'

'I died to get home to my own family in Shepherd Market. We never thought "Coronation Street" would last more than thirteen weeks. In fact it was planned for Coronation Street to be demolished. That was how we were going to end the serial. The trouble was that it went on and on. Of course I had to stay up in Manchester. I lived in the Essex Hotel. In summer I flew home at week-ends or took a sleeper on the night train. After nine months I couldn't stand it any more. My husband, my mother and my aunts needed me. They all lived here in Shepherd Market. So it was decided that Ida Barlow would be run over and killed by a bus. You might say that I died for the love of my real family.'

'From what you tell me you were quite affected by your own death?'

'Of course. Wouldn't you have been? I was still in Manchester while they recorded my funeral, because the same evening we were all going over to Blackpool where Ena Sharples was to turn on the illuminations. The public was not supposed to know that I was dead and we had to be seen as a family.'

'Were you in the studio that afternoon, when it was happening?'

'No, they asked me to keep away. They thought my presence in the flesh might upset the others. But I went to have my hair done in the studio hairdresser's and there I saw a man I didn't know being made up. I asked who he was. "Oh, he's the undertaker," I was told.

'I came back to London the next day, and as I have already told you I watched my funeral from my little flat in Shepherd Market. Poor Frank Barlow looked as if he hadn't slept for a week. I felt almost sorry for him as I sat on the floor with a poodle on my lap. My real husband, Kenneth Edwards, was pretty upset too. Come in and have a drink with us one night. Wednesday next, if you like, and then you can watch the current episode on our TV. set.'

That was how I became momentarily drawn into the vast public that watches 'Coronation Street'. At seven o'clock, half an hour before the episode was due to start, I knocked on the front door of this absurdly small house in Shepherd Market. The poodles all started to bark at the same time, and Noel Dyson (to give Mrs Kenneth Edwards her professional name) came down with a white poodle in her arms and two at her heels. In the tiny first-floor sitting-room her husband was dispensing drinks. This former housemaster of Blundell's (the public school at Tiverton founded by Peter Blundell in 1604) was learning his part for A.T.V.'s series 'Sergeant Cork', while his wife was memorizing her lines for a new play on B.B.C.

The schoolmaster turned actor and the actress Ida Barlow had first met while they were playing in Terence Rattigan's *Playbill* at the Phoenix Theatre, and they were married during the run.

As one of my first books, *A Village in Piccadilly*, was set in Shepherd Market it seemed appropriate that I should find myself with Noel Dyson, who had lived there nearly as long as I had, first next to Andrey, the newsagent in Trebeck Street, then over Webb, the fishmonger, now in the little house in the main square.

'But', I said to her when the dogs stopped barking, 'how is it that you, a Roedean girl, had the right Lancashire accent to be chosen to play Ida Barlow when "Coronation Street" was first introduced to the public?'

'I happened to be born in Newton Heath, a suburb of Manchester,' she answered, 'and my father worked in the Manchester Cotton exchange.'

Was there a real Coronation Street?

Yes, said Noel Dyson, there was, about a mile and a half from the centre of Manchester, down the Ashton Old Road as far as Victoria Street and then the sixth or seventh turning on the left. Of course it had no connection with the TV. serial which, as everybody knew, was more closely identified with Salford, but one street was probably much like another, and why was I asking anyway? There were doubtless lots of Coronation Streets.

I think that at heart I wanted to discover if there were any points of comparison between the streets of my Clichy childhood and those of a present-day Manchester suburb. I wanted to see if children played in the streets as I had once done. The TV. serial was all very well, but it suddenly gave me a desire to see the real thing. I would go to Manchester and find out for myself.

A young man called Ian Gee called for me at the Midland Hotel in his small car. A white fog hung over the city and it was rather cold. The fog smelt of coal gas and made me cough. I had never been to Manchester, but when I was little and January came round my mother and I would set off for the Bon Marché departmental store in Paris, where my mother, who was as provident and as industrious as the proverbial ant, bought thirty yards of madapollam, a cotton cloth made in Manchester, out of which she would make chemises, petticoats, drawers and nightdresses for herself and for me, and which on long winter evenings we embroidered and trimmed with lace.

'There ought to be a shop, a general shop, like Florrie Lindley's in the TV. serial. Do you think there will be?' I asked my companion.

'This is Victoria Street,' he said, turning sharply off the main road. 'Victoria Street . . . Coronation Street. . . . All this must date from Queen Victoria's accession. What makes you think there'll be a shop?'

'There always is,' I said.

There was indeed—the very shop I had dreamed of, a tiny general store, one window facing Victoria Street, the other Coronation Street, the door with its tinkling bell forming the apex of the triangle.

'Stop!' I cried to Mr Gee. 'Park the car somewhere and let's go and buy something.'

'They are probably not open,' he said. 'It's not half past eight yet. I can't think why you wanted to come so early.'

'It's better than the evening,' I said. 'In the evening they'll want to play housey-housey, watch TV. or see relatives.'

The street was little more than fifty yards long, about a dozen one-storeyed houses on either side. It led nowhere, or rather it led into another street, just as short but running at right angles to it, and all these tiny streets arranged criss-cross had alleys running between them at the back leading to outside lavatories and coal cellars. Here and there wisps of smoke were starting to curl up from notched red chimney-pots, and I had seldom seen so many sparrows or heard such a din as they converged on the roof of the general store as if they realized that this was the cornerstone, the heart, the nerve centre of the awakening streets. A green lamp-post of elegant Victorian design, with a gas mantle, stood at each end of the street. Half a dozen workmen sat round a brazier against the wall of an iron foundry on the other side of Victoria Street. The sparrows watched them intently, for the men were throwing crumbs.

Ding, ding.

The bell of the general shop tinkled shrilly as I pushed it open. On the counter in front of me were a machine for slicing ham, some scales, a few loaves, jars of sweets, packets of tea, cigarettes. A white-haired woman wearing a light blue cardigan over a lilac dress came in from the back room. With her was a little girl whose head alone was visible above the counter.

'Just like Florrie Lindley's shop,' I said.

'I hope I'm not as easily flustered as she, love.'

'I'd like to buy a pencil and a pad of paper, and talk to you. I'm not too early, I hope.'

'The fire in the back room has been lit since a quarter to seven,' she said. 'Come through and have a cup of tea, love.'

Chairs were drawn up in front of a coal fire. There were two windows in the small room, one facing Victoria Street, one facing the alley behind Coronation Street. A budgerigar hopped about noisily in its cage, a terrier called Peggy jumped up against me as terriers will, a ginger cat called Timmy purred while Nelly Taylor, the owner of the shop, introduced me to her daughter Doreen Thomas who had come over from her house in nearby Gate Street with her two little girls Jean, aged six, and Pauline, aged three.

The fire, which was raised and which, though small, seemed almost savagely red, had a metal fireguard, and next to it there was an oven with an open door, fire and oven sharing equally the space beneath the mantelshelf of dark polished wood in the centre of which stood a clock that had stopped.

A man's white shirts, starched and ironed, hung on a line stretched across the room from a window to the budgie's cage.

'Your husband's?' I asked Mrs Taylor. 'Does he work on Saturdays?'

'He's upstairs asleep,' she answered, tilting her face upwards as if she could help me to imagine him in the small bedroom immediately above our heads, but when I inquired if we were not in danger of waking him with all our noise, she answered, laughing: 'Don't worry. When Dad sleeps, he sleeps tight. He's in security police at an electrical firm across the canal. When one of his men goes sick he takes his place on nights, which rightly he shouldn't do, being the head one.'

'He is fortunate in having a wife who irons so well.'

'So I should,' she answered. 'Besides, there are no problems with detergents, me keeping so many different kinds for sale in the shop. I couldn't very well run short, could I?'

Her daughter Doreen, hearing the tinkle of the shop bell, slipped out of the room. As soon as she was back her mother asked: 'Who was it?' 'Mrs X.,' said Doreen, 'to say that Mrs Y. had died this morning.'

Mrs Taylor turned to me and her expression was calm, almost beautiful. One read in it fatigue, but infinite patience. Her two grand-daughters were trying to be on their best behaviour, but soon they became restless.

The ginger cat jumped into the oven, curled up and looked at us with wide yellow eyes like those of a mythical creature in the mouth of a dark cavern.

'Won't he burn himself so near the fire?' I asked. But the oven was only warm, not hot.

The postman called and Doreen and the girls ran out to watch him open his sack. Everybody in the street loved him, especially the children. As soon as Doreen was back her mother asked anxiously if the postman had brought anything. She was expecting some papers to sign. Pauline, who at three was already a bundle of energy, brought me a well-rubbed teddy bear. The room was cluttered up, but warm, friendly and spotlessly clean. We fitted into it as comfortably as the ginger cat fitted into his oven home. The wallpaper had a flowered design. By a window an ancient sewing-machine, having lost its lid, was covered by an over-turned wooden case which had the advantage of providing a smooth top surface to act as an extra table.

Pauline went to borrow a pencil from a showcard behind the shop counter, then came to ask me for a page from my pad so that she could draw on it, but she soon tired of this too and dragged me into the shop. Meanwhile her elder sister, Jean, had scribbled 'CLOSED FOR THE WEEK' on the back of an old envelope and had propped it up on a shelf between a bottle of pickles and a pot of of marmalade. A woman came in to buy four rashers of bacon, looked at the notice that the little girl had written, and exclaimed: '"Closed for the week", indeed, and what do you suppose your customers will do!' Mrs Taylor patiently took down the paper and said to me: 'My grand-daughter Jean is a great scribbler, and she just loves going to school.'

The school was a mixed one and was less than a minute away, in a street similar to Coronation Street and forming part of the curious patchwork that had surprised me on arrival. Mrs Taylor, who could look back on nearly fifty years, told of the time when all about were fields and gardens, and she spoke of a wheatfield with cornflowers and poppies and a little brook. There was music in her voice. 'There are no more flowers,' she said sadly, and I saw her eyes turn to a miserable little bundle of plastic roses in a vase. But Pauline in her green dress and red ribbon in her hair looked like a tulip about to unfold its petals.

Most children went to this school at the age of four, and Mrs Taylor claimed that when she herself was little there were not enough to fill it, whereas now there was hardly enough room to accommodate all who wanted to go.

Though by now it was close on nine the street was only just stirring. One could tell this by the wisps of white smoke curling up from chimney pots, first from one house, then from another, but some still had none. The two little girls kept on darting into the street, prancing round the lamp-post, trying to persuade a little boy from across the road to come out and play with them, but he was shy. Ten years ago Doreen had stepped out of this same general shop as a bride in white on the arm of her father, the security policeman, to be married at nearby St Clement's Church to young Trevor Thomas, now a draughtsman with a computer firm. Her mother, this calm, white-haired woman, who, having seen the fire in the back room suddenly lose its fierce redness, had gone to fetch more coal, must have been very proud of her daughter. She had owned the shop since before the war. For twenty years before that it had belonged to an aunt, so that it had been in the family for nearly half a century.

I walked slowly down the street past net-curtained windows, then rang a bell at random. A woman with a comfortable frame and an enormous smile opened the door. She exclaimed: 'Well, this is a time to come visiting, love, but come you in and have a cup of tea and summat to eat. My name is Jesse Gibbons

—a good old-fashioned name, love. Breakfast is laid in the kitchen.'

The room that looked out on the street, the parlour, hiding behind net curtains, was foggy and cold, furnished with ceremonial chairs and settees and an oval watercolour, of a woman dressed in the fashion of a hundred years ago, hanging slightly askew over the empty fireplace. But the back room was as cosy as could be with a coal fire every bit as bright as the one at Mrs Taylor's at the general shop, a budgerigar in a cage and breakfast set out on a white cloth on a table by the window, at which sat Jesse's husband, Louis Gibbons, aged eighty-five and 'as sprightly as he ever were, but only a bit hard of hearing, so just shout, love!'

I think I had never heard the Lancashire accent with more delight, or perhaps I had and this was bringing it back to me, so that I fell utterly under the charm of Jesse Gibbons and basked in it, feeling immensely happy and delightfully relaxed.

She never stopped talking, merely allowing her husband (who clearly doted on her) to beam between eating toast and marmalade and sipping tea. I think this was one of the rare occasions when I would have liked to have a tape-recorder, for I was intrigued by her unquenchable talk, for ever punctuated by the Lancashire 'love'.

Louis (she pronounced it Lewis) had been in gas mains with, so she said, hardly a day's illness in sixty years of work. They had a married daughter, and a grand-daughter Christine aged twelve, who was one of the few pupils who had graduated to grammar school from the one round the corner in well-named Elysian Street. When Jesse revealed her age, seventy-nine come Valentine's Day, I said something about her not looking it, which was indeed the truth, and back came the answer: 'I'm not miserable, love!' and for the first time I understood the old adage that a person can be poor and absolutely contented.

Not that Jesse Gibbons and her husband gave one the slightest impression of being poor, for did they not both enjoy complete good health (one could never quite believe in Louis's deafness) and hadn't they much more than Virginia Woolf's minimum requirement of a room of their own? They had a whole house— front parlour, back parlour (or kitchen if you prefer it), carpeted staircase and two fine bedrooms on the floor above, one facing Coronation Street, the other facing the alley at the back.

'We live in the quietest and nicest street in the neighbourhood, because you can't get nowhere at top or bottom!'

How often I was to hear this, but from her it sounded truer.

'And, oh, love, I've had such a beautiful life! You should have heard the clitter of clogs, when I worked as a cloth looker in the mill—real music!'

'A cloth looker?'

'To see there were no flaws, love—and just at the top of the street a cornfield and a farm. Oh, it was beautiful!'

The clitter of the clogs, I repeated, bemused.

'Yes, and a hat and a shawl—a little round hat, one that wouldn't blow off. Oh, wasn't it nice to go to the mill and hear the clitter of the clogs!'

She kept getting up and sitting down and getting up again. She said that when she was 'coming on for sixty, I fixed up this corner by the fire for slops, and I put a curtain across so that nobody can tell what's behind, love—so I have me gas stove here, me fire there, me slops behind the curtain and me table here with the kettle ready to pour out tea. Everything is handy, love, and I had Louis working till he was past seventy-three'.

She insisted on showing me the family photographs, and though normally I don't much like looking at other peoples' pictures, these were different.

'That's me on a donkey on holiday in the Isle of Man, and here's me in a white blouse on the sands at Blackpool when I was a girl of twenty, and there's me dancing!'

Jesse on the sands at Blackpool with her white blouse, her boater and parasol, looking like the woman in Degas's famous picture called 'La Plage'. How pretty she was! How exasperating this mirage of a long-gone youth! She must indeed have had a happy life—not that there weren't bad patches, notably the time her sister went home with the shopping, put on a frilly nightdress, bolted the door and slipped into bed, and was found three days later—dead. Soon afterwards Louis was knocked down in the street and brought back by the police covered in blood—'but the good Lord sends these things to try us, just as when the bombs dropped and I sat in the parlour with my little dog on my lap and was never for a moment afraid, for I said to myself: "God will help us!"'

'How did you and Louis first meet?'

'In the centre of Manchester, at the Old Piccadilly, over sandwiches and a drink. Meat sandwiches, pickles and a pint of bitter.
'Twas a beautiful pub, and in them days a courting couple could
wander along the canal side as safe as in their homes. There were
none of them terrible bad men knocking about.'

Before leaving Manchester I wanted to see Salford, and asked
Ian Gee to drive me there. I had in mind a scene in *A Taste of
Honey* in which the young sailor standing in the bows of the ship
waves farewell. I wondered if I could recapture, however briefly,
the strange emotion I had experienced at the time. There was also
another reason. For some time past I had watched the drama of a
tall, pretty girl, Muriel-Jane, who had left her home in Salford to
hurl herself into the struggle of life alone in London. She had
arrived full of determination and wonderment, but found especially
at first that the buffeting she got—in part because of just tha
Lancashire accent that in her I had found so enchanting—was
sometimes more than she could bear. Once or twice she must
have felt tempted to give up and go back to the warmth and
friendliness of her own people. I felt for her as I would have felt
for a daughter.

With a little trouble I now remembered the name of the street
in Salford in which her mother lived, even the number of the
house, and decided to call on her to see this mother of whom she
was always speaking with such devotion, and warm myself for a
moment at the coal fire, which seemed to both of them, as to the
people of Coronation Street, such an important part of their lives.

Hafton Road—that was the one, modestly hiding itself in a
small maze of similar streets with houses that appeared much
newer, more coquettish than those I had seen at the other end of
the town. I rang the bell. At first there was no answer. Then, her
husband, John, having opened the door, a tall, slim woman, dark
whereas her daughter is fair, appeared at the top of a tiny staircase,
curiosity and wonderment in her lovely blue eyes. She was draped
in a nylon housecoat, came slowly down two or three steps, then
exclaimed: 'Oh, I know! You must be Mrs Henrey!' She hurried
down and I kissed her. I said: 'I'm sorry to have called at such
a difficult hour. Perhaps I should not have come. It was because of
your daughter and that accent of hers which has endeared h'er to me.'

She led me into the living-room, similar to so many others, with a budgerigar hopping about in its cage and making welcoming noises. She said: 'I was a little tired. That's why I was still in bed. Normally on Saturdays I stack my linen on a little push cart and go to the launderette where I meet some of the neighbours I don't see on other days. It's not hard and we have a good talk.'

I thought of my own mother, when I was little, and the bundles of washing half as big as herself that she took every Sunday morning to the public wash-house outside Paris, one of those public wash-houses with a tricolour flag. Flags on wash-houses in Paris in those days were painted on iron. Vlaminck has handed down such scenes for posterity. These expeditions were for me pure joy. For Matilda they gave rise later to her worst nightmares. She used to say to me: 'I've had another of those dreadful dreams in which, try as I would, I couldn't get through my huge pile of washing before the wash-house closed, and all the other women who washed so much faster than I did were laughing and jeering at me!' For on Sundays the wash-houses in the Paris of those days closed at midday. My mother's arms were too frail and short to allow her to compete against those of the huge sturdy women who pushed their fruit and vegetable carts through the Paris streets.

Lily Shaw had no such problem. She had merely to put her wash on the little push cart and take it with a packet of detergent to the launderette, which magically would do all the work.

'I'm so glad I was a bit tired and stayed in bed,' Lily Shaw was saying. 'How terrible to have missed you, Mrs Henrey.'

We were on a sofa in front of a very shiny modern gas fire.

'What has happened to your coal fire?' I asked. 'Your daughter in her moments of nostalgia cried for her mother and the warmth and friendliness of a Lancashire coal fire.'

'Alas,' said Lily, 'our district has gone up in the world. We have become a smokeless zone, and so we no longer have the right to the cosiness of glowing coals.'

We embraced, and as the car moved away Lily threw me a kiss. This is what I shall remember when next I hear her daughter's accent.

Soon I was being driven along wide, depressing streets. There seemed nothing particular about them, and I was thinking of the journey home, when on my right I saw the bows of a big white ship outlined against the greyness of a warehouse wall. Cargo was being loaded into the hold; men were standing about the deck. Here, I think, were some of those other things I had wanted to see before leaving this great, foggy city—ships, warehouses, docks—symbols, for a woman, of that strength and protection which consciously or not she is for ever seeking.

DATE DUE

GAYLORD   PRINTED IN U.S.A.